YOUR BRAIN ON LATINO COMICS

For our
Friends Saed
Nora, Kclaes
with much
affection
Frederick
Aldrin
Corinne Bruco

Cognitive Approaches to Literature and Culture Series

EDITED BY FREDERICK LUIS ALDAMA, ARTURO J. ALDAMA, AND PATRICK COLM HOGAN

Cognitive Approaches to Literature and Culture includes monographs and edited volumes that incorporate cutting-edge research in cognitive science, neuroscience, psychology, linguistics, narrative theory, and related fields, exploring how this research bears on and illuminates cultural phenomena such as, but not limited to, literature, film, drama, music, dance, visual art, digital media, and comics. The volumes published in this series represent both specialized scholarship and interdisciplinary investigations that are deeply sensitive to cultural specifics and grounded in a cross-cultural understanding of shared emotive and cognitive principles.

YOUR BRAIN

ON LATINO COMICS

From Gus Arriola to Los Bros Hernandez

FREDERICK LUIS ALDAMA

University of Texas Press ◆ Austin

Requests for permission to reproduce material from this work should be sent to:
Permissions
University of Texas Press
P.O. Box 7819
Austin, TX 78713-7819
www.utexas.edu/utpress/about/bpermission.html

♾ The paper used in this book meets the minimum requirements of ANSI/NISO Z39.48-1992 (R1997) (Permanence of Paper).

LIBRARY OF CONGRESS CATALOGING-IN-PUBLICATION DATA

Aldama, Frederick Luis, 1969–
    Your brain on Latino comics : from Gus Arriola to Los Bros Hernandez / Frederick Luis Aldama. — 1st ed.
        p.   cm. — (Cognitive approaches to literature and culture)
    Includes bibliographical references and index.
    ISBN 978-0-292-71934-7 (cloth : alk. paper) — ISBN 978-0-292-71973-6 (pbk. : alk. paper)
    1. Comic books, strips, etc.—United States—History and criticism.   2. Hispanic Americans—Comic books, strips, etc.   3. Hispanic Americans in literature.   I. Title.
    PN6725.A38 2009
    791.5'352968—dc22

                                                                                    2008049356

The interview with Jaime Hernandez was published previously in Frederick Aldama, *Spilling the Beans in Chicanolandia: Conversations with Writers and Artists* (University of Texas Press, 2006).

FOR CORINA ISABEL
AND WITH A SPECIAL THANKS TO
EVAN THOMAS
AND
SHAWN SALER

Contents

YOUR BRAIN ON LATINO COMICS

PART I

AN OVERVIEW OF LATINO COMICS

Author cross-dressed as a *luchador* (wrestler)/superhero

① INTRODUCTION

This book began the moment I decided as a kid to read and reread one comic book and not another. It began when I decided to cross-dress as a Mexican *luchador* (wrestler) and as some sort of Superman-Batman mix. It began the moment that comic book storyworlds allowed me to imagine myself battling foes, indulging in superhuman feats, surmounting gigantesque obstacles, and overcoming looming fears; it began the moment I could step into other worlds and feel another's pain and pleasure; it began the moment I experienced a certain delight in putting together storylines, character attributes, and scenic detail.

This book contains interviews with a number of comic book author-artists, and most of them are not garden-variety enthusiasts, ComiCon aficionados, suburban hipsters, or Marvel fetishist types; they are Latinos who in one way or another were exposed to and enthralled by comic books and comic strips at an early age; some, like Los Bros Hernandez, had ready access to their mother's stacks, and others, like Rafael Navarro, had *tíos* (uncles) with comic book treasure troves.

Studies on comic books seem always to begin in the confessional mode.[1] As the author of a book on Latino comics, then, let me continue to indulge this impulse. Years before developing a hunger for novels and a taste in authors— as a teenager I would return again and again to García Márquez and Salman

Rushdie—I had already begun to develop a discerning taste for comics. I was not drawn to the daily or Sunday funny strips, nor to *Archie*, *Casper*, and *Richie Rich*—some favorites among my friends. No, I unabashedly liked the hyper-masculine Anglo characters as well as the quick lines of movement and color splashes of the superhero comic. More specifically, I was into those superheroes whose muscles were self-sculpted, whose talents were self-engineered, and who kicked ass outside the law: Batman and the super-hunk Captain Marvel. I also preferred those that were set in a recognizable everyday earth-scape—not in some never-never land. This is to say, at an early age I knew I was more a Marvel than a DC guy. At this point I have to confess that ethnic and gendered representational distortions—superhero as Anglo versus supervillain as dark, disfigured, effeminate, "alien" Other—hadn't yet become part of my evaluative vocabulary.

An attraction to those adventuring and self-chiseled superheroes makes up only part of my comic book confessional. Along with U.S. superheroes, I was drawn to Mexican luchadors, especially wrestlers like El Santo and Blue Demon. After various border crossings to visit relatives in Mexico, as well as weekend trips to the local flea market, I would transform into some type of hybrid superhero: blue tights, red shorts, cape, and luchador mask. Super-power battles, rescues, and romances were the order of the day.

While the superhero-luchador sartorial wear was eventually socked away in a bottom drawer (my superpowers were deflated the day I was called a sissy) and the comic books were boxed, this world never fully disappeared. As an adult, I continue to reserve viewings of film adaptations of comic books (no matter how cheesy) as occasions to bond with my father. Generational divides fall by the wayside (he grew up in Mexico City in the '50s) when we share stories of originals versus newly interpreted versions of *Batman*, *The Phantom*, *Flash Gordon*, *The Hulk*, and many others.

In college, word-of-mouth enthusiasm sent me back to the comic books themselves. Three titles visually caught my eye and piqued my intellectual interest: Los Bros Hernandez's *Love and Rockets*, Pat Mills and Carlos Ezquerra's *Third World War*, and Ivan Velez Jr.'s *Blood Syndicate*. One way or another, they were all visually dynamic and textually raw, presenting sophisticated narratives of everyday and epic-dimensioned struggles of characters of all colors, sexual orientations, and walks of life. I knew impressionistically then what I practice now: the study and teaching of comic books.[2]

Even as preverbal children, we notice the interplay between vibrant visuals and word markings on a page. Whether or not we understand the words, we infer and interpret, creating meaning. We have little control over those black markings; their interpretation is left to big people. Then arrives that wondrous moment when we can decipher meaning from those black marks; when we are dazzled by how the visuals and the verbal elements create magnificent narrative choreographs. For many of those interviewed in this book—and for me—this verbal-visual bedazzlement occurred in a first encounter with the comic book or comic strip. It also marked an awakening and sharpening of taste—a rudimentary liking for a certain graphic and lettering style as well as for character and plot. In my day, such a taste led to pocket money being saved for those family outings to the flea market; it meant hours of relishing readings and rereadings of stories I chose to keep, trade, or lend. For the many Latino and Latina comic book and comic strip author-artists heard here, this was a first step in determining which worlds they wanted to imagine and inhabit—which selves they might want to try on for a spell.

As I suggest, and as the Latino author-artists interviewed here forcefully attest, comic books don't go away. They are with you always. They are not, as some suggest, part of a childhood phase; for adults, comic books can stimulate imagination and emotion as much as other storytelling forms. Of course, in the United States (but not in countries like Mexico, France, or Spain), there remains a straightjacket around comic books: they are strictly the domain of young people, and those adults who still gravitate toward their storytelling forms are presumed to suffer from some sort of arrested development. Typically, the novel is considered the domain of the adult, and the comic book that of the child or adolescent; accordingly, the "normal" formative trajectory would mean graduating from comic books to novels. (For an extended discussion of this topic, see *Comic Book Nation* by Bradford W. Wright.)

Many of us read comic books as adults—and not just out of nostalgia for bygone days. We pick up a comic book for the same reasons we might a novel, a short story, or a DVD film. Comic books and comic strips can be as aesthetically complex, self-aware, and emotively engaging as the next storytelling form; and, conversely, they can be as uninteresting, sophomorically self-absorbed, and flat as the next.

Comic books and comic strips are in the storytelling air we breathe. Just as authors can choose from a vast number of storytelling forms—*telenovela* to metafiction, newsstand *Hola!* to Internet short story, to you name it—so, too, can readers choose which form to interface with. And this is the case for all interested readers: Latino and non-Latino women and men, children, adults, and the elderly.

Certainly, one's options may be more or less limited depending on where and when one lives; historical time periods, geographic regions, and cultural contexts affect exposure and choice. If my father had been reading comic books in the United States during the dark era of censorship in the 1950s, instead of in Mexico, he would have had only a sliver of the storyworld experiences that he did have. And, while less so than in my father's day, still today in Mexico City people of all walks of life and in all parts of the city read all sorts of comic books.[3]

This said, I don't ascribe here to the position that comic books are the shapers of history; that they are a discourse that constructs thought, action, and our sense of self; or that their value as an area of scholarly study lies in their uncovering of so-called discursive (historical, cultural, social) forces that intersect to shape the self and society (see Wright, *Comic Book Nation*, and William W. Savage Jr., *Comic Books and America, 1945–1954*).

Comic books don't float free in some ethereal platonic space. Like all cultural phenomena, they are produced and circulate within specific social and historical material conditions. They are not, in my opinion, agents of transformation of their material contexts, however. They can, of course, be manipulated in ways that restrict or unleash the imagination. In the 1960s, the U.S. comic book market struggled back to life after its near death at the hands of the Senate Subcommittee on Juvenile Delinquency and the testimony of psychologist Fredric Wertham, who claimed that the lifestyle of Batman and his "young boy friend" Robin expresses "the wish dream of two homosexuals living together" (*Seduction of the Innocent*, 190).

Largely as a result of the continuing struggle to publish and to shake off the shackles of the Comics Code Authority—a self-regulating board established in 1954 to ensure that only comics that taught good values and morals would be published—by the early 1970s the comic book as an art form found strong expression in what we call the "underground" comic. Comic books could now tell any kind of story—from the most mundane and autobiographical to the most impressionistic and zany-wild—and in the most individualized styles; the comic book conveyer belt gave way to the comic book auteur. During the 1980s and 1990s, under the influence of the "alternative" comics, the Marvel and DC conveyor belts began to churn out revisioned worlds and newly conflicted and psychologically complex characters: racial, gender, ethnic, and sexual concerns entered into the mainstream fray. The format itself shape-shifted: book-length narratives (or "graphic novels") began elbowing the single-issue comic off the shelves.

With these twists and turns in the storytelling form in the '80s and '90s, the opening up of readerly canons, and the pounding on publishers' doors by the author-artists themselves, a path began to clear for the creation and production of Latino comic books and comic strips.[4] As the twenty-one interviewees discuss, great strides have been made. That there is enough material for a book on Latino comics says a lot. Yet the Latino author-artists here also temper their enthusiasm with a sobering sense that the struggle is not over. While much representational turf has been won, there is still much work that needs to be done.

In the Latino graphic narratives, a whole field of artistic accomplishment is being built before our very eyes. Comic books appeared in the United States in the 1890s, and their so-called golden age—at least for those of the mainstream variety—took place between the 1930s and the 1950s. Now, in the twenty-first century, ethnic comics, and particularly their Latino components, are witnessing the arrival of their own golden age.

This is a book about storytelling by Latinos in comic books and comic strips. My exploration is divided into three sections. The first section offers a general view of the subject; the second details how Latino author-artists use and transcend the techniques of mainstream comics to reach the cognitive and emotional faculties of their reader-viewers. This second section looks at a variety of ways in which these author-artists use and fashion anew devices that allow reader-viewers to imagine in particular ways vibrant four-dimensional spaces from markings on a page. The third section prolongs this gesture by offering interviews that allow the artist-authors themselves to express their views on their trade, on their conceptions of the world and human life, on their working techniques, and on the ways they intend to engage their public. This is but the beginning in the texturing of a full and rich picture of Latino comic books—and their authors-artists and reader-viewers.

② SO MANY APPROACHES, SO LITTLE . . .

As has been done in studies of the novel, film, digital video art, and many other cultural phenomena, there has been a critical impulse in studies of comic books and comic strips to identify the uniqueness of these particular storytelling forms. One can follow any number of ways to assert such uniqueness.

One might choose to discuss how their techniques and forms differ from those of other storytelling media, such as films, paintings, and novels. Practitioner-theorists such as Will Eisner and Scott McCloud follow this path, giving primacy to the visual image in comic book storytelling; because the visual is more easily absorbed by the reader-viewer it is more important than the verbal. Yet others tip the balance in favor of the verbal. We see this in the privileging of the verbal over the visual in the work of scholars such as Charles Dierick and Pascal Lefèvre (*Forging a New Medium*), Mario Saraceni (*The Language of Comics*), and Bart Beaty (*Unpopular Culture*).[5] Only in the comic book does the reader infer and decode meaning from both the shape of the visual and shape of the verbal elements. And there are those like Charles Hatfield who give equal weight to the verbal and visual elements and note how their various interactions communicate ideas and meaning (see his *Alternative Comics*).

There are yet others more concerned with identifying a genealogy of comic books or comic strips, showing that one way or another, comics participate in either a verbal or visual narrative tradition that predates their widespread circulation in the late nineteenth and early twentieth centuries. For some, the comic book or comic strip is the last branch of a tree rooted in eighteenth-century illustrated books or in literature generally. Myla Goldberg, for example, speaks of the "electric feeling" when encountering the work of comic book author-artist Chris Ware, who pushes "the limits of his medium beyond established boundaries" ("Exquisite Strangeness," 205), much like the metafictional play seen in the work of Julio Cortázar, Italo Calvino, and John Barth. Thus Ware is not simply telling a story, he is "continually searching for ways to expand what a story is, what it means, and how it engages its reader" (207). And, there are those who take to task the kind of implicit assertion made by Goldberg: that there is a hierarchy and unidirectional flow from literature (from, for example, John Dos Passos) to a comic book or comic strip (to, say, Ware). Hence, a scholar like William Nericcio argues that the comic book–literature influence has always been bidirectional and a process of constant "cross-infiltration." His examples: Chilean author Ariel Dorfman, who is best known for his plays, essays, and longer fictional narratives, but whose early career included the writing of comic books—indeed, his novel *The Last Song of Manuel Sendero* uses freely the speech-balloon technique; the seamless flow between the political cartoons of Eduardo Galeano and his novel *Memory of Fire*; and Jaime Hernandez's self-reflexive comic book stories that extend and complicate a Latin American storytelling tradition. (See Nericcio's article "Artif(r)acture" as well as his book *Tex[t]-Mex: Seductive Hallucinations of the "Mexican" in America*.)

For yet others, the comic book form is the most recent incarnation of a painted medieval triptych. For example, David Carrier argues that narrative painting evolved "naturally" into the comic book, with its "employment of speech balloons and visual sequences" (*The Aesthetics of Comics*, 74). Robert C. Harvey also situates the comic within this "pictorial narrative" ("Describing and Discarding Comics," 21) tradition, but one in which its verbal and visual content are necessarily tied together in ways not seen in other art forms. In comics, he thus states, "words and pictures blend to achieve a meaning that neither conveys alone without the other" (19). Moreover, for Harvey, the possible tensions and harmonies at play in comic book verbal and visual "blends" ultimately free the art form from its next of kin's "doomed wordless posturing and pantomime" (22).

There is an implicit aim here and in other approaches to identify the uniqueness of comics in ways that uplift them from the proverbial storytelling gutter.[6] In this spirit, we see also those who consider comic books a way to understand physics and philosophy, among other fields of scientific and humanistic inquiry. In *The Physics of Superheroes*, James Kakalios describes how the physics employed in superhero comics can be used to teach others physics. He explains, for instance, how a pocket of air can form so that the Flash can breathe even while running at super speeds and why gravity must be fifteen times stronger on Krypton than on earth. I think also of the essays collected in *Comics as Philosophy* (edited by Jeff McLaughlin) and *Superheroes and Philosophy: Truth, Justice, and the Socratic Way* (edited by Tom Morris and Matt Morris). The essayists identify comic books as tools for understanding ethics, notions of truth, existence, and so on. In McLaughlin's collection, for example, transcendental categories of good and evil are complicated when Amy Kiste Nyberg returns us to 1954, when a Senate Subcommittee on Juvenile Delinquency was established to implement a censoring Comic Code. For Nyberg, this not only had an impact on the content and distribution of comic books, but also fundamentally altered how we might understand reality and truth, demonstrating that the "possible worlds" represented in comic books can be a powerful way of understanding reality. For Jeremy Barris, it is the unreality of the "cartoon-picture" that provides the reader with an "experience of the worth of the ideals that world presents" ("Plato, Spider-Man," 79). And when DC decided to bring five fictional worlds into collision and form only one new world to compete with our actual world, then the reader is reminded that superheroes "*are* real but not actual, because they are living lives in real possible worlds but not actual possible worlds" (11).

Before I get too far along, let me offer a couple of observations.

First, I think we are right to identify comic books and comic strips as unique kinds of storytelling forms that require the responsive shaping of a critical set of conceptual tools for analysis. This is why even developing the category "comic book" is useful. It identifies and distinguishes the originality of a medium that uses verbal and visual elements separately and together to tell the story. Jared Gardner remarks of Gilbert Hernandez's *Palomar* and Jaime Hernandez's *Locas*: "These are not novels, and were never meant to be. They offer complex and often brilliant commentary on the limitations of traditional novelistic narrative, particularly in terms of time and complex social spaces" ("Borders and Moments," 120). And by attending to the unique verbal and visual blends and centrifugal separations of comics, we can understand the function of its double narrator. I will discuss this more at length later, but for now, suffice it to say that the ways in which the visual narrator and verbal narrator work (in unison, contradiction, or tension) will engage the reader-viewer in vastly different ways.

By developing critical terms and tools, we can evaluate comic books on their own terms. They give us the tools to turn impressions into critical-evaluative schemas: they allow me to explain why I might gravitate toward a Milestone comic like *Blood Syndicate* rather than to DC's *El Diablo*, or to a strip by Lalo Alcaraz rather than to one by Garry Trudeau. They allow a scholar like Charles Hatfield to identify more specifically why he prefers those comics that push beyond "the limits of formula fiction" and plunge us "into piercingly frank self-examination and powerful sociopolitical argument" (*Alternative Comics*, 163). They allow us to identify how the visuals might play on conventions of realism, whereas the verbal elements address metafictional self-reflexivity; or to understand why too much self-reflexivity or too much verbal or too much visual might push us over cognitive thresholds and lead us to simply turn off. They allow us to understand better why we read some comics only once (those that rely on, say, only the element of suspense) and reread others (those that play with all sorts of elements, such as characterization, time, point of view, textual rhythm, panel pacing, inking, and so on).

Second, there is an overlap between the elements that make up comic books and comic strips as storytelling media and those of pictorial narratives, novels, and films, among others. And so when we develop critical tools for analyzing comic books, we might do well to borrow from advances made in understanding how other media work. For example, in film studies, new concepts were created and tools formed to account for the restrained use or absence of written text as well as the very present elements of sound, noise, and moving image. This said, comic books are not appendages or contemporary incarnations of these various cultural phenomena. In his interview, Javier Hernandez reminds us, "The comic book is its own coherent unit. Each panel has to be composed on its own, but at the same time, it interacts with the panel following it. [. . .] A comic book simply doesn't aspire to the same feeling as film."

This is to say, we can borrow useful concepts and tools, but at the end of the day, comics use different nuts and bolts to move the reader-viewer, and thus require us to develop our own particular set of wrenches and screwdrivers if we are to understand how they work and how they are made.

Third, comic books are neither pictorial narratives nor illustrated books. Books with images aimed at illustrating a text are a phenomenon that have existed since the Middle Ages, when there were all kinds of books being produced, especially on the lives of saints. Later, famed illustrator Gustave Doré put his hand to Dante's *commedia*, and illustrative work appeared in Rabelais's *Gargantua and Pantagruel* and Cervantes's *Don Quixote*, to mention but a few. Here, artwork appears in the pages between described actions; in the case of *Quixote*, the visuals even act to remind the reader of the difference between subjective and objective reality—that Quixote is attacking windmills and not the giants he imagines. In all such cases, the visuals function to illustrate the written narrative. This is to say, books with illustrations are not comic books. They are illustrated books or books with illustrations. As the Latino author-artists of comic books and comic strips make clear here, they are not illustrating novels or using novels to illustrate art. They are actively choosing to tell stories in the comic book or comic strip form—a form that offers them the unique possibility of engaging audiences and redirecting their perspective on reality through a particular interplay of verbal and visual elements.

Comic books and comic strips are relatively new storytelling media. We don't have to make any excuses here, nor try to fold in other visual and verbal art-form traditions. To understand how comic books may or may not provide us with the cognitive and emotive rewards of effectively conveyed worldviews, we must continue to refine and identify new concepts and terms for understanding how their ingredients can and cannot combine in ways that differ, say, from novels, films, or paintings.

Mimesis works differently in films, novels, paintings, and comics, and these different modes affect how we perceive what we imagine holographically as viewer-readers. Lastly, just as a comic book is not a novel, an illustrated book, a painting, or a film, it is not philosophy or scientific proof. While a comic book might deal with philosophical concepts, it is its own unique storytelling form. Trying to make comic books out to be anything but comic books "reeks of status anxiety and an over-earnest bidding for gentrification" (*Alternative Comics*, xii), as Charles Hatfield so pointedly expresses it.

There have been long-standing debates in the mainstream media and within academia about the value of studying certain cultural phenomena rather than others. This "good culture versus bad culture" debate plays itself out in many different ways. Besides fearing Robin and Batman, Dr. Wertham also deems Wonder Woman bad, for being "anti-masculinist" and lesbian (*Seduction of the Innocent*, 193), but finds Donald Duck (albeit without a gun) good (64). During the so-called culture wars of the 1980s, the flavor of the day for then–secretary of education William Bennett was Western canonical (good) versus "ethnic" noncanonical (bad) literature. Battling it out with the likes of Jesse Jackson, Bennett declared in so many words that opening the door to authors like Alice Walker and Toni Morrison would mark the end of Western civilization. Recently, this "good versus bad culture" dichotomy has appeared when the media blames video games, goth-rock (Marilyn Manson), or rap for social ills; for example, the artist Mars's song "Go Suicidal" was blamed as the cause of a Minnesota high school shooting in 2005.

While the debates will continue—and inevitably lead nowhere—what is true is that comic books have increasingly been moving off the cultural sidelines. This result is attributable to author-artists' pounding on publisher's doors, to capitalist profiteering, and to academic innovation. For example, in the twilight of the academic culture wars, we began to see in the academy a scholarly interest in comic books—along with other nontraditional visual-culture phenomena. With disciplinary borders and cultural hierarchies seemingly melting away, Shakespeare tomes and H. W. Janson's *History of Art* doorstoppers were being traded in for Alan Moore's *Watchmen*, Los Bros Hernandez's *Love and Rockets*, and Art Spiegelman's *Maus*.[7]

Today's media and academy reflect such shifts. The *New York Times* followed Chris Ware's comic series *Building Stories* with Jaime Hernandez's *La Maggie La Loca* (April 23, 2006–September 3, 2006). And we are seeing increasing numbers of dissertations filed on comics and such topics as masculinity, queer sexuality, gender, and globalization. (A random sample of dissertation titles includes "Read Junk! It's good For You," "Super Black Macho," "Globalizing Comics," and "Coming Out in Comics.") And more of those writing these dissertations are finding tenure-line spaces in humanities departments across the country. In response to demand, the University of Mississippi Press is dedicating a book series to scholarly monographs on comic books; and venues like *ImageTexT: Interdisciplinary Comic Studies*, published by the University of Florida, as well as special issues of journals such as *Modern Fiction Studies* and *MELUS* allow one to publish shorter scholarly work on comics. Professors like me can teach courses on American literature that focus almost exclusively on comics; others can teach courses titled, for example, Gutter Stories: Contemporary Graphic Novels. Money and space are given to preserving archives of comic books and comic strips, as at the Cartoon Research Library at Ohio State University. Symposia and conferences on comics—comics as literacy, comics as social justice, and comics as the future—abound.

With centers off-kilter and disciplinary straightjackets unbuckled, just as literature, film, and visual art could be mined for topical intellectual concerns, so too could comic books.[8] From Hergé's *Tintin* to Disney's Mickey Mouse, comic books and characters could be deciphered in ways that would reveal their participation in the construction of restrictive gender, racial, sexual, and ethnic ways of existing; they could reveal anything from capitalist imperialism to the affirmation of a resistant subjectivity; their tradition of depict-

ing women as dimensionless characters could be revealed as a commentary on patriarchal oppression, the creating of male-fantasy object, and the normalizing of a white masculinity.[9] (See Lillian S. Robinson, *Wonder Women: Feminisms and Superheroes*, and also Trina Robbins, *From Girls to Girrrlz* and *The Great Women Superheroes*.)

The rather idealistic claims aside, there is, of course, something to such critiques. Robbins and others do important work in recovering a "womyn's" comic book tradition that has been over-shadowed by a DC/Marvel male-oriented tradition. There has been a long tradition of representing women and people of color in derogatory and

Sheena 3-D Special, Issue 1

denigrating ways in comics. Consider some of those Editors Press Service (EPS) comics like Jerry Iger's Tarzan knockoff, *Sheena*. The blonde, blue-eyed, leggy superhero dressed to the nines in her leopard-print one-piece battles primeval monsters to save tribal peoples from harm: "Hail! Our leader bows humbly before the golden one who has returned from death. She shall be our queen and the treasure of the Taurs skull is hers" (issue 1, 12). Alongside *Sheena*, EPS would publish stories like *Jo-Jo, Congo King*, which featured a muscled white beefcake, also in leopard-print, who vanquishes villains like the evil Krang to save helpless and hapless others.

These are only two images from a massive canvas filled with simplistic and rather unpleasant representations, so it is not surprising that scholars have given energy to both its critique and also to excavating alternative comic-book traditions. Jeffrey Brown, in his book-length study *Black Superheroes, Milestone Comics, and Their Fans*, details the way an African American–run publisher like Milestone created racially and ethnically identified comic book superheroes who not only didn't need saving from a leopard-print-wearing blond, but were strong, smart, complex, and even contradictory.[10] Milestone comic series such as *Blood Syndicate*, *Hardware*, and *Static*, maintain the "fundamental conventions of comic book heroism at the same time that they expand the traditional definitions of the medium" (188). Positively valued ways of representing black masculinity ultimately provide readers with powerful ways, as Brown argues, "to negotiate their own lives" (2).

Along with African American excavations and critical studies on representation, there has been some scholarly attention paid to Latino comic books and comic strips and to their texturing of identities and experiences. In 1995, a special issue of the journal the *Americas Review*, titled "Cartooning and Other Graphic Arts," published essays and political and satirical comic strip art by Lalo Lopez, Alejandro Sánchez, and Jaime Crespo. In their introduction, Rosaura Sánchez and Beatrice Pita locate Latino visual art, cartoons, and comics as part of a Latin American (and Third World) tradition of "unmaking of dominant systems of representation" (7). They reflect on the Chicano murals of Ybarra-Frausto, the performance art of Asco, *fotonovelas*, 1960s-'70s *raza* art, as well as that of Mexican artists José Guadalupe Posada, José Clemente Orozco, and Rius, as part of the large portfolio that makes up a Latino counteraesthetic. Just as Rius uses his comic books to critique and satirize the Mexican bourgeoisie, so too do Chicanos like Oscar "The Oz" Madrigal in his strip *"Los Borrados": A Chicano Quest for Identity in a Post-Apocalyptic, Culturally Defunct Hispanic Utopia (a Reinterpretive Chicano Comic)*. Madrigal's comic strip (included in this special issue of the *Americas Review* and later in *Velvet Barrios*, edited by Alicia Gaspar de Alba) is an allegory of the United States today with its border patrols and political disenfranchisement of Latinos. It is set in 2039, just after the "Great Salsa Wars," when New Hispanica is formed and tyrannically led by the dictator Luna. The "malfunctioning" *cholo*, Jonathan Martinez, is a member of the resistance, Los Borrados; he ultimately takes down Luna.

Other scholars have chosen to approach Latino comics from the perspective of sexuality. Darieck Scott's article on Los Bros Hernandez that also appeared in this special issue of the *Americas Review* focuses on the fan mail responses to Jaime's bisexual and lesbian characters. Laura Laffrado focused on Erika Lopez's use of cartoon art and storyboard style layout in her novel

Hoochie Mama; for Laffrado, such hybridizing of forms is a self-reflexive gesture that signals an awareness of Lopez's own hybrid ethnic and sexual identity; it is Lopez's way of shaking up in form and content "social norms of fem-
ininity" ("Postings," 410) as well as affirming a more complex racial, sexual,
and gendered identity (426). And we can add to this Deanna Shoemaker, who
celebrates Deborah Kuetzpalin Vasquez's invention of the "unruly macha-
femme" Chicana superhero Citlali. Shoemaker reads this Chicana superhero's
rootedness in indigenous myth and cultural tradition, her English-Spanish-
Nahuatl code switching, "terroristic drag," and vocalized anger and rage as a
radical revision of the "white male-dominated spaces of comic book superheroes" ("Cartoon Transgressions," 5). She disrupts "signs of authority and
provokes fear and insurrection" (5). Accordingly, her code switchings force
English-only readers to engage with her culture on her terms. Given that
Vasquez paints Citlali on rough wood and cheap newsprint paper, she enacts
a form, as Shoemaker writes, of "guerrilla art" that does battle with the dominant colonizing culture. Its production and style speak to a feminist and
"mexla" (mixed-race) activism and resistance to neocolonialists and *"vendido*
cultural brokers who profit from stereotypes" (10) as well as to sexist Latinos
within the community.[11]

Other scholars have chosen to focus on issues of gender, race, ethnicity, and
sexuality in comics south of the tortilla curtain. I think of David William Foster's sociopolitical approach to Latin American comic books in *From Mafalda
to Los Supermachos* as well as Anne Rubenstein's *Bad Language*. Rubenstein
considers comic books part of a popular culture that includes *fotonovelas*, the
serialized satirical short stories known as *historietas*, and the comic strip *dom-
incales*, which offer a "politics-by-any-other-means" (165) within an oppressive Mexican administration. For Rubenstein, even though comic books are
produced within a capitalist system, that they are so easily available and read
by the masses in Mexico is evidence of their potential to shape (regressively
and progressively) the political landscape. For example, because comic books
like *Pepín* or *Los Super-locos* push at representational limits and offer up social
and political satire, they keep alive a revolutionary and "oppositional" spirit in
Mexico (165).

Comic books and comic strips, Latino or otherwise, circulate within a huge
moneymaking industry dominated by U.S. capitalists who manipulate and
artificially create (with the help of appendages like newspapers, magazines,
even big-name prizes like the Pulitzer) audiences and target markets to maximize profits. Notwithstanding the exploitation and oppression of capital-

ism, there are some beneficial side effects. In capitalism, as Marx noticed in the nineteenth century, the drive to profit requires producers to identify and make products that will sell to larger and larger numbers of consumers. Once sniffed out as a potential profit-making object, even the most radically independent and alternative comic book will receive wide marketing and distribution attention. So Art Spiegelman's hard-hitting *Maus* and Eric Drooker's controversial wordless comic *Flood!* suddenly move into high-gear production runs when they pick up big awards like the Pulitzer Prize or the American Book Award. The radically alternative and unconventional becomes a meal ticket in the capitalist marketplace. Moreover, once the profit-making object is identified, then there is no need to spend money diversifying—at least until such comic books fail to turn a profit. I suspect this is why even some of the most independent and alternative comics can feel repetitive: black and white, autobiographical, or day-in-the-life-ish with characters who experience subtle (if any) epiphanies.

To a much lesser degree, of course, we see this play out with, say, Los Bros Hernandez's *Love and Rockets*; its profits mean that until it flags in the marketplace, it will take the spot of dozens of other Latino comic books. This is not Los Bros Hernandez's doing. It is simply the way capitalism works. And we see this at work in DC's funding of Milestone. While funded under the umbrella of DC Comics, and therefore required to share its profits, Milestone retained total creative control and copyrights for characters. Of course, DC's investment in Milestone also meant an expectation of profitable returns. It wasn't the quality of the Milestone issues like *Blood Syndicate*, *Xombi*, *Shadow Cabinet*, *Kobalt*, *Icon*, and *Static* that led to its closure, but its failure to meet quarterly dollar gains. An epigraph to issue 35 of *Blood Syndicate* reads: "The current comics market is beginning to resemble the economic situation in Paris Island: There's an abundance of talented people ready to accomplish great things, but where there used to be an infrastructure, there's only hope" (31).

Capitalism works in this constant open-close motion: diversify for profit, then reductively single out. And Latino comic books circulate within a system in which the push for diversity is ultimately only a push to identify the profitable; once the profitable product is obtained, all others fall by the wayside.

Latino comic books or comic strips do not exist in a vacuum. They are made by authors who work, eat, live, and breathe in a world dominated by capitalism. Whether or not the author-artist creates a so-identified politically resistant story, and whether or not they can make a living out of their craft, at the end of the day they all exist within this economic system. There is no way around the fact that all those interviewed here create a "product" (in Carlos

Saldaña's words) with the aim of selling to a wide audience of readers. There is no getting around the fact that I can pull at random a comic book off my shelf and see that while it might be U.S. Latino made, it was produced by cheaper laboring hands in China.

That Los Bros Hernandez, Javier Hernandez, Laura Molina, Richard Dominguez, Peter Ramirez, Frank Espinosa, and many others interviewed here, exist in a capitalist world economy doesn't mean that they should cease writing and drawing; nor does it in any way mean that they should stop publishing their work and wishing for larger distributions and more readers. Because Ivan Velez Jr. can't make a living writing and drawing *Tales of the Closet*, he must devote great amounts of time and energy to a nine-to-five job. And while Peter Ramirez speaks of the disability check that subsidizes his income, and gives him more time to work on *Raising Hector*, he too wishes that he could make a living from the strip. Anthony Oropeza dreams of one day being able to support himself and his child by not working a day job for the forestry department, but rather by drawing and writing *Amigoman*. And while Javier Hernandez has made giant leaps forward from 1998 when he first produced a photocopied and stapled issue of *El Muerto*—it has now been made into a movie directed by Brian Cox and starring Wilmer Valderrama as El Muerto—he still has to hold down a day job. While the remarkably low production cost

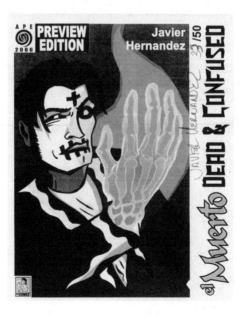

El Muerto Dead and Confused, Preview Edition

of comics allows these artists to be able to fulfill their vision—much more difficult in film—they still have to be able to sustain themselves in a capitalist economy. So they work day jobs to support their craft.

And these Latino author-artists should have the choice to tell whatever kinds of stories they want, including, if they choose, to critique corporate greed and the capitalist way. Among the many villainous characters that Richard Dominguez's community-oriented Latino superhero, El Gato Negro, battles and vanquishes is El Graduado, the eventual heir of the exploitative Val-Tex. And Steve Ross is free to invent a story that complicates the "community versus corporate" opposition; although his eponymous Latina superhero, Chesty Sanchez, brings down villains who profit from biochemical weapon sales, we discover that she works for a corporate-run outfit called the Frijoles del Oro Company. In *Ultra*, the Luna Brothers invent superheroes like Pearl and Liv, who fly around saving the people of Spring City, but who worry about their public poll ratings, appear on billboards selling cigarettes, and receive paychecks from Heroine, Inc. and Olympus, Inc.—corporate capitalist powerhouses in their world. Gilbert Hernandez can choose to invent whatever type of character he wants: in his *Palomar* series, he creates the gringo character, Howard Miller, who arrives in Palomar with his camera in tow to capture images of the "primitive" Other, à la *National Geographic*;[12] in *Sloth*, he creates the teenagers Miguel, Lita, and Romeo, who identify more as angst-filled adolescents living in anywhere suburbia than as Latinos. The plot, along with Hernandez's sparse background visual detail and stark black-and-white con-

Palomar: The Heartbreak Soup Stories

Burrito: Jack of All Trades, Issue 1

trasts, emphasizes how, as Tom Crippen writes, "these teens remain a bit tied down to broad, familiar mannerisms, because in terms of story they never can quite escape themselves" ("Sauntering through," 100).

Perhaps, then, it is not so much excavating for how a given comic book resists capitalism, imperialism, or patriarchal oppression, but rather how it might choose to represent and reframe all aspects of our everyday world.[13] Nothing is alien to narrative fiction, comic books included. Because Latino comic books are free to incorporate any and all elements of our world—including even Carlos Saldaña's invention of a burrito (little donkey) as his serape-wearing crusader—we should be open to how they tell stories that speak to and represent all varieties of other phenomena. So we might find references, as in Gilbert Hernandez's *Palomar,* to *One Hundred Years of Solitude,* Mexican wrestlers, Bruce Lee, Jerry Lewis, Aztec myth, and Sophia Loren. Latino comic book author-artists can choose to incorporate, reframe and complicate our engagement with all cultural phenomena. And very often such references not only particularize but also comment on the general. Among many themes and issues covered in the *Palomar* series there is a sense of how its characters, living in a very remote village, experience the negative and positive side effects of global capitalism: Hong Kong's Bruce Lee films are screened at the village cinema, and the book-worm character Heraclio gets his hands on all sorts of

Chance in Hell

world literature. Gilbert Hernandez's *Chance in Hell* tells the coming-of-age story of Empress—a young girl abandoned along with other forgotten ones in a dump at the edge of an unnamed city. About to go to sleep in the middle of the dump, a boy turns to Empress, drawn tucked in under a blanket with a raggedy doll: "I'll take care of you, Empress. Nobody'll rape you no more" (14). As we follow her coming of age, it is her movement out of the dump and through various parts of the city—from apartment to street to brothel to upper-middle-class beach house—that particularizes the degenerative state of existence under capitalism.

There are author-artists who choose to create stories that are more socially critical (Alcaraz's *La Cucaracha* and Molina's *The Jaguar*, say), just as there are those who choose mostly to entertain (Saldaña's *Burrito* and Alvarez's *Yenny*, say). Lalo Alcaraz readily identifies his allegiance, dedicating *La Cucaracha* to "Gus Arriola, Sergio Aragonés, Rius, Los Hernandez Bros, Quino, and all the unsung *cartoonistas* in Latin America." But he also announces an affiliation with a tradition of metafictional play.[14] Author-artists can choose to use Homer's *Odyssey* as a story substructure, as with Espinosa's *Rocketo*, or Bernal Díaz's chronicles of pre-Columbian Mexico as with Montijo's *Pablo's Inferno*. There are also those comics that are easily consumed—and even used to sell products, like the appearance of the Perry Ellis comic strip (www.perryellis. com.) Comic books have the capacity to open readers' eyes to social injustice, but they also have the power simply to make us imagine running at the speed of light, battling foes, and laughing uproariously.[15] It is important for us to keep centrally in mind the idea that nothing is off-limits to Latino comic book author-artists.

Scholarly approaches to the study of Latino comic books can reveal how a given comic might challenge dominant social, sexual, and cultural codes of conduct. They might even help identify how a capitalist world economic system determines who is published and where the comic books are distributed and received—which voices are heard. And Latino comic books can certainly move people to act: to laugh or cry or get angry. Perhaps we would do well to heed Trina Robbins's caution: to not overly "exaggerate their importance in either reflecting or shaping our culture" (*The Great Women Superheroes*, 7).

If we lean too heavily on arguments of influence—the ultimate being that comic books are themselves sites of political resistance—we fail to account for how the comic book author-artists distill (systematically eliminate that which is redundant or dispensable) then distort and exaggerate in ways that create pleasing effects for their reader-viewers' brains. As Martin Barker soberly declares, "Just because a witch-doctor appears, it does not mean he can be directly related to the mythical witch-doctor of racist legend; he is a witch-doctor within the transforming laws and structure of [the comics]. Therefore he can 'reinforce' nothing" (*Comics*, 127).

CONCERNED COMICS

As already mentioned, there has been a long-standing debate about just how much cultural phenomena influence behavior; how much they can construct subjectivity; how much they can alter reality; how much they can even create a nation. As we have seen with other cultural-studies investigations, approaches that gravitate around the influence of comic books move back and forth between asserting that they do or do not shape and move us to think and act. One way or another, this has lead to ethical concerns. If they do move us to think and act, then shouldn't we promote certain comic book stories over others? This is most clearly seen in Fredric Wertham's *Seduction of the Innocent* (1954), which identified comic books as sources of increased teen suicide, queer sexuality, and procommunist sentiment; the study led to the establishment of a self-censoring machine—there would be no more Batman or Robin, sexual innuendo, scantily clad women, or violence under the 1950s Comics Code.

However, we see this also in one form or another in scholarly discussions and fan-mail responses, or when a Latino author-artist like Richard Dominguez declares an urgent need for the circulation of positive Latino role models. On the back jacket of *Team Tejas* appears a description of El Gato Negro: he "gives us something badly needed in the comics world: a real super-hero of Hispanic origin. Not a thug. Not a drug dealer. Not a terrorist. An honest-to-God role model" (issue 1). Likewise, Anthony Oropeza announces on the inside back cover of *Amigoman: The Latin Avenger* (issue 1) that he hopes his "artwork and characters will hopefully entertain," but intends his story to "touch issues our society faces on a daily basis and still tell the story of Antonio Alvarado and his alter ego, Amigoman. You might see issues on crime, school dropouts, drugs, teen pregnancy, war, gangs, homelessness, racism, and many more issues that face our communities that those like Señorita Sin, Mad Mex, Ed Ex, DJ Kill or anybody else may bring about to the city of Del Oro."

Latino comic books tell us big and small things about the world; they can show us that Latinos aren't all dark, stubble-chinned, heavily accented, wicked evildoers. And they do so by relying on certain identifiable traits and iconographic types; if this were not so, each would require, as Philip Sills rightfully

El Gato Negro: Nocturnal Warrior, Issue 1

points out, "paragraphs of text and much more detailed drawings to transmit information" ("Illusions," 59). If, say, certain types of gestures were not used, we would not be able to infer the interior states of the characters. But of course, when only one or two traits or types are represented—good or bad—then the characters become more superficial and less interesting; this flattens out and makes monotonous the representational landscape.[16] This is to say, there are comic books that simplify and those that complicate different aspects of our identities and experiences, but they ultimately rely on certain recognizable types. Of course, these types can be played with in ways that allow, for example, the visual and the verbal elements to undermine stereotypes; in the work of the many Latino author-artists discussed here, we see how they use identifiable types—even if simply round faces instead of triangular ones—to more interestingly engage reader-viewers and to complicate our evaluation of their character's actions in complex worlds.

④ THE GOOD, BAD, AND . . . BEAUTIFUL

Latino comic book author-artists can complicate characters and their storyworlds in how they present values—in how a character's individual values conflict or align with those of the collective, for example. Rafael Navarro invests his eponymous character Sonambulo with a certain 1950s machismo that rubs up against the values of the twenty-first century. At the same time, the complexity of such a character as Sonambulo (who betrays his own bitterness over not being college educated) increases the reader's evaluative engagement: we are sometimes with him and sometimes against him. And Gilbert Hernandez creates certain tensions in *Palomar* between the narrator—whereby, for example, we see an implicit critique of a racist, heterosexist, queer-phobic world— and Latino characters who themselves uncritically perpetuate prejudice. We see a like confusion and tension in the noir-driven *100 Bullets*: Brian Azzarello and Eduardo Risso foreground a strong and smart Latina (issue 1) living in an urban dystopia where the line between good and bad action, immoral and moral obligation, is completely gone. Dizzy Cordova does the job of the "Five-Ohs," avenging her family by using the 100 untraceable bullets to shoot down local gangbangers, her brother Emilio included. Here, Dizzy's will to avenge clashes with the sense of her responsibility to family and society—a conflict that is never fully resolved.

The comic book can of course provide more or less readable moral and ethical compasses. For instance, in issue 17 of *Blood Syndicate*, Velez takes the opportunity to critique history textbooks that glorify Columbus and denigrate native New Worlders. And while told in a lighter comedic form, Bobby Rubio's *Alcatraz High* follows the adventures of Chicano teen Miguel Castillo and his constant negotiation of a society of surveillance: force-field fences, laser-barred classrooms, security robots, sweep drones and their entrapment webs; here the narrator pauses to make sure we know that we are to align ourselves not with the adult world of high-tech surveillance, but rather with rebellion and ancient myth and tradition. In Carlos Saldaña's *Burrito: Jack-of-All-Trades*, he chooses as his protagonist a quick-witted and strong burro (good) to reschematize preconceptions of Mexicans as slow and lethargic

Burrito: Jack of All Trades, Issue 1

(bad). Quick of feet and mind as well as richly imaginative, the Chicano Burrito stands in sharp contrast to a California that polices the movement of brown bodies and delimits the dreams of Latinos. Fernando Rodriguez's *Aztec of the City* makes sure that the reader understands the social consequences of ignoring the homeless issue as well as the evils of U.S. border patrols, Texas-Arizona minutemen, and coyotes (smugglers) who exploit the innocent.

Laura Molina's *Cihualyaomiquiz, the Jaguar* also lands us squarely on the U.S.-Mexico border issue, opening her story with a panel depicting a *Los Angeles Times* headline reading, "Wilson Re-Elected 187 Passes" (issue 1, 1). As the story unfolds, we see how anti-immigration laws (such as Proposition 187) turn California into a land filled with xenophobic vigilantes. Linda Rivera is by

Cihualyaomiquiz, the Jaguar, Issue 1

Cihualyaomiquiz, the Jaguar, Issue 1

day a law student and by night a superhero warrior known as the Jaguar, who does her bit to fight racism in the community when she kicks some neo-Nazi butt: "Viva la raza! Nazi punks, see ya later" (issue 1, 9).

Yet others seek to texture good and bad within a mythological story space. For instance, in Rhode Montijo's *Pablo's Inferno*, the narrative asks the reader-viewer to align herself with the innocent child protagonist, Pablo, and learn through his eyes and ears of the evils of the Euro-Spanish genocide and conquest of the Americas. Offering an alternative, insider perspective of the conquest, Montijo's character Quetzal informs Pablo, "Most of the knowledge we have of the Aztecs was learned from books of those who came to conquer us" (86). Then Quetzal announces, "I am the last link to our past. I am writing so that our history will live on" (153).

Pablo's Inferno

Others, like Wilfred Santiago and Ivan Velez Jr., choose to convey and complicate the reader's ethical engagement by their use of social realism. In Velez's *Tales of the Closet*, we follow the story of a handful of gay teen characters and their everyday struggles in and out of school. Here the reader enters a world where teenagers are made to feel bad about being queer; we experience the pains of their closeted life as well as the very real pain of their physical victimization. *Tales of the Closet* crescendos with the juxtaposition of the main character, Tony, recently orphaned and hustling his body on the street, with a violent scene of gay bashing and the murder of his friend Imelda. Careful not to put those like Tony and Imelda up on the martyr pedestal (good), Velez makes it clear that this is not so much the "tragic downfall" of one or two characters in his story, but an everyday occurrence for a regular "bunch of kids with nothing in common but their fears and hopes and growing love for each other" (*Tales of the Closet: Volume 1*, 95). And, finally, while there is a certain affirmation of teen-gay coalition building in the story— Tony, Imelda, and a handful of others discover their common closeted experience—Velez reminds us that such a sense of solidarity (good) versus a threatening homophobic world (bad) is fictional: the "gay world" outside *Tales of the Closet* "isn't as accepting as one might think" (95). And in Santiago's social-realist *In My Darkest Hour*, the protagonist, Omar Guerrero, struggles to keep his sense of well-being in an alienating, consumer-driven society. In this capitalist world, one eats, works, sleeps, and pops pills. The story pauses, and Santiago introduces a splash page with a portrayal of an obese amputee with breasts stitched on and a crucified Jesus hanging in the crotch. Santiago leaves little for the reader to wonder about what we are to identify as bad.

And Lalo Alcaraz chooses social satire as his preferred form for conveying values, as in his collection of strips *Migra Mouse: Political Cartoons on Immigration* (originally published in the *LA Weekly* between 1992 and 2004), a no-holds-barred critique of many of the issues that Latinos face in today's United States, including Operation Gatekeeper and other militarizing responses to border and immigration issues. He also takes shots at mainstreamed Latinos such as English-only proponent Richard Rodriguez as well as archconservative and former Reagan official Linda Chavez. In his introduction, he writes,

> Immigration is a powerful force which also brings much friction and conflict. I have tried to explore these contradictions in this cartoon collection through critical analysis and satire. [. . .] I hope readers can take the cartoons in this collection and use them to educate themselves or others on the immigration issue. Bilingualism and biculturalism are elements in many of these cartoons, certainly topics worthy of study. Perhaps readers can explore the attitudes and emotions that many in the Latino community felt over the last decade, as expressed through my work. (9)

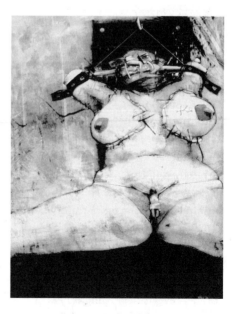

Tales of the Closet, Volume 1   *In My Darkest Hour*

Migra Mouse: Political Cartoons on Immigration

Alcaraz, however, also complicates the representational map; for instance, he pokes fun at Latinos in the strip "How to Spot a Mexican Dad," which depicts a tattooed Chicano drinking a beer and eating stale chicharrones in a La-Z-Boy (22).

The comic book's visual narrator and verbal narrator can work in tension or harmony, but their individual parts are taken up by the reader as a whole; this double narrator, along with the character narrator, can work to convey an ethically conflicted storyworld. In the case of more individual-focused comics like Dominguez's *El Gato Negro*, we see a strong resemblance between the verbal narrator's first-person voice and that of the character narrator; even though there is still a felt difference in the distance of the "I" narrating—the voice in the story and the voice outside—the author's purpose and that of the narrative would appear to coincide. Conversely, in Gilbert Hernandez's *Palomar*, we see a lot of play among the storytellings of the verbal narrator, visual narrator, and character narrator; extended flashbacks focalized through the character's framing of the world conflict with that of the verbal and visual narrators' telling, not only unseating the reader (we no longer have a reliable sense of story events) but also communicating a different ethical perspective. For example, our overhearing and overviewing of the character narration of Carmen reveals her telling others of her ultraconservatism, which conflicts with the more liberal verbal and visual telling of the narrator.

Others, like Rhode Montijo, contrast narration with what a character tells another character in order to communicate several worldviews to multiple audiences. For example, in *Pablo's Inferno*, when Quetzal tells another character, the Rain God, about the Toltecs' wearing of butterflies, he is relaying information that would already be known to the Rain God, given that he wears a butterfly and is Toltec. That is, this is superfluous information within the storyworld. Quetzal, as the character telling the story to another character, the Rain God, is telling this character something that he already knows. However, it is implied that the reader doesn't know about Toltec beliefs. Accordingly, in this brief intrusion, the reader of *Pablo's Inferno* can know only what the author-artist is telling him or her through the character narrator. That is, the

Pablo's Inferno

author-artist of *Pablo's Inferno* conveys a worldview (an ethical position, even) via the character narrator's telling of information that another character would already know, but that is essential for the ideal reader-viewer to overhear in order to understand the story's worldview—one that conflicts with that of the overall narration, which conveys a more twisted and gnarled landscape of good and bad. We see this art of indirection in many Latino comic books, including Steve Ross's *Chesty Sanchez*, in which he often has the eponymous character discuss in detail with her sidekick, Torpedo, something that Torpedo would clearly already know because of shared cultural experience.

Of course, this split between narration and what a character tells another character is a completely constructed narrative device. But it is necessary in the comic book world because it allows the author to convey certain informa-

Rocketo Vol. 1: The Journey to the Hidden Sea

tion via a character-narrator as opposed to the narrator present in the caption box. In *Rocketo*, this is the moment when we get that strong sense of the difference or uniformity between the worldview of the character and that of the narrator. Frank Espinosa chooses both a third-person omniscient narrator and a character narrator, and his choices lead us to feel more directly a storytelling purpose when his character narrator tells the story than when his third-person narrator does. But this is always a choice, and is not limited to this type of narrative configuration. We can know the story through the first-person limited or the omniscient narrator's visual and verbal narrative, or through a character narrator, or through an infinite combination of these narrator positions. It is also important to keep in mind here that the purpose of the author-artist is not only to tell a story, but also to make the telling engaging. It is the rhetorical power of Hernandez or Montijo or Ross that allows us to swallow something rather unbelievable (unnatural), as when the character narrator tells the story to another character who shares the same experience or is already in the know.

It is absolutely true that a narrator and a character narrator can convey different or similar values, and it is important to be able to identify those structures in a comic book narrative that allow for the conveying of values. Ultimately, however, the reader's range of experience can lead him or her in any direction. Those with their own set of political and ethical preferences might read *Chesty Sanchez* completely differently from me or from the narrative's narratorial signposts; they might read it as a positive example of the individualistic ambition to climb the social ladder and change one's social status at all costs—without seeing that Chesty is selfless and community oriented. Someone might read *Pablo's Inferno* as being only about death and destruction and miss out on its life-affirming values. Or someone might come down hard on the violence in Navarro's *Sonambulo* and yet generally not talk about how unethical or immoral it is to kill thousands of children, women, and men in Iraq.

So while Velez, Alcaraz, Montijo, Molina, Saldaña, Risso, or Dominguez might guide the reader to evaluate their worlds in particular ways, the reader of course has the last say. We may or may not follow the author-artists' ethical signposts. For example, many Latino readers didn't respond well to Alcaraz's poking fun at Latinos. There were also those readers who responded to his strips with things like the following: "'To you and people like you, I say, get the f*** out of this country if you don't like it here. Go back to Mexico, or Africa, or wherever the F***. Don't let me, the f****** honkey, hold you back from leaving'—J.B., Phoenix, Arizona" (jacket cover). And another reads: "You advance my cause. I want the entire country to see how you filthy *mestizo* animals feel about your superior White Masters. Your cartoons are pathetic, but what can you expect from a filthy illiterate Mexican?" (jacket cover). Clearly, Alcaraz chose to put these misreadings on the jacket cover to show how racism can prevent a reader from recognizing a narrative blueprint that uses devices and signposts to satirize contemporary society as well as to poke fun at identity politics generally.

 ## MAINSTREAMED COMPADRES

The Latino comic book and comic strip author-artists interviewed here speak of a variety of cultural influences: film, literature, music, mythology, alternative comic books, and so on. Most don't recall any childhood awareness of the absence of Latinos in comic books. Many simply enjoyed the other worlds the mainstream comics presented; many considered such mainstream characters, settings, and adventures to be escapes from their very real and ragged everyday environs. Not surprisingly, such first encounters with a DC or Marvel superhero acted as formative impulses and initial influences in their work.

Without a doubt, few Latino superheroes were saving the day. However, there was a (minor) presence of African American superheroes—some more interesting than others, and some more subtly present than others.[17] Not surprisingly, the mid-1960s civil rights era saw the arrival of an African protagonist: Stan Lee and Jack Kirby introduced the Black Panther in *Fantastic Four* (volume 1, issue 52, 1966). He reappeared more consistently in the series *Jungle Action* (volume 2, issues 5–24, 1973–1976), and was finally given his own eponymously titled series in 1977; in the latter, we see a character of color not just providing background filler or an easily outwitted nemesis, but rather the central protagonist and generator of the story. In 1969, Stan Lee and Gene Colan introduced in Marvel's *Captain America* series (volume 1, issue 117) the African American character Sam "Snap" Wilson—a Harlem street thug turned superhero, the Falcon. At Marvel in 1972, Archie Goodwin and John Romita, Sr., introduced a comic book that center-staged an African American character: Carl Lucas in *Luke Cage, Hero for Hire* (issue 1). In 1975, Len Wein and Dave Cockrum introduced a female African American superhero, Storm, to the Marvel universe in *Giant-Size X-Men #1*. Marvel's *X-Men* titles notably introduced several other African American mutant characters, including Lucas Bishop and Everett Thomas (Synch).

Whether social worker, gangbanger, or African prince, several of these Other-identified characters lacked psychological complexity; and while Luke Cage had a fourteen-year run in his own title, most had less time on their clock. That is, until the arrival of other comic book publishers in the 1990s. Milestone comics, founded in 1993 by African American artists and authors with the goal of diversifying the superheroes terrain, had a more extended and extensive portrayal of African Americans in its various series. I have already mentioned *Blood Syndicate*, but there was also *Icon*. An alien starship jettisons a life pod that crashes in the Deep South in 1839; the infant is raised by the slave character Miriam to become Icon—a superhero who becomes a leader for the "Downtrodden" (issue 1, 31). Milestone's *Static* follows the story of a fifteen-year-old working-class geek, Virgil Hawkins, who transforms into a charismatic wiseguy superhero. There is also Big City Comics, which published *Brotherman*, and Image Comics, which published Todd McFarlane's *Spawn*—a comic book whose protagonist is a former CIA agent (a special ops soldier) who returns to life as an agent of hell. It is less his phenotype—his flesh is literally seared off—than his background story that identifies him as African American.

If there is a yawning gap in the representations of African American superheroes in comics, there is an even larger one when it comes to Latinos, Native Americans, Asian Americans, and other nonwhites. A quick glance at the 1,500 entries in *The World Encyclopedia of Comics* (revised) reveals such a scarcity. As already mentioned, there are many factors that determine whether conglomerates like DC or Marvel will try out nonwhite superhero characters and why, once introduced, they don't seem to last; among many other factors, this can be partly due to consumer demographics and demand, the hiring of author-artists who create one-dimensional characters, the type of editor assigned to a title, and the vision of a comic book publisher. The bottom line: while Latinos, Native Americans, and Asians had filled in the background of white-adventurer and cowboy comics since the 1930s and 1940s (I think of Rodrigo "Rod" Elwood Gaynor, who dresses up in mariachi outfits and speaks a heavily accented Spanglish as the Whip in DC's *Flash Comics*, for example), it was not until the 1970s that such ethnic-identified figures began to appear somewhat on their own.[18] Several such superheroes are still with us, like the Japanese Sunfire (*X-Men* [volume 1, issue 64]) and Warpath (*New Mutants*, issue 16). Others, like Warpath's brother, Thunderbird (*Giant-Size X-Men*, issue 1), and Red Wolf (*Avengers*, [volume 1, issue 80]), are no longer around.

⑥ SLIPSTREAMED LATINOS

In 1977, the Latino superhero El Dorado was introduced on the television show *Super Friends*—a show based on DC's *Justice League of America*. Named after the mythical city of gold, El Dorado sports an Aztec solar calendar on his chest, speaks in a heavily accented Spanglish, and acts as a south-of-the-border tour guide for his Anglo team of Super Friends. In 1975, Marvel introduced its first Latino superhero, Hector Ayala, the White Tiger, in a story by Bill Mantlo and George Perez that appeared in *Deadly Hands of Kung-Fu* (issue 19). In 1979, Marvel's introduction of an urban crime fighter, the criollo swashbuckler Alejandro Montoya as El Águila (the Eagle), didn't much improve the representation of Latinos (*Power Man and Iron Fist*, issue 58).

In 1981, Marvel introduced to the series *The Incredible Hulk* (volume 2, issue 265) a north-of-the-border Latina superhero, the devoutly Catholic social worker Bonita Juarez, known as Firebird, in a story by Bill Mantlo and Sal Buscema. The readers learn via an interior monologue that she acquired her superpowers when struck by a fireball that dropped from "the heavens" (issue 265, 6). Catholic through and through, she considers her power, sent from God, a "force for good" (6). The story unfolds in various parts of the Southwest and follows the rescue of the all-Anglo Teen Brigade, which is being held hostage by the Corruptor in a secret lab hidden under an old Spanish mission. Rescuing at-risk youth in her hometown, Buenavista—"an optimistic name for a dirt-poor Mexican American village on the outskirts of Albuquerque, New Mexico" (5)—Firebird transforms into "a great blazing bird-form"(6) to help save the day. Juarez as Firebird and Will Talltrees as Red Wolf (fully

The Incredible Hulk, Volume 2, Issue 265

The Incredible Hulk, Volume 2, Issue 265

Justice League of America, Volume 1, Issue 233

tapped into his lupine spirit power) are outwitted and outperformed when the Anglo superheroes Night Rider, Texas Twister, and Shooting Star arrive on the scene; Firebird and Red Wolf are referred to here as "the Mex-Chick"(16) and "Redskin" (14) and are asked to stand aside while Night Rider and the others rescue their Anglo team members.

Latino representations didn't much improve in later DC lines. In the mid-1980s, after a first appearance in DC's *Justice League of America* (annual issue 2, 1984) by Gerry Conway and Chuck Patton, Paco Ramone as Vibe—a Puerto Rican gang leader turned break-dancer extraordinaire—appeared more regularly in the series. On the cover of the first regular issue of *Justice League of America* in which he appeared (volume 1, issue 233, 1984), he is dressed to the nines in break-dancing regalia: baggy yellow pants, a *V* lettered vest top, a red bandanna around his neck, green gloves, and yellow wraparound sunglasses. For that finishing ethnic touch, he sports a "soul patch" and is colored a slight shade of brown. Splashed across the cover: "He's going to *shake things up!*"

Justice League of America, Volume 1, Issue 233

Set in Detroit, the story begins with Vibe snapping his fingers and moving his feet to a "Do-Da-DA-Do" rhythm. The narrator announces: "They call him Vibe. He's special" (2). After an African American villain, Crowbar, calls him a greaseball, Vibe responds: "Whatchu think chu *doin*" (8). Vibe's ability to control a "single vibration wave—a pulse of energy like a one-man earthquake" (11) overpowers Crowbar and other villains he encounters—at least until he is strangled to death by Professor Ivo (volume 1, issue 258).

In 1987, DC buried Vibe. In 1988, it introduced readers to a team of immortals called the Chosen as part of the series *Millennium*, by Steve Englehart and Joe Staton. Recruited to "advance the human race" (issue 1, 4), the team includes, among others, an Australian aboriginal woman, Betty Clawman; a Maoist from mainland China, Xiang Po; an Inuit, Tom Kalmaku; an Afro-Caribbean Brit, Celia Windward; and Gregorio de la Vega, born and raised Peruvian. The story conveys an explicit critique of U.S. imperialism, and the characters are for the most part interestingly fleshed out. On one occasion, Celia remarks, "What futures *dat, mon*? No future 'roun' *here!* Jus' waitin' for

Millennium, Issue 1

da end oo' da *world*, mon—cmin' any day, day way bloody America carries on!" (issue 1, 16). However, when it comes to Gregorio de la Vega, known as Extraño (Stranger), much is to be desired. He is presented as a limp-wristed Latino who speaks in truncated half sentences, refers to his team members as "Honey," and is more concerned with color coordina-

Millennium, Issue 1

tion than with using his superpower—illusionism—to fight Western imperialism. De la Vega doesn't last long; he is bitten by the villain Hemo-Goblin, contracts HIV, and soon dies.[19]

In 1989, DC tried the Latino superhero once again with the introduction of Rafael Sandoval as El Diablo in his own self-titled comic. There was an attempt on the part of writer Gerard Jones to root him in the community as a public defender in Dos Rios, Texas (other community-based roles like that of social worker are reserved for Latinas like Bonita Juarez). As a public defender, he moves easily between different social scenes: he hobnobs with

El Diablo, Issue 1

the wealthy elite in Standard English, and on the streets he code switches: *órale*, *vato*, and *ese* easily fall from his tongue, for example. Like Bonita Juarez, he too is connected to the Catholic Church; he was trained by Father Guzman to avenge the poor. On one occasion, he confronts a big capitalist, the owner of Muhlbach Imports, for "lying to the artesanos about the resale of their work" and for "supporting non-union factories in the guise of cottage industries" (issue 1, 17).

El Diablo, Issue 1

However, that he is both hot-tempered and lusty for the blonde, blue-eyed, and leggy Virginia triggers all sorts of clichéd stereotypes. His brown tint does little to offset his chiseled, Caucasian-superhero features. And the visuals that describe a southwestern landscape—cactus, brown dusty roads, and adobe buildings aplenty—fall short in a world full of taquerias, jails, and check-cashing buildings. It doesn't help that other Latino characters who appear, like the arch-villain El Eskeleto's love interest, Yolanda Ybarra, speak with heavy accents. When she first meets El Diablo she says, "nice to mee-tchoo" (31). Finally, there is a certain conservative element to El Diablo's waxing nostalgic about bygone times when kids could play in parks without being accosted by drug dealers and the homeless. That is, as much as he acts in the present to vanquish crime, there is a certain conservative inflection to his yearning for the days when people knew their place in the socioeconomic hierarchy. Regardless of political sensibility, *El Diablo* only made it to issue sixteen before being canned.

The hot-tempered Latin lover (El Diablo) or selfless Latina (Firebird) gave way to more of the barrio-born gangbanger type in the 1990s. In the series *Avengers West Coast* (by Roy Thomas, Dann Thomas, and Paul Ryan), for instance, we see the appearance of Miguel Santos as Living Lightning (issue 63, 1990). He is born and raised in East LA, comes into his super power (he wears a containment suit that allows him to control electrical energy and hurl lightning bolts), attempts to avenge his father's death, breaks his bonds of enslavement to Doctor Demonicus, and returns to East LA to help his family: his brother, José, has joined a street gang, the Jaguars, and his sister Lisa is murdered by a rival gang, the Snakes. Living Lightning is later revealed to be gay. And in 1994, Scott Lobdell and Joe Madureira introduced in their *Uncanny X-Men* (issue 317) the smooth-talking car-thieving Angelo Espinosa as Skin. Here it is not skin that identifies him as Latino. He remarks, "About a year ago, my skin started turning grey—sagging . . . Growing! For the most part I can control it . . . when I concentrate" (issue 318, 14). He uses his skin to suffocate foes, for example. Marvel let us know that he is Latino by his use of Spanglish (he mixes phrases like *Madre de Dios*, *chica*, and *buenos días* into his English) and by his background story: his father was murdered in a drive-by in East LA; his girlfriend, Tores, is a *chola* (Latina gangbanger); his overprotective mother forced Skin to become a member of Father Miguel's Catholic Youth; and he has always been at the edge of gangbanging. Skin was a major protagonist in the series *Generation X*, and was later killed in a mutant hate crime (*Uncanny X-Men*, issue 423). In *X-Men* (volume 2, issue 65), Scott Lobdell and Carlos Pacheco introduced a Puerto Rican doctor, Cecilia Reyes, who has mutant energy-field powers. In *X-Factor* (volume 1, issue 17), Louise Simonson and Walt Simonson gave life to Julio Esteban Richter as Rictor—a former mutant who recently admitted his bisexuality.

In the new millennium, Marvel began introducing readers to mixed-race Latinos. In 2001, Marvel's series *X-Force*, by Peter Milligan and Mike Allred, introduced a mixed Irish and Latina superhero, the green-eyed Anna (issue 117). They provided some background to her character: she was conceived when an Argentinean priest crossed the line with an orphaned Irish girl in a mission. Anna's superpower: to heal the "sick and sad" as well as to move objects with her mind. In no time, however, Anna was killed off. She died during an X-Force mission to rescue Paco Perez, a character whose parents were killed by a truck when they tried to cross the U.S.-Mexico border. While *X-Force* killed off Anna pretty swiftly, the comic book is deliberately self-conscious about identity politics and racial tokenizing: when a second African American character is introduced, the first starts to feel for his life.

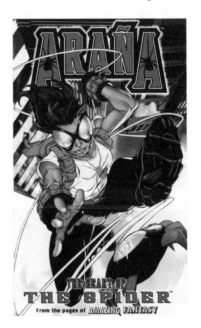

In 2004, Marvel introduced a Latina superhero called Araña (Anya Corazon) in a new title, *Amazing Fantasy* (volume 2, issue 1), that recalled the magazine in which Spider-Man originally debuted. After six issues she was given her own self-titled comic book. Written by Fiona Avery and illustrated by Mark Brooks, *Araña: The Heart of the Spider* aimed to appeal to a fast-rising middle-class Latino demographic (young and old). Not only is the character more fully

Araña Volume 1: The Heart of the Spider

fleshed out than her mainstream Latina predecessors—she stays connected to her cultural roots via the memory of her Mexican mother, Sofia, and she learns much from her smart, sensitive, and strong Puerto Rican father, an investigative reporter for the *New York Herald*—but she is the central protagonist of her own generously expansive story. She is smart, strong, culturally aware, determined. In high school by day, she crosses all sorts of racial, gender, and faith-based lines in her friendships, including the heavily charged one of Islam. By night, as Araña, she sports urban baggy street wear (rather than the usual spandex) and spider-exoskeleton armor, and she wields heavy industrial throw discs in her battles with the Sisterhood of the Wasp. Just as her story brings the worlds of adults and teenagers into contact, so too does it rub her contemporary urban New York up against a mythically dimensioned past: she is recruited by the Spider Society—a nine-hundred-year matrilineal line of fighters of Wasp supervillains—to become their hunter to fight to preserve world peace. Upon ending her story after a twelve-issue run, Marvel republished the issues of *Araña* in three manga-sized pocket volumes, most likely in an attempt to capture a teenage audience that tends to gravitate toward Japanese manga. She continues to guest star in Spider-Man comics and has a recurring role in *Ms. Marvel*.

In 2005, second-generation Cuban American author-artist Joe Quesada (Marvel's editor in chief) introduced *Daredevil: Father* (issue 2)—and with it the Latino superhero team the Santerians. The team leader, Nestor Rodriguez, or NeRo, is by day a multibillion-dollar entrepreneur with a successful hip-hop label and cologne line for men, and by night he is Eleggua, with

Daredevil: Father, Issue 2

superpowers, like those of his Yoruban-deity namesake, that include being able to scramble thoughts and communication. (Notably, during the day, he sports a distinctive goatee, but by night he is smooth shaven, with a slick of hair over one eye.) NeRo's motivation to set up a vigilante superteam spins out of his disillusionment with civil rights activism—his own activism as a young teen was overshadowed by his father's before he was murdered. And the others of his team also derive their powers from the orisha (deities identified with Catholic saints) of Santeria. They include the Afro-Hispanic, cornrowed, massive Ogun (deity of war), with his superhuman strength; the mischievous Chango (deity of fire and passion), who can throw thunder from his fingertips; the light-skinned Latina Oshun (deity of rivers and streams), clad in a fur-collared cape and sneaker boots, who can manipulate any form of liquid; and the Afro-Hispanic-featured Latina Oya (deity of storms), who can fly and control the weather. At the end of the book that collects issues 1–6 of *Daredevil: Father*, Quesada provides his readers with a glossary of the different traits that characterize the orisha. (We also learn that Quesada's mother practiced Santeria.) As this Latino vigilante-superhero team fights crime and tangles with Daredevil, they code-switch: "Levantate, Diablo. Rise and shine, baby," Eleggua tells Daredevil (*Daredevil: Father*, 67).

And on January 1, 2007, Marvel released a reinvented *White Tiger*. Fantasy and young-adult fiction writer Tamora Pierce coauthors with Timothy Liebe the story of a street- and book-smart, Bronx-born, gutsy Latina, Angela Del Toro, as White Tiger. She has a BA in political science and an MA in criminology. The niece of the original White Tiger, Del Toro was introduced as an FBI agent tracking the superhero Daredevil (*Daredevil*, volume 2, issue 58, by Brian Michael Bendis and Alex Maleev). She inherited the artifacts that gave her uncle his powers after he was killed. Her own adventure begins with bringing down Sano Orii, the killer of her uncle Hector. Orii works for the transnational cartel Chaeyi, peddling contraband passports and green cards. Del Toro as White Tiger struggles with her own identity issues, both expected and unexpected. For instance, when street thugs dare to call her a "Mutie," she reminds them with a drop kick: "Superhuman, estúpido! I'm superhuman!" (issue 1, 31). Pierce and Liebe reflect on contemporary concerns regarding Latinos and immigration in the U.S. by having Angela pass a newsstand with newspapers headlined: "House Debates Registration Act." She reflects, "Great, I was born in the Bronx—but if I put on a costume, I still have to get a green card" (issue 1, 20).

DC has also shown a renewed interest in creating Latino superheroes. Paul Dini's Dominican police detective, Renee Montoya, moved from the backdrop

Blue Beetle, Volume 7, Issue 1

of the 1992 *Batman* (issue 475) to the foreground in *Gotham Central* (2003). (She also appeared in 1992 in *Batman: The Animated Series*.) In addition to being a central protagonist in *Gotham Central*, she is one of the protagonists of DC's best-selling comic 52 in which she takes up the mantle of the Question. In DC's major publishing event of 2006, Geoff Johns and Phil Jiminez's *Infinite Crisis* (issue 3) debuted the new Blue Beetle as the Texas-born and Texas-raised teenager Jaime Reyes. In May 2006, *Blue Beetle* appeared (created by Keith Giffen and John Rogers, and Cully Hamner). As the issues of this self-titled comic unfold, we discover a more and more complex everyday life of Jaime, his mom (nurse), father (mechanic), and sister Milagro, but also the day-to-day existence of those living along the U.S.-Mexico border. In issue 5, Jaime crosses over to Mexico, where he learns that his nemesis is his Tia Ampero, otherwise known as La Dama. She makes high-interest loans to undocumented people, who use the money to pay coyotes to get them across the border; she is using the profits to build a superarmy of "Magic-Metas" (issue 6, 28).

The series makes several moves to complicate Latino identity and experience. For instance, not only do the writers create a Latina, La Dama, as the big capitalist exploiter of the economic imbalance between Mexico and the United States, but we learn in issue 8 that Jaime's sidekick, Paco, has to take a makeup class because he flunked Spanish for speaking Spanglish. There is also a stretched panel depicting Jaime and Paco crossing the border from the United States. They walk without much ado in the foreground into Mexico; in

Blue Beetle, Volume 7, Issue 5

Blue Beetle, Volume 7, Issue 5

the background appears a seemingly immovable cluster of people waiting to go the other way (issue 5).[20]

Comic book publishers other than DC and Marvel have created Latino characters—even some complete storyworlds. I think of Italian creator George O. DeLorenzo and his 1996 bilingual flip comic book, *Justicia*. Here we meet Angel Lopez as the Lost Angel, who uses his power to fly to save kids from gangs, drugs, and all varieties of temptations in the barrio. In 2001, Daerick Gröss used a bilingual flip book to introduce his readers to the eponymous character Murciélaga, or She-Bat. Here we follow the adventures of a light-skinned social worker, Mega, who by night uses her supersonic hearing and martial-arts training to clean up the crime-ridden streets of her barrio. Along with fighting street criminals, she combats the likes of Scorch, a pyromaniac hired by the mobster Baboso to burn buildings in the barrio so he can buy up the real estate on the cheap.

Certainly some strides have been made in the mainstream world of comic book storytelling. However, there are still many uninteresting Latino stereotypes in circulation. A case in point: in 2006, Ed Brubaker and Michael Lark's *Daredevil* (volume 2, issue 82) visually describes a chiseled, clean-cut, and buff Matt Murdock, who encounters in prison an unshaven, slick-haired, and tattooed-to-the-nines Latino: Carlos LaMuerto as Black Tarantula. LaMuerto speaks only in laundry lists made up of "*ese*," "*vato*," "*dawg*," "you off the hook," and "knowhut I'm sayin" (18).

So we might ask, why do some mainstream comic books like *Araña* and the *Blue Beetle* work more effectively to depict and tell stories about Latinos? Is

Daredevil, Volume 2, Issue 82

there a certain ingredient that allows their comic books to engage audiences more completely? Is it that they don't situate their stories only in a trashed-out barrio? Is it a question of having more variety of representations, so that it isn't just the gangbanger-made-good superhero, but also the social worker, the family man, the schoolteacher, the aristocrat? Is it that their characters have more complexity? Is it that they employ more storytelling elements than those that came before? Is it that mainstream comic-book creators—just like the independents—have the choice and freedom to create complex characters and stories as well as use and reshape more storytelling ingredients to more intricately engage audiences? Is it a sense of commitment to detailing Latino cultural particularities?[21]

7 LATINOS STRIKE BACK

The year 1977 saw the making of the first Latino superhero by a Latino: Texas judge Margarito C. Garza and his comic book, *Relampago*. Garza inked the black-and-white adventures of the morally complex, Texas-born and Texas-raised Marcos Zapata. Raised from the dead and given superpowers by a local *bruja* (witch), he turns his thieving ways around once she is out of the picture and he finds guidance from a local priest. By day, he uses law books to

Relampago, Issue 3

YOUR BRAIN ON LATINO COMICS

defend his community. And by night, fully embracing truth, justice, and the Latino way, and wearing form-fitting spandex from head to toe (and a cape), he keeps an eye on the community, sweeping in to help the underdog, the stranded child, even endangered birds (issue 3). However, *Relampago* was a proverbial flash in the pan. It was not until the 1990s that readers would begin to see the appearance of other Latino caped crusaders. One of the main catalysts: Milestone.

Milestone created not only *Blood Syndicate*, but also, riding on its coattails, *Kobalt*—a sixteen-issue series introduced in 1994 that ran for sixteen months. Milestone editor Dwayne McDuffie brought together writer John Rozum and artist Arvell Jones (Robert Quijano joined as inker beginning with issue 8) to add to their city of Dakota universe (which also included the African American Static and the characters from *Hardware* and *Blood Syndicate*) the psychologically compelling beefcake Kobalt, a long-haired, masked vigilante who battles street thugs and multinational corporate evildoers with fists and a steel pole weapon.

In the final panels of the last issue of *Kobalt*, we discover his true identity. After a near-death battle with a nonmortal villain—"I'm just an ordinary man with a number of tricks up my sleeve. Gimmicks. They're no match for someone with inherent powers" (issue 16, 43)—he arrives in Mexico City, where for the first time we see him out of mask, tinted brown, and identified as

Kobalt, Issue 1

Kobalt, Issue 16

"Miguel" (46). He is home to rest and retrain in order to return to save the city of Dakota. This final striptease enlarges retrospectively the reader's understanding of Kobalt: his unstated but strongly felt sense of alienation; his deep empathy for the racially victimized and down-and-outs; his deep distaste for underworld kings like Milton St. Cloud and for capitalist ventures like the turning of the barrio into Utopia Park. Perhaps, too, it is this Latino identity that gives him a not-so-Superman-like sense of right and wrong. Kobalt himself often finds himself on the wrong side of the law.

Latino unmaskings happen much more swiftly in Milestone's *Blood Syndicate*, which ran from 1993 to 1996. Here, Ivan Velez Jr., along with cowriter Dwayne McDuffie and artists Denys Cowan and CrisCross, introduced readers to a series of gritty, barrio-made, blaxploitation-style multiethnic superheroes: "a street gang like no other," as one character announces (issue 1, 3), they are bound to one another in their defense of "turf and loyalty" (26). Reflecting on the lack of adequate social representation in comic books, Velez writes at the end of issue 2 that if one can "do anything in a comic book, then why not put a mirror up to American society and show it the way it 'really is?'" (28). As the Milestone editors announced:

> We like the world inside our books, and we want everybody to know about it. Why? Because we feel that the City of Dakota resembles the real world more than other comics do. Diversity's our story, and we're sticking with it. The variety of cultures and experiences Out There make for better comics In Here. When people get excited about the diversity In Here, they'll get just as excited about the diversity Out There. (issue 1, 13)

But *Blood Syndicate* is not a mirror held up to the world; it is not exactly social realism. It is still all comic-book-superhero epic-adventure stuff. The characters use their super powers—supercharged electricity and the ability to go back in time, among many others—to battle archenemies like the hybrid voodoo-digital, technologically savvy Soul Breaker; the local mob; and corporate elites who send drugs into the barrio to kill off the poor so that they can buy and develop the land. Indeed, since Milestone considers the superhero genre a means for mixing "drama, humor, adventure and fantasy" but also for reflecting on what it means to be human, it seeks to represent in its superheroes a diversity and range that reflect "different backgrounds, different experiences and world views" (issue 28, 11). Thus, each of its superheroes also comes with a unique set of problems; enemies materialize in the form of crack addiction, greed, religious fundamentalism, sexism, racism, and so on.[22] And the team members struggle with their ethnic identities—and some even struggle with sexual desire and orientation. Wise Son must learn to temper his African American Islamic-nationalist zeal; Korean American Third Rail becomes more inclusive; the Afro-Hispanic, Dominican-identified sister and brother Sara (Flashback) and Carlos Quiñones (Fade) "deal with the reality of being black and Latino at the same time" (issue 2, 28). Flashback often steals crack to feed her addiction; Fade struggles with his closeted gay

Blood Syndicate, Issue 1

sexuality; the Puerto Rican Brickhouse struggles to remember her past; and the other Puerto Rican character, Rolando Texador as Tech9, drowns his abusive upbringing in alcohol.[23] There is a Haitian American, Masquerade. And in issue 8 there is the Chinese superhero Nina Lam as Kwai, who struggles with her family's strict cultural values.

Diversity is not just skin deep; it is also how one self-identifies and how one uses language to announce group affiliation. For example, Boogieman struggles to fit in as an Anglo who identifies with the street and as African American. After an initial upset—the others discover that he is an Anglo posing as an African American—he tells them: "I am down with all of you. That's the way I talk!" (issue 23, 25). Yet in the end, all his ethnic posturing is forgiven. The characters quite naturally code-switch between English and Spanish (*que mierda*, *coño*, *puñeta*, and *pendejito*)—and not in the broken English of DC's Vibe.

In *Blood Syndicate*, Velez also revises the reader's expectation of gender. Issue 1 bends gender expectations when it opens with a blonde-haired, purse-toting reporter for the *Dakota Chronicle* who is identified as Rob Chaplik. While from the clothes and accessories we might infer the character to be a woman, her physique, angularly structured facial features, muscled legs, and name suggest otherwise. CrisCross's visual portrayal and Velez's text work together

Blood Syndicate, Issue 23

to bend the reader's gender expectation. Likewise, when Velez and CrisCross introduce the character Brickhouse, the visuals and text work together to obscure the reader's identification of gender: Brickhouse is built like the Fantastic Four's Thing, has cornrowed hair, and a penchant for romance. Finally, the author and artist interweave into their visual and verbal play with gender (and sexuality and race) complex interior states of mind. Brickhouse, for example, struggles to overcome a deep denial over her past as a slave; Fade eventually overcomes his fear of being gay in a straight, macho, superhero world; Wise Son works through an Islamic-nationalist zealotry that becomes a form of bigotry.

Milestone was not the only publisher in the early 1990s that was creating complex Latino superheroes and compelling stories. In 1993, Richard Dominguez introduced the first edition of *El Gato Negro*, published by Azteca Productions. Set in everyday Edinburg, Texas, the protagonist, Francisco Guerrero, works as a public defendant by day (he also mentors young parolees of color) and busts U.S.-Mexico drug cartels by night as the masked El Gato Negro. And in homage to Judge Garza's Relampago, Dominguez's El Gato Negro also has a priest as his consigliere. (As Dominguez reveals in his interview, he was to collaborate on a series with Judge Garza; unfortunately, Judge Garza died before they could do so.) He is deeply rooted in his culture and is bilingual, speaking to the priest in Spanish. That El Gato Negro is middle-class and Catholic doesn't mean he is above using Chicano slang, often peppering his phrases with *pendejo* and *ese*, and the like. The bad guys buy rocket launchers over the counter; El Gato Negro trains in the ways of the ancient fighting arts, using only in self-defense (and in defense of the community) the power of his sharply focused mind, kinetic body action, and martial-arts weapons (shurikens, or flying cat's claws) to battle evil. During an epic battle with a muscled, goateed, dark-glasses-wearing El Graduado, and just before he blows up the Val-Tech weapons factory, he makes a last attempt to reach out to this fellow Latino who has turned to the dark side: "Why? Why you couldn't use your college educated knowledge to help your own community in other investments?" (issue 2, 1994, 2).

When not fighting the likes of El Graduado or the capoeira-trained villain El Observador, El Gato Negro is helping documented and undocumented Latinos in the community. But Dominguez doesn't make him an undefeated, saintly do-gooder. El Gato Negro is often defeated—and often calls on the power of the Virgin Mary to help him out of a tough situation—and his nice-guy front with the character Narci is merely a means to an end: to woo her to the bedroom.

El Gato Negro, Issue 2

Also in 1994, José Martinez made a splash with *The Chosen*, or *The Americanos*, published by his creator-owned company, Chosen Comics. Independent minded and ethnic driven, Martinez's *The Chosen* first appeared—alongside Carlos Saldaña's *Burrito* and Richard Dominguez's *El Gato Negro*—at the 1995 San Diego ComiCon. Soon after, with funding funneled through the Los Angeles district attorney, he was able to produce a high-quality full-color hardback (intended for libraries) of a four-issue set as well as a spin-off comic titled *Sombra*. While not quite as gritty or grim as *Blood Syndicate*, *The Chosen* features a compelling multiethnic team. LA-based freelance reporter Santana, after being shot in a drive-by, writes from a wheelchair on blue-collar and gangbanger criminal activities; he gains his superpowers by tapping into ancestral spirits and flies the skies to safeguard the innocent. Martinez also invents the mixed American Indian and New Mexican Latino professor of history, Apache, who combines expansive knowledge with extreme agility and physical speed to disarm and vanquish his enemies. And there is the Texas bull rider Joe Lopez as the Rattler, who is superpowered by the venom that runs through his veins, using his razor claws to slice through wrongdoers. There is J. J. Montoya, an Afro-Latino University of Miami student by day, who becomes the shape-shifting superhero Santo by night. Finally, there is the young Puerto Rican Rico Chico who has a dog, Piloto, and who builds

YOUR BRAIN ON LATINO COMICS

The Chosen, Issue 1

The Chosen, Issue 1

The Chosen, Issue 1

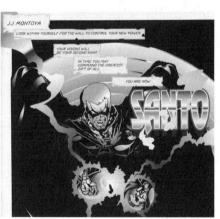

The Chosen, Issue 1

The Chosen, Issue 2

radio-controlled cars and then uses his power to miniaturize in order to drive and fly these special vehicles.

The Chosen travel across big spans of time. For example, in issue 2 we see them travel back to the year 1525, as the Apache estimates; here they encounter Nahuatl-speaking *indios* and discover the deep roots of their own indigenous ancestry, an ancient culture "free of the horrors of modern technology—the folly of civilization" (1). As a Maya god informs them, they are rooted in deep Maya culture and have an obligation to follow their destiny: to protect the people. They begin by saving the Maya peoples along with Moctezuma and Marina, his scantily clad mistress, translator, and diplomat, from the evil Toro. Finally, in a last reminder of the importance of community and collective solidarity, the story emphasizes that it is not so much their individual strengths that allow them to save the day, but it is their working together that makes them superheroes.

In a turn from a middle-class to a blue-collar superhero, in 1993 Fernando B. Rodriguez created *Aztec of the City*, from El Salto Comics. Here the reader-viewer meets nineteen-year-old Chicano construction worker Tony Avalos, eking out a living in San Jose, California. After a life-threatening accident on the work site, Avalos wakes from a month-long sleep, a journey to the Aztec underworld: "No recuerdo . . . Can't remember nothing" (issue 2, 5). While he doesn't recall details of his journey, he does discover from his hospital bed his pre-Columbian-rooted shape-shift-

Aztec of the City, Issue 2

Aztec of the City, Issue 2

ing superpower—Cuauhtémoc reincarnate. Newly self-identified as Aztec of the City, he battles various community-threatening enemies—from mobsters to more mythologically dimensioned foes. For example, in issue 2, "Enter La Llorona," Aztec of the City, or AOC, uses his street smarts to sleuth out the villain behind a recent spate of homeless killings and orphaned-girl disappearances: La Llorona (the Howling Woman), otherwise known as the Cryptic Queen of Creekside Chaos (23).

In 1997, Richard Dominguez added to the Latino superhero universe members of *Team Tejas*, published, like *El Gato Negro*, by Azteca Productions. Just as Dominguez's El Gato Negro is not a gangbanger-born superhero, but one who has entered the middle class, so too is his chisel-bodied Jonathan Gonzalez, assistant mayor of Dallas and leader of Team Tejas, which also includes the twenty-something college student Abel Castillo as Calibre, young fashion designer and Spanish-only-speaking Vanessa Castillo as Reata, and American Indian astronomer Daniel Brightfeather as Plainsman, who is deeply connected to the earth: "Speak to me, mother. . . . I am part of you, and I can feel your pain" (issue 1, 17). Like the power of the characters in Velez's *Blood Syndicate* and Martinez's *The Chosen*, theirs springs from their working together as a team, and not out of selfish individualism. They are invested with individual psychological dilemmas (Jonathan has abandonment and trust issues), but they must overcome their psychological obstacles to be able to fight as a team

Team Tejas, Issue 1

Team Tejas, Issue 1

Team Tejas, Issue 1

for justice, truth, and the Latino way. And Dominguez creates villains that are as complicated as the superheroes. For example, when Team Tejas is battling in Bosnia, it encounters a rebel Slav who strikes a deep chord with the team members when he reminds them: "You know what it is like to have your country taken away from you!" (issue 1, 5).

In 2002, even the great corn-swept plains of the Midwest saw the arrival of a Latino superhero. A third-generation Chicano from Kansas City, Kansas, Anthony Oropeza created and published his first issue of *Amigoman: The Latin Avenger*. Oropeza opens the story with a black-and-white-shaded visual of a colonial church sitting in the middle of a desert wasteland, and then cuts to a panel that introduces the protagonist, Antonio Fitzgerald Alvarado, who is wondering if he had seen an apparition—his murdered *abuelo* (grandfather) back from the dead. As the story unfolds, we learn that Antonio is by day a high-school history teacher; on one occasion, he tells his students, "Our very expensive textbooks do not tell us the whole story. They basically tell us what they want us to know. And if we want more information, like the truth, we need to do research" (issue 1, 6). By night, Antonio is Amigoman, training in the art of combat so that he can safeguard the community against drug dealers and other criminals as well as avenge his abuelo's murder. To play up his superhero charms with the ladies, he deliberately speaks with a "sexy Spanish accent" (3).

With the publication of Eli Hernandez's *Americo* in 2005, we see a push to attract younger reader-viewers. Published in the bilingual children's magazine

Amigoman: The Latin Avenger, Issue 1

Amigoman: The Latin Avenger, Issue 1

Iguana, Americo follows the story of a man of mixed Venezuelan and Mexican parentage, Amador Mercado, whose life-transforming visit to the Aztec Pyramids of the Sun and the Moon forever alters his immoral gambling and philandering ways. For Hernandez, it is important that Mercado's superpowers don't result from an accident (industrial or otherwise) but from the deep history and spirit of the people and land, and that they reflect the power of the pyramids. As Americo, Mercado sports a dark green, gold, and silver costume (symbolic of his ecological sympathies, the narrator informs) with a pyramid icon planted squarely on his chest. He is a Latino superhero created for children and young adult readers, and his PG-rated crime-busting adventures (keeping drugs out of playgrounds and violence out of the community) aim to provide a positive role model and celebrate *la raza*.

8 SPANDEXED LATINAS, WHERE ART THOU?

Certainly, there have been some interesting complications of Latina superheroes since the 1981 appearance of Bonita Juarez (Firebird) and Murciélaga, mentioned above. Yet the representations of Latinas are still few and far between. Since the early 1980s, we have seen the mainstream dabble in a few radically feminist or queer characters: Marvel's X-Men-Othered bisexual Mystique and her lesbian lover, Destiny; the (mostly) closeted lesbian Amy Chen of Silver Sable's Wild Pack; DC's Legion of Super-Heroes team members Shrinking Violet, Lightning Lass, and Element Lad. In Greg Rucka and Michael Lark's *Gotham Central* (issue 6), Renee Montoya is involuntarily outed to her family and coworkers in a revenge plot by the villain, Two-Face. Later, in issues 7 and 11 of DC's event comic, *52*, it is revealed that Montoya had a former relationship with the Jewish heiress Kate Kane, the new Batwoman. In DC's *Outsiders* (volume 3, issue 1, 2003) writer Judd Winick introduced the superstrong, feminist, and superpower-regenerative Chinese American superhero Grace Choi, a survivor of a sexploitation ring. And in 2001, Winick introduced to Marvel's series *Exiles* (issue 2), the smart, funny, and fireball-hurling Japanese lesbian superhero Sunfire—an alternate-reality counterpart to a male Japanese superhero and to the hero Wolverine's fiancée; she was killed off three years after her introduction.[24] In 2006, DC gave the superhero the Atom an Asian makeover as the Hong Kong émigré Dr. Ryan Choi, introducing him in a *DCU: Brave New World* special before launching him in a series by Gail Simone and John Byrne. (This is the fourth incarnation of the Atom, who first appeared as the Anglo Al Pratt in *All-American Comics* issue 19, 1940.)

In the 1990s, Vertigo/DC's *The Invisibles* (created by Grant Morrison) included in its antisuperhero team the Brazilian transsexual Lord Fanny, whose patron goddess is Tlazolteotl (deity of filth and lust).

While there are still wide gaps in the representation of smart, strong, ethnically identified superheroes, there have been a handful of writer-artists who have created significant Latina superheroes. (See Trina Robbins' *The Great Women Superheroes*.) I have already mentioned Velez's creation of the Puerto Rican Brickhouse—who literally embodies strength and pushes it in your face—as well as his psychologically dynamic Dominican Flashback. There are others too.

I mentioned earlier Steve Ross's *Chesty Sanchez* (Antarctic Press, 1995). The narrator describes the twenty-three-year-old Maria Sanchez from Cuernavaca, Mexico, as a good superhero candidate: she is tall, she rose to wrestling fame as Chesty Sanchez, "she lived clean, she was good to her parents, and she always fought fair" (issue 1, 5). This retired Latina *luchador* is hired by the Frijoles del Oro Company to fight dictators, desperadoes, exploitative capitalists, and drug lords. She is smart and witty, and she packs a punch. In a playfully tongue-in-cheek manner, the Frijoles del Oro Company wants Chesty Sanchez to wear a costume that says "'Mexico' to Americans" (issue 1, 25).

When she does appear in costume, she is sporting a short mariachi jacket that reveals her ripped abs; her tight hip-hugging pants don't get in the way of her strapped-on whip and double-barreled machine gun; she has brains and brawn. The short, mustachioed, Latino-identified Torpedo in full mariachi regalia acts as her sidekick; weaponless, he helps out by blasting enemies with

Chesty Sanchez, Issue 1

Chesty Sanchez, Issue 1

environmentally sound gas bombs: "The natural kind," Torpedo tells Chesty (issue 1, 9). Finally, in spite of her upward mobility, Chesty never loses sight of her family and cultural roots.

And as mentioned above, there is Laura Molina's *Cihualyaomiquiz, the Jaguar* (originally published by Insurgent Comix in 1996, and recently in negotiation for rerelease by WorkHorse). On the inside of the front cover, Molina announces:

> ¡Orale! Gente, It takes near super-human strength to get through these oppressive/regressive times. [. . .] This little book is dedicated to those of you who have experienced and survived racism and discrimination. (No, I'm not talking about White boys whining about women and minorities 'taking over.') If you've ever been denied a job, a promotion or a fair trial because of the color of your skin or if you've ever been pissed on because you're poor, you know what I'm talking about.

Indeed, Molina's Xicana-empowered protagonist, Linda Rivera, is driven to study law to help defend her community against a militarized police and INS as well as corporate capitalists. By night, as the Jaguar, empowered by her Xicana ancestral roots, she takes down local neo-Nazi villains.

And more recently, the Luna Brothers gave reader-viewers a superdynamic, multiethnic, superheroic female trio in the miniseries *Ultra* (Image Comics,

2004): the Latina Pearl, Penalosa, as Ultra, the Italian American Olivia "Liv" Arancina as Aphrodite, and Anglo-Texan cowgirl Jen Pederson as Janus. And while they all have superheroic powers, and are hired by Spring City to serve and protect, the Luna Brothers invest each with a psychological struggle. Liv struggles with a dangerous addiction to sex; Jen tries to quash her love and sexual desire for women, especially Ultra. On one occasion, when Ultra begins to lead little more than a stereotypical superhero life, she faces the stigma of a fallen-from-grace Latina. On the streets, she runs into some Latino gangbangers who tell her, "Yeah, you messed up. You went Gringo when you shoulda went Latino [. . .] for real. You need to keep it *Brown*, chica. We vatos know how to treat our bitches" (issue 6, 9).

Ultra, Issue 6

9 MORE SUPERHEROES REVEALED

We can add to the Latinos and Latinas in spandex other nonmainstream superheroes. Since the 1990s, we have seen ecofriendly, Polynesian, Arabic, and queer-identified crusaders.

Ivan Velez Jr.'s *Blood Syndicate* was of course a huge milestone for queer superheroes of color; he created several compelling gay and transvestite characters who were psychologically complex—and smart and swift and strong. When Dwayne McDuffie's comic *Static*, another series with a Milestone pedigree, became the WB cartoon series *Static Shock*, McDuffie introduced several new characters, including the gay superhero Gear.

While not a character of color, Marvel's French-Canadian Northstar (introduced in *X-Men*, volume 1, issue 120, 1979) was hinted to be gay (in *Alpha Flight* in 1983), an identification later confirmed in issue 106 of *Alpha Flight* (1992) in a story scripted by Scott Lobdell. (According to *Alpha Flight* creator John Byrne, he always intended Northstar to be gay, but was prohibited from making this identification by editorial policy at the time.) And, in a similar coming-out trajectory, in his *Starman* series, James Robinson revealed in the 1990s that another character called Starman, an alien named Mikaal Tomas, who was created in 1976, is bisexual. In 1998, Warren Ellis and Bryan Hitch introduced the gay-partnered dynamic duo Midnighter and Apollo in *Stormwatch* (volume 2, issue 4). In 2003, Marvel MAX (an adult-oriented imprint of Marvel) published a five-issue series of *Rawhide Kid* by Ron Zimmerman and John Severin that revealed Johnny Bart—introduced in 1960 by Stan Lee and Jack Kirby in *Rawhide Kid* (volume 1, issue 17)—to be a gay cowboy. Other gay-friendly characters include DC's Green Arrow, who, after becoming the liberal mayor of Star City, pushes to legalize gay marriage (*Green Arrow*, volume 2, issue 65, 2006).

Among ecofriendly superhero series, there is Sam Campos's ecologically minded, yet more ethnic and native-rooted *Pineapple Man* (SoloGraphics, 1997). Told in a radically reworked and kinetically faster manga style, the comic lays out the adventures of Hawaiian Sam Pahoa as the monolithically massive, native-weapon-wielding Pineapple Man and his battles to save his people and their earth against mythically dimensioned, pro-global-warming archvillains like Luk Fun.[25]

In 1995, even a bicultural-identifying Anglo superhero took flight. Mark Shainblum (writer) and Gabriel Morrissette (illustrator) introduced Eaton M. McGill as the eponymous satirical hero Angloman, a white Canadian who fights for bilingual laws and racial tolerance. Along with others in this comic book world, like the deeply patriotic country-club denizen Canadaman, Angloman appeared first in comic book form, then, in 1997, migrated to the *Montreal Gazette* and the *Montreal Mirror* as a weekly strip.

As far as American Indians in comics go, four years later Peter Schmidt, along with an American Indian creative advisory team, published the comic book *Peace Party*. While Schmidt is not himself American Indian, he has advisers on board like Cherokee Steve Russell, who make sure he gets his history and cultural act right when throwing his land-preserving superhero tribal team in the deep end of the capitalist usurpation of native territories.

We have yet to see if this diversity is here to stay, or even becomes a trend that follows dollar-bill trails. What we have seen for sure is that each author-artist has the choice to create complex characters and worlds as well as to engage readers with a sophistication of style for a greater cognitive muscle workout.

⑩ SPANDEX ALTERNATIVES

Superhero-driven comics are one of many routes Latino (and non-Latino) author-artists can choose to follow. Latino author-artists such as Wilfred Santiago, Roberta Gregory, Los Bros Hernandez, Mark Campos, and Ivan

Velez Jr. have radically extended what is known as the alternative comic-book storytelling mode. The alternative (Art Spiegelman and Eric Drooker) took up where the underground (Harvey Pekar and R. Crumb) left off, following day-in-the-life stories of characters otherwise invisible to the mainstream.[26] It is the backbone of Peter Kuper's stenciled style in his wordless urban melodrama *The System*, which follows a day in the lives of strippers, crooked cops, street artists, and Pakistani cab drivers. We see this alternative mode vividly expressed in the stories Ho Che Anderson and Wilfred Santiago include in their coedited *Pop Life*, in which they mix up photomontage realism with that of more iconographic cartoon and comic book characterizations. Anderson writes on the inside of the front cover of issue 2:

> Frankly, I have no idea why *any* of us are here. I have no idea why Fantagraphics agreed to publish this rag. I have no idea why you agreed to buy it. Nonetheless, despite my lack of understanding, these anomalous variables have conspired to create our current reality. I can only offer theories as to *my* participation in this enterprise: I'm assuming certain rewards are accrued from vicious comic book labor—in lieu of money we are perhaps offered such intangibles as the exorcising of creative demons, the joy of playing God, of constructing worlds from the ground up. Those rewards may even extend to *touching* your readers, to creating something that allows them to invest portions of their hearts and souls ordinarily reserved for living, breathing human beings. A side note: I would tend to recommend investing in *Pop Life* over living, breathing human beings—*we* need your money and real people are messy: they have thought and wills of their own which can be problematic. Real People can *hurt* you.

We see this alternative mode weave itself into the work of many Latino comic book author-artists. In Mark Campos's written and edited *Moxie, My Sweet* (2005), he collects nine stories that follow the ins and outs of such marginalized characters as, for instance, kitchen appliances that revolt against their human owners. We see this mode in Jaime Hernandez's stories that follow, for decades, a panoply of characters who age, gain and lose pounds, have straight and queer romances, and grow apart and together again. For example, the back cover of Hernandez's *Locas in Love* appropriately reads: "Stories range from the despair of daily existence to the comfort of friendships and the pleasures of sex." And in an extratextual blurb, Alan Moore writes, "Jaime's art balances big white and black spaces to create a world of nuance in between, just as his writing balances our big human feelings and our small human trivias to generate its incredible emotional power." *Locas* follows the everyday life of Maggie, Hopey, Norma, Negra, Izzy, and Penny Century, living in a "Shithole town."

Issues of race, gender, and sexuality powerfully murmur in the background: we learn of Hopey's frustration at not being able to fit in as a young Latina by way of a flashback of her decapitating a blonde Barbie; we learn of the difference between her carefree approach to her lesbian sexual identity versus that of the more uptight Maggie. And, we recognize an underlying frustration in most of the characters as they grow older and realize they haven't fulfilled their dreams. (During the twenty-five years that Hernandez has been creating these characters, they have all been transformed by their many experiences of growing older.) In Gilbert Hernandez's *Palomar* and *Luba* storyworlds, we see a microscopic detailing of several generations of Latinos south and north of the U.S.-Mexico border; the reader-viewer is invited into the lives of characters like Luba, Ofelia, Pipo, Fortunato, Tonantzin, Casmira, and many others, who also age, struggle with life-changing events, even transform into their total opposites. Many react violently to Pipo's coming out of the closet; happy-go-lucky Tonantzin becomes a lost soul who commits suicide by flame; Sergio and Gato become so green with jealousy that they beat their longtime childhood friend Fortunato to death.

And we see the alternative mode also in the shaping of strong female comic-book characters by and about Latinas. For example, we see it informing Erika Lopez's various comic-book-inspired long narratives like *Flaming Iguanas*. And when mixed Mexican-Anglo-identifying Roberta Gregory shapes a strong, sexually diverse range of female characters: from her parody of the romance genre in *Comic Books Aren't Just for Boys Anymore* (collected in *Click: Becoming Feminists*, edited by Lynn Crosbie) to her more recent issues of *Bitchy Bitch*, collected as *Life's a Bitch* (2005). Indeed, in the interview with Roberta Gregory included in this book, she describes growing up in Wilmington, California, in the 1950s and 1960s, very much aware of her Mexican-ness; she could swim in the public pool only on certain days as a Mexican American, for instance.

The alternative form allows Gregory to create the protagonist Midge of her *Bitchy Bitch* series—a character who comes face to face with questions of racism. In a flashback sequence, we see Midge as a young girl who passes on learned prejudice to another young girl: "You're not gonna sit next to a nigger girl, are you? They eat weird food an' they smell funny" (*Life's a Bitch*, 167); she learns as well that Mexicans are "nothing but trouble" (199). However, it is the creative latitude offered by the alternative-comic-book frame that allows

Gregory the freedom to create a non-Latina character like Midge, who as an adult hates all walks of life: lesbian, white southern blonde bimbos, abusive uncles, PC yuppies, feminists, you name it.[27] Midge declares, "Now, thanks to this women's lib crap we gotta do all that and go to work!!! And, above all, give you sex on demand" (147). In an episode in which Midge, after Dumpster diving to retrieve her winning ticket, goes on a free vacation to "Rosarita Shores Resort," located, as she says, "in some . . . Third World hell hole . . . Shit!!!" (19), her prejudice comes out in full force: "I knew it . . . all the people here are . . . colored or something . . ." (37), and she asks herself, "are they Mexican . . . are they black? or, both?" (38). The alternative mode gives Gregory the vehicle to shape the most non-politically correct of characters—to give us a unique insight into a mind that still considers those south of the border primitive and not "genetically as smart as Americans? Shit" (38).

The alternative mode finds unique expression in Ivan Velez Jr.'s *Tales of the Closet* (volume 1). Set in Queens in 1987, this story follows the lives of a handful of closeted Latino, Anglo, and Asian teens struggling with either unsympathetic or absent parent figures, school bullies, and hormone-driven desires; Velez's use of a series of filtered narrations through the eyes of Ramona, Kyle, Mary, Jenny Chin, Scotty, and the jock Ben immerse the reader-viewer deeply in the minds of these characters, serving up less a voyeuristic thrill than a deeply moving portrait. On one occasion, we overhear Ben's thoughts: "No college is gonna give a sports scholarship to some fag! God I hate lying! It feels so damn wrong! I got no choice. I either act straight or don't play!" (11) In a postscript, Velez tells of the impulse to not write so "pretty or polished" a story about the different ways of sexually identifying as a gay or lesbian urban teenager (95).

Tales of the Closet: Volume 1

In My Darkest Hour

In Wilfred Santiago's *In My Darkest Hour*, the alternative mode takes the shape of a highly self-aware, bitingly paranoid, and often drug-induced first-person account of the urban life of the twenty-something Latino Omar Guerrero. A hopeless Omar reflects: "Everyone's on their own little orbit within an orbit, round 'n' round, over and over again without losin' a beat, close but distanced from the other, until we go out with a whimper or with a bang . . . we think that beats the hell out of being alone . . . but we all go alone. And that's the end of it" (8). At a turn of a page, Santiago joltingly breaks up an already psychologically disturbing and debilitating story with a series of full-page panels that hit hard with allegorical meaning: an amputated, bound and gagged, headless blubbery body with a Christ figure strapped between its legs; a grotesquely gargantuan, muscled, bald Captain America who doesn't use his shield to protect, but rather as a holder for bombs that he spills willy-nilly on a diminutive land. The text reads: "Living countdown servants and spectators of the slave drivers' masquerade ball" (109).

Los Bros Hernandez also break up their more straightforwardly visual and verbal storytelling with other modes. They vary their realistic plot rhythms and characterizations by throwing in curve balls of fantasy, sci-fi, or even a superhero fly-by—but always, of course, with a twist. For example, even in the more character-driven dramatic work of Gilbert and Jaime Hernandez, we see them variously break up story sequences with appearances by alien creatures, anthropomorphic monoliths, anxiety-driven supershrinking or gigantic-growing women (Izzy Ortiz in *Locas*), hyper-libidinous little Hinkenfoffers, and Latina superheroes like Cheetah Torpeda; she tries to relieve her boredom by watching telenovelas and flying around looking for something to do, someone to save, or an enemy to fight (*Love and Rockets Collection: Locas in Love*, 13).[28]

In another issue, "One More Lady's Man," we even see Cheetah try out a day job as a stripper. And in the first issue of the series, *Love and Rockets* (1982), we see Jaime use not only the epistolary form—"Well, here we are. Sorry I've taken so long to write" (9), in which we learn of Maggie's obsession with her weight—but also a self-reflexive and playful sci-fi mode. La Maggie is a mechanic hired to travel the world and fix otherworldly machines, like the "Legendary Saturn Stilletto," used during the "Zymbodian Revolution" to transport the "biggest load of pito in the world out of Zhato" (10).

Alternative Latino comic-book possibilities are wide open. We see in Mario Hernandez's work (Jaime and Gilbert's older brother churned out a couple

Locas in Love

of stories in the early days of *Love and Rockets*) the texturing of more politically charged stories set in tropical-identified countries run by U.S.-imperialist-funded dictators. The narrator of one such story, "Somewhere in the Tropics," begins: "The eve of the union elections in Comprachico . . . The first step, many hope, toward loosening the heavy grip of neighboring Marzipan, itself dependent on Comprachico for the production of its official state soft drink, Blik!" (*Hernandez Satyricon: Love and Rockets, Book 15*, 20). His visually bold realism and thickly drawn mise-en-page, along with the crowding of verbal text, depict a suffocating and chaotic world where beneficent gringo volunteers put a happy face on capitalist exploitation and oppression.

Such alternatives might also weigh more heavily on the story-about-a-story, self-reflexive device. We see also in *Hernandez Satyricon: Love and Rockets, Book 15* that any narrative technique goes. Here we see Los Bros Mario, Gilbert, and Jaime play with the verbal and visual comic-book storytelling conventions when, for example, in one panel, there appears a photographic image of Jaime along with a cartoon balloon in which he remarks, "That's right! [. . .] No Hinkenfoffers, no elders . . .! None of it exists without me!!! For I am the puppet master! I pull the strings! I am life and death!" (15). And in Mario Hernandez's story "Life and Rockets . . . When the Muse Is not Amused," after the appearance of an in media res establishing splash page—Mario-as-character falling into the ocean—the visuals depict a bald mermaid, who remarks, "Maybe you should try again . . ."; bubbling underwater, the Mario-as-character responds, "Hey, c'mon! This is gonna be good! Gimme a chance!" (49). Later the bald mermaid appears again, berating Mario-as-author-inker: "You did that same story last time with the same old weird for weirdness sake sequence" (51). In Gilbert's story "The Artist," the visuals depict an eyeglasses-wearing, supermuscled artist-author penciling in panels and wondering whether he should "draw in a more neo-primitive style," since this might get him "more attention as a serious artist!" (64); here, too, Gilbert fleshes out characters who speak back to their artist-author creator: "Hey! We like us better this way. Yeah, no giant boobs, no exaggeration, no childish fetishism" (64).

Latino author-artists have radically extended the alternative-comic-book storytelling mode in various ways while they detail the everyday firmly located within a larger society and world.[29] Finally, working within the alternative tradition doesn't preclude the use of more conventional modes of storytelling, such as melodrama or noir.

11 ALL THAT IS WHITE TURNS NOIR

This leads me to another storytelling container used by Latino comic book author-artists: the gumshoe or noir-driven storytelling mode.[30] I have mentioned how Brian Azzarello and Eduardo Risso use the hardboiled genre in *100 Bullets* as a vehicle for telling a story that complicates the reader-viewer's ethical evaluative schema. While Azzarello and Risso stick to hardboiled conventions fairly closely, Rafael Navarro's *Sonambulo* intermixes more readily the conventions of horror, gothic, even the heroic-epic. As the reader-viewer follows the various sleuthing adventures of its luchador-masked eponymous hero, the comic book defies the genre's plot and character expectations. Yes, a crime is committed and a dame in distress seeks out Sonambulo's help; however, Navarro intermixes horror with the superheroic, the banal with the epic, to defy readerly expectations. So when Navarro first introduces Sonambulo, he appears in a suit, holding a gun and standing next to a window with vertical blinds that cast shadowed lines across the scene; splashed across the bottom of the first page is the announcement that we are about to read "48 Manly Pages!" In the next series of panels, a woman knocks on the office door, enters, expresses her distress, and the character Sonambulo remarks to himself, "She is tragedy cleverly disguised as lust" (2). The noir conventions are established, but exaggeratedly so. The playfulness with the genre, of course, is readily apparent when we notice that this private dick is wearing a luchador mask and that he drops Spanish slang (*cojones* [balls], say) into his phrases. And more than a sleuthing instinct, Navarro gives Sonambulo a power to overhear other people's thoughts and dreams; after his journey to an ancestral, Aztec-identified underworld, he returns with this superpower.

In Argentinean author-artists Carlos Trillo and Eduardo Risso's *Chicanos*, there is the topsy-turvy urban dystopian mood, but also much revision, including the most central: gender. Their private dick is a Chicana: Alejandrina Yolanda Jalisco. She is visually portrayed as small, big-breasted, and curiously

Sonambulo's Strange Tales, Issue 1

Chicanos, Issue 1

Chicanos, Issue 1

featured. We know, too, from the first series of panels in issue 1—visually describing the mob boss, Mr. Walken, with his sidekick Monkey, getting a shave and fellatio—that this isn't going to be your regular hardboiled story. Indeed, as the story unfolds, we learn more and more about Alejandrina; the authors push the reader-viewer to invest less in the traditional puzzle-solving aspect of the genre and more in her character. She doesn't really ever solve any crimes or fully figure out mysteries; what is compelling are her everyday psychological ups and downs; her awkward attempts at romancing women and men; her jealousies of friends like Sonia, Marita and her queer brother, Guadalupe; her ins and outs with her mother; and her various struggles in a racist world. For example, when she tries to flag down a taxi, the driver yells abusively, "Sure, I'll stop traffic for you, Chicana bitch! So you can stick a knife in my back from the back seat, broken ass!" (issue 1, 18). Others tell her that she stinks and that she is "half-deformed," (issue 1, 6) like all Chicanos. Trillo and Risso's Alejandrina uses these stereotypes to her advantage: being racially marked as smelly, dark, and deformed provides a kind of social invisibility that she takes advantage of, passing into otherwise white-privileged private and prohibited spaces to sleuth out and at least partially solve crimes.

⑫ OTHER À LA MODES

For Latino comic book author-artists, the sky is the limit. One can reenvision any mode: the superhero, the noir, the playfully anthropomorphic (recall Saldaña's bulletproof, serape-wearing, time-traveling Burrito), the goth-horror (Javier Hernandez's angsty El Muerto), the alternative everyday (Santiago's overmedicated Omar), to you name it. There are also those who tell a story, but do so to teach audiences about history, culture, and myth. In the case of Ilan Stavans and Lalo Alcaraz's *Latino U.S.A.: A Cartoon History*, the comic book's visual and verbal narrators function to educate; here, facts are given primacy over fiction. And we see this impulse also in Andrea M. Gaudiano's bilingual flipbook *Azteca: The Story of a Jaguar Warrior*, in which plot and adventure are subordinate to details of Aztec mythological gods such as Coatlicue, historical figures like Hernán Cortés, and early chronicles of the conquest by the likes of Bernal Díaz del Castillo and Miguel León-Portilla. There is an adventure story here: the birth of Xochiquetzal and twin brother Xochipilli, the arrival of Cortés on Mexico's shores, his duping of Moctezuma, and the epic battles of gods like Quetzalcoatl and Tlaloc. However, the overwhelming presence of a verbal narrator—in one panel, for example, we learn that "The eagle is associated with the sun, Huitzilopochtli, and the pictorial glyph symbolizing Tenochtitlan is an eagle perched atop a prickly pear cactus on a rock" (77)—makes for a comic book that primarily aims to educate its audience. (The inclusion of a glossary of terms and a chronology of events also strongly pushes it in this direction.)

This is not to suggest that elements of history, myth, and cultural lore do not find their way into comic book stories that emphasize fiction. In fact, as we see in many of the abovementioned comics—El Muerto's and Sonambulo's journeys into their ancestral underworlds, the returns to a pre-Columbian Latin America by team members of the Chosen and Burrito, Pablo's encounter with a dynamic Aztec underworld, to name but a few—there is the active inclusion of such elements. Rather, it is to emphasize once again that Latino comic book artist-authors can choose among many possible storytelling modes and conventions.

This goes for Frank Espinosa, who chooses a blended retro sci-fi mode for *Rocketo*—a story set roughly 2,000 years after the earth is nearly obliterated; new hybrid species—Dogmen like Spiro, Fishmen, Earthmen, and Mappers like Rocketo—roam the fragmented planet. Rocketo informs: "I was born in 1887 N.W on Kova, a small island measuring just 90 square miles" (*Rocketo Vol. 1: The Journey to the Hidden Sea*, 24). Within this genre, Espinosa can create a character whose raison d'etre is that of remembering where places like Kova ("Cuba") are on the planet and keeping in his memory stories of times past. He can imagine new spaces and new hybrid villains like the mouthless Turnstiles who live on the continent of Venedicto. Espinosa bends the genre also with his retro-expressionist, stylized visuals; a heavy dose of Homeric allusions; and an allegorical interface with the pre- and post-Castro Cuba.[31]

Rocketo Vol. 1: The Journey to the Hidden Sea

13 STRIPS WITH NEW STRIPES

Just as one might choose to tell a story in the form of a novel, a film, a comic book, and so on, one might also choose that of the comic strip. Indeed, this is a tried-and-tested form that dates back at least to the first appearance in 1867 of *Ally Sloper* in the magazine *Judy* in Britain. Following on its heels in the United States was *Hogan's Alley*, and its most memorable character, the Yellow Kid, which first appeared in *Truth* in black-and-white in 1894, and took off when it was published in color in the *New York World* in 1895. While some of the more memorable comic strips have been *Krazy Kat* and *Dick Tracy*, thousands upon thousands of lesser- and better-knowns have filled many a newspaper—too many to catalogue here. (See Maurice Horn's *The World Encyclopedia of Comics*.)

In an attempt to understand its form, scholars have traced the comic strip's origins to a moment in European art when figures like William Hogarth added linear narrative and caricature to painting. Most agree, however, that its solidification into a unique storytelling form was spurred on by the introduction of the Sunday supplement in the late nineteenth century—especially in the United States, where the mass media grew rapidly. Indeed, while inspired by those circulating in Europe, the U.S. strip was shaped more deliberately, according to Ian Gordon, as a "mass market product" (*Comic Strips*, 7) and was more firmly tied to the ideological shaping of a "national identity" (11). It is important to remember, too, that the comic book storytelling form grew out of the comic strip.

There are other scholars who seek to uncover the damage done by stereotypes mediated by the mass media; Latino characters (often in dog or mouse form) were portrayed as lazy, dirty, double-crossing, thieving, hypersexual, or illiterate. In "Autopsy of a Rat," William Anthony Nericcio considers, for example, the Speedy Gonzales cartoon character a kind of "pre-recorded visual memory byte [that etches itself] onto the contours of the collective psyche" (219); for Nericcio, Speedy functions within a larger propaganda machine that seeks to make normal the everyday exploitation of and violence against Latinos. So while one might laugh at the characters and gags, Nericcio reminds us to always critically engage with and contextualize such images within larger policy making moves.

For others, comic strips function less as a mirror of society or a shaper of a national imagination than as the focus of taxonomic inquiry: how comic strips use particular narrative devices and formal elements to tell a quick story, convey a moral, or get a laugh; how their visual or verbal narrative elements must lead quickly to that final gag or that social, ethical, or moral insight; how their physical restriction to a small space on a newspaper page means that they necessarily lean more heavily on readily consumable iconographic and simple caricatures than, say, comic books.

The Latino comic strip authors interviewed here speak of issues of form as well as social, historical, and readerly contexts; of how industry pressures and societal expectations restrict comic strip expression; of how social shifts have allowed for a greater range of expressivity; of how specific uses of narrative devices aim to move readers in specific ways. The author-artists speak of choosing to tell their stories in the comic strip form; they don't wander into the comic book form. Likewise, when author-artists choose to tell their stories in the longer comic book form, with few exceptions they tend not to venture into the realm of the strip. Javier Hernandez and Los Bros Hernandez occasionally use the comic strip form, but only to vary the rhythm of their longer comic book narratives.

Indeed, the late Gus Arriola chose to tell his stories in comic strip form. In 1950, when he introduced the south-of-the-border Mexican bean farmer (later turned tour guide) Gordo, Arriola wanted to reach as many readers as possible, so he chose the comic strip form. He knew that people had a limited amount of reading time and that the form delivered via newspapers could potentially reach a large audience—and he wanted this especially in order to put a human face on Latinos. While he chose the comic strip form, he envisioned from the beginning a story with wide, sweeping character arcs—a Latino character's adventures that his readers could follow in short, quick bursts, but that would develop over long stretches of time.

Arriola was the first to break through with a Latino comic strip, which meant that he was a creator of his time (as he discusses in his interview here). He had to take baby steps in using Gordo to complicate representations of Latinos. At first, Gordo was represented as lazy, and spoke broken English. In *Accidental Ambassador Gordo*, Robert C. Harvey discusses at length the many decisions Arriola faced in this process: first, identifying Gordo as a Mexican bandit, then as a farmer, and finally as a tour guide (32). And while Arriola wanted to situate Gordo in the United States, he finally located Gordo and his setting, as Robert C. Harvey writes, "in Mexico rather than in the southwestern United States because he didn't want Gordo to have the second-class citizenship status often accorded to Americans of Mexican descent" (33). As the Gordo strip became more and more popular, syndicated in over three hundred newspapers during a thirty-plus-year run, Arriola was able to complicate

 YOUR BRAIN ON LATINO COMICS

Gordo's identity as well as the storytelling form. After moving out of black-and-white, the *Gordo* strips became "fiestas of color" (111) and were framed by new panel shapes (round, oval, or diamond, for instance), and even on occasion had Mexican folk art drawn around their borders (111). With this experiment in form, we also see the making of a socially aware, non-broken-English-speaking Gordo.

As Arriola brought Gordo's story to a final close in 1984, there appeared a lesser known strip, *Dupie: The Life and Times of a College Student as Seen through the Pen of Campus Cartoonist, Gil Morales*. The black-and-white strip ran in the *Stanford Daily* from 1978 through 1981 while Morales was a Stanford undergraduate. Again, rather than choose an animal to represent Latinos, Morales created the Chicano college-going character Dupie and his Anglo sidekick, Ian. Cartooning in a very different historical moment from, say, Arriola's 1950s *Gordo*, Morales showed how radically different the story terrain can be. Dupie and Ian indulge in women and mind-altering drugs; they discuss the intricacies of mathematics, how best to procrastinate, what to do after graduation; they mull over the inability of the older generation to sympathize with the younger set. The brief background sketch and the dark-haired inking of Dupie (versus a nonshaded, non-dark-haired Ian), along with the author's name, biographical sketch, and photograph included at the end of the collection, tag Dupie as Chicano; however, the activities and problems of a middle-class undergraduate within a hermetically sealed university campus are the real focus. Morales invests his Chicano character Dupie with the full-fledged markings of the educated middle class.

There has been a strong tradition since the late 1960s of Chicanos inking political cartoons and strips. I think of the Los Angeles–based Asco and the publishing of *Con Safos*, for example. Indeed, contemporary comic strip author-artists like Lalo Alcaraz acknowledge the massive influence of the satirical political work of predecessors like Gronk of Asco and also Oscar "Zeta" Acosta; he also dedicates his collection *La Cucaracha* to "Gus Arriola, Sergio Aragonés, Rius, Los Hernandez Bros, Quino, and all the unsung cartoonistas in Latin America." However, much of this remained at best a cottage industry, reaching a rather limited audience. It wasn't until 1993 that a more socially biting and politically savvy Latino-spun black-and-white strip came to the attention of a wider audience. While Lalo Alcaraz, formerly of the Chicano Secret Service comedy troupe, had inked satirical cartoons for the *Daily Aztec* at San Diego State University, in the early 1990s his work began to appear in the *LA Weekly*.

Recently, many such strips have been collected and published in *Migra*

Migra Mouse: Political Cartoons on Immigration

Mouse: Political Cartoons on Immigration* and *La Cucaracha*. As mentioned earlier, we see here how Alcaraz holds little back, hitting hard such issues as English-only laws, immigration policy, militarization of the border, and the exploitation of Latino workers. He titles one such single-panel strip "A remake of the 1950s classic The Bracero Program. Tonight's episode: 'Indentured Servitude'" (*Migra Mouse*, 62). He titles another strip "Schwarzenegger The Mexterminator" (*Migra Mouse*, 111). Alcaraz's aim is clear: to use his pen to make strips (single and multiple) that will open his readers' eyes to issues

Migra Mouse: Political Cartoons on Immigration

of immigration, exploitation, racism, bilingualism, and education. His bottom line: "All people should be treated fairly regardless of when they got here. Besides, my ancestors were right here when the only border was the ocean" (*Migra Mouse*, 23). As he remarks in his introduction to *Migra Mouse*: "Perhaps readers can explore the attitudes and emotions that many in the Latino community felt over the last decade, as expressed through my work" (9).

Anglos and racist policy making are not the only targets. Alcaraz also pokes fun at Latinos on both sides of the liberal and conservative divide: *raza*-power nationalists as well as darlings of the establishment like Richard Rodriguez and Linda Chavez (mentioned above). And in a series of panels in *Migra Mouse*, he uses his own life and family background to playfully complicate the Latino representational map: from his birth during the year of JFK's assassination, to his parents meeting in an ESL (English as a second language) class, to his early love of drawing, to his joining MEChA (Movimiento Estudiantil Chicano de Aztlán) in college, to his socially conscious stand-up comedy work with the Chicano Secret Service, an experience that "turned me back on to the concept of art as a living" (19). For Alcaraz, then, the comic strip is a carefully honed art form and a viable venue for social critique. It can be at once playful and bitingly satirical, self-reflexive and realistic, because at the end of the day, it is a form for telling any and all kinds of stories. A case in point: In an opening panel of *La Cucaracha*, the reader encounters a cartoonist character,

Migra Mouse: Political Cartoons on Immigration

"Lalo," who is drawing the character La Cucaracha. The former says, "Wait a sec—you're not real! You're just a cartoon cockroach—this is no place for you!" (7). And La Cucaracha responds, "As your alter ego, it's my duty to explain that I've leapt off the page and right into your boring life. What a cheap story device! Eddie, you're Latino, right? Just say it's Magical Realism" (7).

Alcaraz's full commitment to his craft and a no-holds-barred approach to issues and subjects—including the refusal to sugarcoat representations of Latinos—certainly ruffled feathers, especially of those who couldn't tell the difference between story and reality. As noted earlier, many Latino reader-viewers sent hate mail denouncing his representations of Chicanos—like that of the beer-drinking Mexican dad. And many more Anglos attacked Alcaraz, calling him "a filthy illiterate Mexican" or telling him to "Get the f*** out of this country if you don't like it here. Go back to Mexico, or Africa, or wherever the f***" (*La Cucaracha*, jacket cover).

In another move to radically shake up singular representations of Latinos, David Gonzalez transformed characters from his *Homies* comic strip, which first appeared in *Lowrider Magazine*, into a series of Chicano plastic figurines. Although less satirically driven, Gonzalez's *Homies* aims to upset mainstream preconceptions of Latinos: in one series of panels, the bandanna-wearing character Smiley remarks, "Eh what's all this caca I'm hearing on t.v. about us Homies being gangstas?" Gonzalez has his character Hollywood respond: "That's the L.A.P.D. showing they know nothing about the lowrider lifestyle. You a gangsta Smiley?" In another panel, the pancho- and sunglasses-wearing Mr. Barrio says: "Being brown and from the barrio is not a crime! The nega-tive profiles and stereotypes being perpetuated on all of our Chicano brothers and sisters by certain law enforcement officials only intensifies the problem-atic racial and social barriers existing within the very communities they are sworn to protect and serve. [. . .] I in fact represent the system's worst fear, an educated homey with an attitude!" (http://www.homies.tv/comics_har-ras_01.htm). Gonzalez's panoply of caló-speaking Chicano characters, each with his or her own set of issues and day-to-day activities—including attend-ing lowrider conventions, community organizing, and actively participating in Mexican cultural celebrations like Cinco de Mayo parades—aims to positively depict and normalize the lives and experiences of these East LA Chicanos.

Other recent Latino comic strip author-artists exhibit a more domes-tic sensibility. Puerto Rican Peter Ramirez's bilingual strip *Raising Hector* had a short run in the *Odessa (Texas) American* and has recently been syn-dicated. (See his interview here.) Ramirez tells a series of adventures in the life of retired policeman Hector Sanchez and his transition to become a stay-at-home dad. Chicano Hector Cantú and Cuban American Carlos Castella-nos's *Baldo* follows the everyday foibles of the pubescent Baldo Bermudez; his "Viva Che" and Frida Kahlo–loving younger sister, Gracie; the *curandera*, lotto-playing Tía Carmen; and his *guayabera*-wearing father. (See their inter-views here.) Rob Cabrera's strip *Silo Roberts* asks questions of the world from the point of view of the multiracial-identifying fourth grader Silo Roberts. Raised by a single professional mother along with his sharp-tongued and can-did younger sister, Lisa, and his rather dimwitted jock older brother, Donny,

Silo struggles to find a place for himself in a society that forces black-white racial divisions. On one occasion, Silo reflects: "On dad's side, grandpa is half Native American and half Afro-American. Grandma's half Spanish and half Japanese. On mom's side, abuelo's full blooded Italian and abuela's half Puerto Rican and half Irish." And in a comment that reveals much about racialized representations in the mainstream, Lisa asks her mother, "How come I have a nappy noggin—instead of your long, flowing, shampoo commercial-like hair?" (The strip had its final run on December 10, 2006, and is unfortunately no longer available.)

Another of the more domestically oriented comic strips is David Alvarez's *Yenny*, which takes place in Puerto Rico and follows the lives of the voluptuous, wide-eyed, big-thighed, model-aspiring Yenny; her pet iguana, Zacha; her friends Jake and Kelso; and her young single mother, Juana, who is as concerned with her looks and the boys as with her daughter. The strip is lighthearted, playing also with cultural perceptions. For instance, in the episode "Nieve in Puerto Rico," Alvarez has fun with readerly preconceptions about geography, culture, and identity: "It's snowing in Puerto Rico. I w-wonder how this c-can change our culture . . . our traditions, o-our thoughts as tropical d-dwellers" (issue 4, 2). And Alvarez deliberately draws Yenny with big feet, not only to foreground Yenny's internalized idealized notions of beauty, but also to root her firmly in the land (culture and nation) of Puerto Rico. No matter how much she thinks about clothes and her good looks, her gigantesque feet make her immovably Puerto Rican. (See the interview with Alvarez here.)

Of course, such Latino comic strips don't exist in a vacuum. Many author-artists reflect on the influences not only of those south of the border like Rius

Yenny, Issue 4

and Sergio Aragonés, but also the work of Bill de la Torre (*Little Pedro*), Bill Watterson (*Calvin and Hobbes*), G. B. Trudeau (*Doonesbury*), Charles Schulz (*Peanuts*), Elzie Segar (*Thimble Theater*), Chester Gould (*Dick Tracy*), George Herriman (*Krazy Kat*), Berkeley Breathed (*Bloom County*), and Frank Cho (*Liberty Meadows*), among many others. Latino comic strips grab from anywhere and everywhere when lightly or boldly texturing issues of race, ethnic, and gender identities.

There are many others currently storytelling from other racial and ethnic perspectives. African American Aaron McGruder authors the series *Boondocks*. And in *Candorville*, African American–Jewish author-artist Darrin Bell charts the everyday activities of a mocha-brown African American protagonist, Lemont Brown; his Latina friend, Susan Garcia; and an African American nationalist, Clyde. While the strip is playful and lightweight, it nonetheless reminds those reader-viewers who may have forgotten that race matters— and sometimes in less obvious ways. Even before the strip begins to unfold, Bell has Lemont ask, "Why do I get pulled over all the time when I don't speed? Why do so many minorities either believe they have no business commenting on politics or feel the only politics they should concern themselves with are matters of race? Why do so many Americans not care about politics at all when politics determine the amount of freedom they can enjoy and the quality of their lives? [. . .] Why do so many young minorities accuse those who choose to study, who are polite, and who speak proper English of 'acting White'?" (*Candorville*, 5). And, as the story unfolds we see Lemont, Susan, and Clyde chew over issues and express discontents: Susan mentions how, under the multicultural sensitivity training at work, her Anglo boss brought her a pillow in case she wants to take a siesta, and calls her "Súsaña Gárcías" (24). He takes her out to "Chevo's Fresh Mex" and orders the "Cesar Chavez Nachos. Extra cheese" (24).

Latino comic strip author-artists like Alvarez, Arriola, Cantú, Castellanos, Alcaraz, Ramirez, and others seek to question and rough up any smooth, one way of being an ethnic or racialized person. There are more ingredients to being Latino than speaking Spanish (or Spanglish), eating tacos, or being connected to your pre-Columbian roots. The author-artists remind their readers that eating at a Mexican taqueria and not at Denny's doesn't make you more Latino than the next guy. We are these things, even in contradictory ways, and much more—and that is what these comic strip author-artists convey with their characters and stories.

PART II

BRAINS A-SIZZLE ON LATINO COMICS

The recovery of a Latino comic book and comic strip tradition that flows within and against mainstream currents is more than informative. The more we know of its details, the greater pleasure we reap as reader-viewers. When such a genealogy is identified, it becomes more visibly a part of the social memory we categorize as comics: comic books and comic strips. The more conscious we are of its conventions, the more readily we can access how its devices make meaning in our brains. Of course, as the Latino comic book and comic strip ingredients become a part of this social memory in the writing of a book like this one, the more reader-viewers who have not directly experienced and encoded these ingredients in their neural networks can discover and take delight in the creative reorganizing and deploying of comic book and comic strip techniques, props, characters, and prototype narratives. The more we familiarize (schematize) ourselves with the Latino ingredients that make up the whole pie, the greater the cognitive and emotive pay off for the reader-viewer.[1]

To further deepen our knowledge of Latino comics, we can study the different narrative elements that make up Latino comic books and comic strips: point of view, width of gutter, voice, balloon type, font size and format, and so on. Many have done this well. Will Eisner, for instance, considers the repetitive use of devices, images, and symbols as forming a grammar of sequential art. (See Eisner's *Comics and Sequential Art*.) Indeed, a focus on such narrative elements can help clarify and distinguish between the goings-on within a given story's content (event, characterization, theme) and the activity that takes place at the level of form (play with time, style, point of view, tempo). This is important, since it helps direct reader-viewers away from interpretations that reduce the given narrative to only its content or thematic message. Of course, the reader-viewer's experience of the narrative is finally one in which form and content are one. And as the interviews attest, comic book author-artists are aware of this.

Latino comic book author-artists distill (systematically eliminate whatever is redundant or dispensable) their stories, then distort and exaggerate them in ways that create pleasing and even shocking effects in the brain. We see this clearly when a Latino comic book author-artist uses only a few brush strokes to represent a character's face, as Frank Espinosa does in *Rocketo*. It is also why ballet can be so moving: it distills everyday body motions and movements, and then reframes and distorts them on the stage. We feel its beauty because it is unnatural—even though the movements are possible and perfectly natural. As readers and viewers, we find our perceptual problem-solving faculty triggered by this distilling and distorting.

A Latino comic book artist's distilling and distorting can trigger a like process in the reader-viewer. When we figure out that Wilfred Santiago employs the device of frame narration in *In My Darkest Hour* to present the experiences of a young Puerto Rican character living in a twenty-first-century society chewed up and spit out by capitalism, our brains go: "Aha." That feeling of being puzzled by something anew provides a cognitive and emotive payoff for solving the puzzle. The use of a six-panel grid style coupled with a break into a splash page might work best to introduce a significant character, or raise our pulses for a thundering crescendo. The cross-hatching (intersecting lines) might provide just the right gradations of light to texture a Latino character's skin color.

This is to say, we need to keep in mind always how the particular vision of any given Latino comic book narrative moves its reader-viewers—and authors as reader-viewers. And this is where cognitive science can be useful. It can begin to help us account for our making or engaging with Latino comic books. For example, why author-artists and reader-viewers know (intuitively or consciously) that a bold-faced word is louder than a nonbold word. Why a handwritten typeface effectively conveys feeling. Why comic books lettered in a more uniform typeface feel cold and calculated. Why the specific shape of a line over a character's head can convey anger or confusion. Why big eyes can convey anxiety. Why such visual devices work together with textual elements to nudge us to infer one thing and not another. Cognitive science can help us understand how far an author-artist can go in putting distance between a series of panels before pushing reader-viewers over their critical cognitive threshold. Why our minds can infer the passage of time by linking characters who appear as children in one series of panels and then in another series as adults, as is often seen in the work of Los Bros Hernandez. Why we can know that it is the same character from panel to panel even when her shirt or pants are not drawn identically in each. Why reader-viewers can move from one panel to another and connect disparate scenes through inference—hold in short-term memory—in order to create coherent wholes. Why the frequency of gutter placement (more or fewer panels on a page) can slow down or speed up the reader-viewer's sense of the story's pacing. Why the size of the gap between the panels (and their distribution) might require more, or less, imaginative filling-in in the making of the story. Why a series of distant or close-up shots can create specific moods. Why the frame's bordered shape (or the absence of one) can heighten or diminish our mood. Why a panel shot from below can trigger a sensation of fear or anxiety. Why we can read characters' interior states of mind from the stylization of a body gesture. Why we can create four-dimensional holographic spaces in our mind from two-dimensional visuals and text. Why, for that matter, we can create a sense of motion, time, and space from rather simple and static images.

To understand the particulars of each Latino comic book expression, we need to keep in mind the universals: how we are moved by their comic book storytelling devices. Thus, an approach to Latino comic books and comic strips requires an accounting of genealogy (as was provided in Part I of this book) as well as some nuts-and-bolts comic-book narrative theory (above and below) and some insight from the brain sciences. This will help us understand how each Latino comic book works to engage reader-viewers specifically—and universally.

I will discuss in this section how Latino comic book and comic strip author-artists use certain techniques, narrative devices, styles, universal prototypes, and story innovations to reframe in new and interesting ways not just day-in-the-life experiences but a variety of story types, such as the autobiographical, superheroic, epic, fantastic, realistic, and metafictional.[2] In choosing to reframe real and fictional worlds, they also ask the reader-viewer to look upon this newly reframed object from a new angle of vision; in so doing, they amplify the reader-viewer's everyday cognitive and emotive activities. Necessarily, then, I will also include a discussion of how these author-artists pleasurably engage both our capacity to infer interior states from outward gestures and our fictional-world-making ability.

Let's first look into this idea of the reshaping of genre. I mentioned the idea of a Latino comic book tradition—a storehouse of sorts filled with passageways lined with rows of shelves packed with types of stories, boxes filled with tools, and folders filled with characters. Indeed, the shelves extend beyond themselves, touching those built in all other storehouses that collectively make up world fiction. Gilbert Hernandez's *Palomar* stories both elbow their way onto certain shelves within the Latino-identified storehouse and necessarily rub up against those that lie adjacent and share, say, storytelling in the romantic-tragicomic mode.

If we take yet another step back, Hernandez's use of the romantic-tragicomic mode (one of three prototypical genres that Patrick Colm Hogan identifies in *The Mind and Its Stories*) is an outward manifestation of something going on more deeply within our cognitive and emotive architecture. I will speak to this more at length later, but suffice it to say that, as a species, we strive for fulfillment, and have been doing so ever since we walked out of Africa.[3] Storytelling genres themselves are constrained manifestations of this universal drive. In this circular loop-back system, a given emotion prototype governs what types of stories are tellable and determines what is interesting to the reader-author; the prototype also works as a guide to what is ultimately, as Hogan states, "effective and engaging" (88). So when Gilbert Hernandez pitches *Palomar* in the romantic-tragicomic mode, he is putting into play a story type that guides our cognitive processes and emotions.

Of course, while we all have prototype emotions and a hard-wired cognitive architecture (the brain's thought, language, and memory modules), this doesn't mean that there isn't room for creative play. Within such prototypical constraints, there are numerous (infinite even) ways that a given genre can be freshened up to engage us anew. This could be seen, for example, when Gilbert Hernandez decides to employ the romantic-tragicomic mode and yet innovates this genre by altering its conventions, infusing the story with a good dose of self-reflexivity to reform the conventions of the romantic tragicomedy and thus readjust the reader-viewer's expectation of and emotional engagement with this prototype genre. This is why a critic like Jared Gardner can identify in Gilbert's stories a move to "ultimately sacrifice their original romance for the characters for an almost existential cynicism" ("Borders and Moments," 121).

Latino comic book and comic strip innovation spins out of our universal capacity to imagine other worlds. We share the capacity to exist temporally in a past and a future as constructed by another in the present as well as to propose and share hypothetical situations with others. When Rhode Montijo takes up the sacrificial story prototype in *Pablo's Inferno*, he tweaks and amplifies this everyday ability to imagine outside ourselves. Montijo, like the author-artists interviewed here, dedicates a huge portion of his day to becoming an expert at plot, dialogue, drawing, panel layout, and so on in ways that non-comic-book authors have not. He is familiar with enough contents of the storehouse—themes, forms, traditions, techniques, plots, characters, and narrators—to be able to mix and match them and create something novel for a readership. He also looks to storehouses outside of the comic book tradition, to those of art, music, history, and many others. He has an aptness that allows him to engage with prototype and schema sets to reach beyond his own set of narrative prototypes in the crafting of *Pablo's Inferno*.[4]

Latino comic book and comic strip authors often reach beyond a specific domain (say, the techniques and plots that characterize the epic-superheroic prototype) and into other domains (say, the metafictional) to innovate their comic book forms. In *Sonambulo*, for instance, Rafael Navarro variously reaches outside of his dominant domain—the techniques that characterize noir—into that of fantasy, horror, and even gothic to create what we might call a fabulous noirism; in his *Palomar* stories, Gilbert Hernandez reaches beyond the domain of realism and into that of metafiction to create an invigorating self-reflexive suprarealism.

Innovation is a cognitive process, not the result of divine inspiration. It entails not only that a Latino comic book and strip author-artist know well how his or her prototype or schema set allows for an evaluation of what he or she might employ in the shaping of imagery and point of view, but also how it will appear in relation to other forms that constitute the comic book genre. Finally, innovation also entails a sense of how the reader-viewer carries certain domain-specific baggage that will need to be reshaped. That is, author-

Palomar: The Heartbreak Soup Stories

artists can't reach too far from a given prototype or schema set in their innovation, or they risk losing their audience. And here it is usually the Latino comic book author-artist's built-in sense of what "feels right" that helps govern how far he or she can innovate, how far he or she can push the reader to re-form given prototypes and schemata.

⑮ COMIC, TRAGIC, EPIC — REDUX

Latino comic book and comic strip author-artists work with a finite range of prototypical narratives, which spin out of a finite number of cross-culturally universal aspirations: happiness and fulfillment, for instance. These authors often (and to varying degrees) mix up the prototypical narratives to vary storytelling rhythms and complicate character types and plots. After exhaustive research in oral and written narratives from all over the world, Hogan identifies three recurring universal narrative prototypes that can be combined and individually shaped in an infinite variety of ways.[5] I summarize them as follows:

1. Romantic tragicomedy: characterized by conflict, usually between lovers, the parents of the lovers, or the society in which the lovers live; by the subsequent separation and exile of the lovers; and by their final unification.
2. Heroic tragicomedy: characterized by an individual like King Lear, who is usurped (politically, economically, etc.); by territories invaded by an Other; and by the final defeat of the invader and the usurper.
3. Sacrificial tragicomedy: characterized by a character or entity whose hubris leads to the punishing of the community (by drought, for example); harmony and plenitude are restored only once the offending character or entity has been punished.

Each prototypical narrative (the romantic and heroic are the most prominent worldwide) is based on our emotion concepts and prototypical emotion scenarios, which function "to prime or activate personal memories along with their associated feelings" (*The Mind and Its Stories*, 65).[6] For example, a reunion with a lover equals happiness and implies the previous experiences of falling in love and being separated.

A Latino comic book author-artist like Gilbert Hernandez can combine different prototypical narratives with their affiliated dominant-emotion scenarios (say, those of either happiness or sadness) to intensify specific sequences of events in the story of *Palomar*. In his series *Birdland*, he can combine the prototypical narrative of the heroic epic—a large part of the plot parallels the structure of epic journeys like those of Ulysses, Gilgamesh, and Daedalus—with that of the romantic (multiple characters falling in love, conflicts, separations and reunions) to texture this more erotically driven story: it ends in the realizing of fulfillment and happiness for the characters, but in a polymorphous smorgasbord of sexual interpenetrations and biological transformations (female characters with penises, and males with vaginas).

Ivan Velez Jr.'s violent, heroic-dimensioned *Blood Syndicate* not only mixes in the sacrificial prototype, but ends on a romantic note. Going against interracial taboos, Korean American superhero Third Rail couples with Afro-Latino Brick to realize goals of fulfillment—powerfully embodied in the birth of their multiracial, electrically charged, and epidermally bricked child. Romance wins the storytelling day in *Blood Syndicate*; when closing the final page of the final issue, the reader-viewer feels not sadness or tragedy but a sense of having encountered something new and vital. As Velez puts it: "Milestone got me interested in superhero comics in a way no other comics did. Reading of characters who looked like me, talked like me, grew up around the sort of people I did and felt the need to make a difference was something I very much needed and, perhaps, still need" (issue 35, 31).

Of course, the coupling convention is not the only road to fulfillment. As we see in Wilfred Santiago's *In My Darkest Hour*, Omar ends up reuniting with his girlfriend, but tragedy and sadness permeates the air at the comic book's close. He returns to his love interest not in search of fulfillment, but rather to deaden feelings of deep estrangement from the world, to temporarily sidetrack his thoughts from an acute sense of his life as a "big waiting room; waiting for a sand nigger to blow himself up, waiting for religious prophecies and ancient predictions to not be right, waiting for old age, waiting

for the death of the woman I love, waiting for my turn to rot" (112). *In My Darkest Hour* ends with Omar and his girlfriend's coupling, but the narrative leaves the reader feeling something other than the newness that accompanies the end of Velez's *Blood Syndicate*. Once again, the universal prototype narratives are in play, but have been combined in ways that innovate cognitively and emotively.

In My Darkest Hour

Pablo's Inferno

The sacrificial and heroic-epic prototype narratives also abound. We see in Montijo's *Pablo's Inferno* the emphasis on the sacrificial. Pablo becomes a stand-in for a society ignorant of its history. His journey into the underworld is one in which he learns of his ancestral roots and the bloody history of conquest. His final battle leads to a self-knowledge that ultimately restores a barren earth. The final panels describe Pablo planting corn seeds, and then rain comes—a sense of balance has been restored.

Many other Latino author-artists choose the epic-heroic—the superhero route—and subordinate romance to heroic tragicomedy. The Luna Brothers' Pearl, Oropeza's Amigoman, Javier Hernandez's El Muerto, Rodriguez's Aztec of the City, Saldaña's anthropomorphic Burrito, Molina's Jaguar, and many others are heroes who are marked off from society as special and who constantly face threats of being usurped by invading villains. The characters prevail, vanquishing villainous invaders and restoring communal social harmony.[7]

Each of the Latino comic book authors combines tragic moments with happy moments. They create the prototypical conditions for happiness and for sorrow. That is, each uses different emotion scenarios as ways to intensify the goals of the dominant prototype narrative. Doing otherwise would make for some rather boring comic book reading.

16 PROOF'S IN THE PUDDING

Even before we open to a Latino comic book's first series of panels—the story proper—we as reader-viewers are already doing cognitive work. The title, author name, jacket-cover blurbs, plot summaries, color schemes, fonts, and drawing style orient us toward certain generic paths and expectations. The author-artist can introduce here certain signposts that will create deliberate tensions or harmonies with what is to follow within the storyworld. Not surprisingly, and those interviewed here confirm this, it is the goal of the comic book author-artist to have as much control as possible over all elements of the comic book, including cover art, titles, blurbs, and the like. Sometimes publishers add blurbs and so on after the fact. However, even in those cases we see how an author-artist like Gilbert Hernandez creates a story so richly textured that it necessarily leads to interesting, even tense, interfaces.

This extratextual signposting can work rather straightforwardly. On the cover of Steve Ross's *Chesty Sanchez*, we see, from a low-angle shot, an epically proportioned, gun-toting, muscled Chesty Sanchez, along with her mariachi-outfit-wearing sidekick, Torpedo. The reader immediately positions the story not within, say, the mode of the everyday, but of the superheroic epic. That is what the story turns out to be: the superheroic adventures of a Latina. Jacket blurbs often identify story elements, as with *Latina Magazine*'s blurb of Cantú and Castellanos's *The Lower You Ride, the Cooler You Are: A Baldo Collection*: "Hot pick of the year—*Baldo* follows its teen hero on his cross-cultural suburban adventures. The funny papers are richer for it." In both *Baldo* and *Chesty*, the stories do little to complicate the extratextual signs.

The extratextual signposts can work to build expectations and situate the story in more complex ways as well. Before opening Gilbert's *Love and Rockets X*, we find a back-cover blurb that reads:

> Set in Los Angeles shortly before the Simi Valley riots, it tells a *Rules of the Game*-style story interlinking every stratum of L.A. society—a gay documentary filmmaker, his anorexic daughter, a group of skinheads who've beaten an elderly black woman, a punk rock band and Luba's Maricela, working as an undocumented street-corner flower girl as she makes her way in the north. Gilbert manages to break down the usual barriers in class- and race-segregated L.A., and to reveal links between characters from North and South and places in between.—*The Nation*

Along with a seal of approval from the liberal-identified *Nation*, the reader-viewer is given a sense of social setting and historical context as well as a sense of the style and the story's content. The crowded cast of variously colored, differently shaped and featured characters on the cover reinforces the expectation that we will enter a world filled with all sorts of types. Words and visuals cue the reader-viewer to frame the story as multicultural and sexually venturesome. Once in the storyworld, however, we find many of these types turned upside down. The story events, along with deeply contradictory char-

acters, set in motion racial, sexual, and gender schemas other than those suggested visually and verbally on the cover.

Extratextual elements can retroactively work (often in the form of published fan mail and the creator's response or an explanatory narrative) in a
contrary fashion to reduce the scope of the reader-viewer's imaginative horizon. For example, at the end of *El Diablo* (issue 1, 1989), writer Gerard Jones
leaves little room for ambiguity: "We wanted a character who got into this
'hero' business out of a desire to serve the public, as an adjunct to the political work he does during the day time. We wanted a hero who is consciously
and emphatically a part of his community" (39). And in case the reader wondered why El Diablo is depicted as flawed and not always in costume, it is to
play against "absurd super-hero clichés" (39). Such a straightforward overview
risks, of course, whittling down to nothing the reader-viewer's puzzle-solv-
ing-induced cognitive pleasure. We no longer get that feeling of fulfillment
from having put all the pieces of the story together or from putting all the
fragments of character into a whole personality.

The discussion of jacket-cover visual and verbal elements and those of
the story might appear to simplify our engagement with Latino comics to a
quasi-Pavlovian response. It is and isn't the case. While the elements both on
the cover and in the story's panels might cue, trigger, and even modify certain cognitive and emotive schemas, each reader-viewer has his or her own
distinct experiences. As cognitive science shows, such experiences leave two
types of memory traces in the mind: one representational and one emotive.
At any given moment, one sort of trace might be more active than another.
That is, the reader-viewer isn't in a constant state of amplified sensitivity to
both, but rather more conscious of one than the other at any given moment.
The colors, composition, background-foreground relationship, text font, and
angled view that present the multicultural cast of characters on the cover of
Love and Rockets X are orchestrated in a specific way to activate social memory traces (more than individual memory) that trigger certain emotions and
thoughts.[8] And in the continual use of a certain device, the author-artist creates a social memory of how we are to read and interpret. In *Love and Rockets
X*, Hernandez consistently places angle brackets ("< >") around sentences to
indicate that what we are reading (actually, listening to in our speech memory) are the words of a character speaking in Spanish or Arabic as translated
for the Anglophone reader-viewer. (He uses double quotation marks to identify Arabic.) And Hernandez uses the margin space at the bottom of the page
to footnote, often in exaggerated ways, single-word translations or pronun-
ciations of Spanish words (*esa*, *pendejo*, and *hijo*, for instance).

YOUR BRAIN ON LATINO COMICS

While there are many signposts that author-artists like Los Bros Hernandez use to cue and trigger our emotive and cognitive responses, each reader-viewer isn't going to be moved in exactly the same way. In the case of the footnotes about the pronunciation of Spanish, rather than see this as playful exaggeration, the reader-viewer might consider this a distraction. In the case of a crowded and chaotic panel composition, the reader-viewer might experience only a fleeting, fuzzy feeling of discontent. Of course, the greater the clarity of our affect, the more we are aware of how individual and social memory are interacting while we read the story.

The Latino comic book author shares this awareness also, wittingly or not. When an author-artist reads his or her work out loud or takes a step back to look at his or her drawing (and this distancing process also happens without any physical movement), he or she is hearing and seeing if it makes sense as well as how it feels. The processes of writing, drawing, and revising include this sense of fine-tuning how to move the reader—and this occurs whether or not the author-artist is aware of it.

On a most general level, then, a Latino comic book author works within a finite range of cognitive processes. He or she uses a finite range of visual and verbal techniques and devices that interact in specific ways to identify the narrative as a comic book. They choose from a finite range of prototypical narratives, but recombine them in infinite ways. And these elements work at the level of both idea (representation) and emotion to prime a reader-viewer's individual and social memories in a loop-back system that further guides his or her meaning-making process.

GETTING EMOTIONAL

We know well that visuals like color, black-and-white, lighting, shading, points of view, panel size, and so on all have some emotional effect on the reader-viewer. When Bobby Rubio, author-artist of *Alcatraz High*, makes Miguel's face triangular, and his sidekick Steve's round, he is doing so to arouse certain subcortical emotional responses. And our emotions will vary in intensity: we could feel annoyed, but this feeling might not overwhelm us and lead to action. It might simply be a mood that whispers in the background. Or sometimes we can be overwhelmed to such a degree that our body acts of its own accord. Hogan identifies this response as being "innately sensitized to particular environmental features," (175). Such responses include automatic, limbic-system reactions to such things as size (large animals), motion type (the slithering of reptiles), sounds (growling), and so on. The reader of a Latino comic book like *Azteca of the City* knows that the archvillain La Llorona is not "real," but the way Fernando Rodriguez chooses to draw her (oversized and predatory), along with the pacing of the panel layout when she is visually described, triggers subcortical responses of fear. Even before she does something nasty, and without a narrator telling us explicitly, we know she is to be feared.

And there is a similar subcortical emotional arousal that takes place at the level of character action. Here I don't mean the sort of action punctuated by *POW! WHAM!* or *BAM!* but rather the action of a reader-viewer closely following the characters as they take paths and make choices that may or may not lead to positive outcomes. As reader-viewers of Latino comics, we are constantly evaluating, considering whether a given event, behavior, or action will

The Incredible Hulk, Volume 2, Issue 265

further a character's goals. The degree to which we are invited in to the story and characters determines the degree of our emotional arousal.

There is another layer of emotional response that is more cognitive than that triggered by the appearance of an oversized animal-like villain (or the close-up of a panicked face, or a tragic turn of events). It occurs when a given Latino comic book author-artist defies certain formal conventions: omitting gutters, using an elongated page (*Rocketo*), drawing a character in different styles, and so on. Such play with convention activates (to different degrees, depending on the reader and his or her comic-book storehouse) our social memory of the norms of the convention and how they work in relation to the author-artist's current modification—all this also elicits an emotional response.

While the Latino comic book narratives move us from one cortically or subcortically aroused peak of emotion (short-duration effects of anger, hate, sadness, or laughter) to another as the stories unfold, there is an overall mood that persists. The mood is the gel that fills in between different peak emotions; the mood can reinforce such emotions (allowing them to persist in attenuated form over long periods of time) or run counter to them. The mood can be maintained either by how the character is expressed or by how the artist-author leans heavily on one type of panel layout (squashed together or spread apart), one type of color wash or schema (black-and-white or color), one type of line weight (heavy or light), and so on. So while we move from one peak emotion to the next, depending on the dominant visual and verbal elements used, each author-artist infuses his or her story with an overall mood.

Now, a story that lacks logic or internal coherence will not engender an emotional response. We invest emotionally (wittingly or not) in stories that make sense—that can make sense, too, in their carefully orchestrated incoherence, as with some of Los Bros Hernandez's more metafictional work. If there isn't a logic governing perspective, color palette, and characterization, then we tend not to invest emotionally in the story. Indeed, when we enter the world of, say, Frank Espinosa's *Rocketo*, we don't really suspend disbelief, as many would have us believe. What really happens is that we constantly evaluate its logic system, deciding whether its world works and is coherent, whether its smoking guns have been fired. If the logic system works, then we will immerse ourselves in (and only ever partially, since our minds are aware always of our actual surroundings) and be moved by the fictional worlds served up.[9]

We might jump at the action; we might vocalize delight or disgust, sadness or the like. The comic book author-artist uses different techniques coherently in ways that trigger our limbic reflexes. We really notice this when watching films whose verisimilitude creates a strong illusion of reality. However, no matter how much an author-artist tries to erase our sense of the difference between reality and fiction, if the internal logic of the story doesn't work, we're not going to invest in it emotionally. We won't cringe, close our eyes, jerk our legs, or tear up; we will simply turn off.

18 ABRACADABRA . . . THE MIND-READING TRICK

I mentioned how I used to dress up as some sort of luchador-Superman-Batman mix when I was a kid. Something about these particular strong, heroic figures moved me more than others. This phenomenon of identifying with a fictional character has been taking place since time immemorial. I think here of all those young men who dressed up in black after reading Goethe's *Sorrows of Young Werther*, or of today's children and teens who dress up as their favorite superhero on Halloween. In these cases, as with comic books generally, the reader-viewer actively empathizes with the character. Through this sense of identification, we wish to become like the character; we feel for the character in ways that we don't for others.

This phenomenon of empathy is limited, whether we are reading a novel like *The Sorrows of Young Werther* or a Latino comic book. We know that, whoever we are, we are not superheroes living in Gotham City. We know that when reading *Rocketo*, while we may adopt temporarily the life and goals of the character, Rocketo, we are Rocketo only in "an as-if way," as Katja Mellmann states of this identification process generally ("E-Motion: Being Moved by Fiction and Media?").

So when I say that I identify with El Santo and Batman, what I actually mean is that I feel for these characters. The coherence of their actions and goals leads me to invest empathetically in them. This identification can even lead to a strong sense that we know them as we might a real friend whose company we long for. Certainly, Latino comic book author-artists are adept at triggering this feeling for characters in an "as-if way." But this process requires reader-viewers who are able to read the interior states of others, who are able to formulate complex hypotheses of the workings of another's mind.

When we read a Latino comic book story, we are not only putting ourselves in another's shoes, but also imagining, from the visual and verbal fragments and signposts provided, a character in a whole world. The same process goes for the author-artists. For example, even though Carlos Trillo and Eduardo Risso don't live in Brooklyn or New York City (both live in Argentina), in their series *Chicanos* they can imagine, distill, and distort in such a way that a powerful sense of the city can come alive—for themselves and their reader-viewers. The visual cues allow us to feel the protagonist Alejandrina's movement in and through the differently textured and inhabited space of the city. The precise visual markings trigger a process whereby specifics of character, time, and place form in the reader-viewer's mind. This also reinforces our emotional investment in Alejandrina. We feel for her when romances fail, crushes shatter, sleuthing leads to dead ends. And when she asks the reader directly, "Do you wanna hear how the story ended?" (issue 6, 24), we nod our heads. We are given just enough information to allow us to imagine fully these worlds. If we lacked the capacity for empathy and its crucial "mind-reading" component, we would find it very difficult to read the interior state of a character from exterior gestures and cues. (And, in fact, sociopaths, who lack consciences,

Chicanos, Issue 6

are distinguished precisely by their complete lack of empathy.) We would find it nearly impossible to make the imaginative and as-if emotional leaps necessary for such comic book worlds to captivate us.

Almost everyone can, to varying degrees, infer the interior state of mind of another human being from exterior gestures, behaviors, and attitudes. Without this capacity, we would be psychologically crippled, resembling severe autistics, who lack this mind-reading capacity. Even if it is not always accurate (we have all had experiences of misreading interior states), this capacity, as Lisa Zunshine sums up, allows us to "construct and navigate our social environment" (*Why We Read Fiction*, 6).

Latino author-artists can direct this mind-reading faculty of ours in pleasurable and complex ways. By reading the author-artist's cues, we can correctly infer causality, identity, perspective, temporal and spatial relations, and character interactions. And Latino author-artists can play, tease, and even push to its limits, our mind-reading capacity in order to intensify our emotional and cognitive responses. Visual signposts may seem to be cuing us to infer a character's frustration, yet the verbal elements suggest contentment and happiness. Maybe character A doesn't want character B to know that he or she is, in fact, unhappy. In the case of Trillo and Risso's *Chicanos*, Alejandrina doesn't want her friend Marita to know that she has a crush on her, so upon hearing of Marita's sexual exploits, she acts nonchalant. The reader-viewer, however, is given enough information to infer Alejandrina's more complex state of mind. And this can become even more complicated when author-artists supply yet another level of interpretation—say, that of a third-person narrator's telling us that Alejandrina is not aware that Marita is aware of her faking emotional indifference.

Chicanos, Issue 2

Palomar: The Heartbreak Soup Stories

For Zunshine, our mind-reading capacity is the bread and butter of all fictional narrative. It is used by authors to "titillate our tendency to keep track of *who* thought, wanted, and felt what and *when* (*Why We Read Fiction*, 5). This can be complicated by racial scripts. For example, in *Palomar*, when Luba ventures into the town of San Fideo to have her movie projector fixed, the guys infer from her gestures (and accent) that she is "a dumb Indian" (95). But it can also be very complicated. I think here of Gilbert Hernandez's *Luba: The Book of Ofelia*, which presents us with a cast of nineteen fully fleshed-out characters. The reader-viewer must keep track of a dumbfounding number of individual interior states of mind whenever a character reads another character's interior state and acts on it. This often leads to a snowballing of misreadings and affiliated chain reactions. Hernandez plays with this by adding multiple dimensions of verbal gestures that conflict with verbal articulations of interior thoughts, leading to both humorous and tragic misreadings. For example, Pipo acts in ways to cover up her romance with her son's girlfriend, Fritz, but this action leads the son and Pipo's ex-husband, Gato, to infer incorrectly her love of Fortunato; in their jealous rage, they kill the innocent Fortunato.

The more of a character's personality the reader-viewer comes to know, the more the author-artist can complicate our reading of the character's interior state of mind. If we know a character like Casmira to be prudent and rational, when she acts histrionic in front of one character but not another, we infer that a strategic manipulation is at work. And when Hernandez describes Ofelia as dressed in black and lying on a bed with her eyes closed, we infer from the preceding visual and verbal elements that she is dead; however, as in the next sequence of panels, we discover that she is simply taking a nap while waiting for a taxi to arrive. Hernandez knows that the reader-viewer is storing information (in episodic memory) about the character's personality, gestures, and context. And that he can constantly add and subtract from this information as well as send the reader on a wild-goose chase. He can create scenes in which the visual and verbal narrative elements lead us to misread a character's interior state. And in so doing, he constantly tantalizes and titillates.

It is important to keep in mind that when we read or view a comic book, it is the author-artist who deliberately guides us to read or misread interior states of mind. This is to say, in comic book narrative fiction, there is no guesswork. As in dreams, so too in comic books: we are not guessing at what is going on in the mind of a character—as we often do in our everyday life when we try to read another person to know if he or she is being sarcastic, joking, aggressive, or affectionate. There is no guesswork, because it has already been done entirely by an author-artist like Gilbert Hernandez. His verbal and visual narration provides all sorts of information about how the characters feel and think.

19   DOUBLE TROUBLE: THE VISUAL AND VERBAL NARRATOR

Unthreading layers of intentionality in a comic book or comic strip involves much more than employing a fully functioning theory of mind. It is a cognitively complex feat that relies on visual and verbal senses to stimulate memories, feelings, thoughts, tastes, smells, and sensations of touch. A comic book or comic strip cues and triggers these memories, feelings, and sensations by its unique configuration of verbal and visual elements. The emphasis on one feeling over another, the tension between our reliable or unreliable reading of interior states, is determined—and this is uniquely so with comic books and comic strips—by the way the visual and verbal elements interact as well as by which is dominant in a particular panel. As Mila Bongco succinctly remarks: "Reading comics involves the pictures and their meanings in relations to the language, and the key to understanding comics does not lie in the words or pictures themselves but in the interaction and relationship between them" (*Reading Comics*, 49). Indeed, just as there can be a tension between the verbal and visual narration, so too can there be tensions between the individual visual or verbal elements that make up a panel.

The narration of a Latino comic book—its most salient feature—uses simultaneously image and text to show and describe its storyworld. I would go so far as to say that for it to be a comic book, it must contain both verbal (speech and thought balloons) and visual elements. The verbal and visual narration works as a gestalt, even when the reader-viewer sees first the image then the verbal text. Given that comic book narration is both verbal and visual, Latino author-artists can play with varying degrees of presence of one or the other to control the rhythm and flow of the story—the pace at which a reader-viewer constructs a narrative gestalt. Of course, some comic book author-artists choose to tip the balance toward the visual, like Peter Kuper in his *The System* and *Sticks and Stones*. Such stories read more like those painted triptychs of the Middle Ages or a pre-Hispanic codex in which the narration is only visual. Conversely, there can be a superabundance of verbal narration, as with Andrea M. Gaudiano's *Azteca: The Story of a Jaguar Warrior* and Michael Perry's *Daniel's Ride / El Paseo de Daniel*. In both, the visuals act as background filler, giving the storytelling role exclusively to the verbal register. In both, the visuals work only as distractions. Frank Espinosa's *Rocketo* takes reader-viewers to the limit of visual narration. Here, however, both the verbal and visual in their various pendular swings are fundamental for moving the story forward. Since the visuals are at the limits of representation—they are very abstract and expressionist—it is difficult for the reader-viewer to fuse the visual narration with the verbal. While this contributes to a viewing or reading of the visuals as being more independent than those in mainstream comic books, Espinosa doesn't push us so far that we no longer move between the verbal and the visual. The verbal and visual narration is still working together to guide and form the reader's gestalt.

How the Latino author-artist chooses to put into motion the verbal and visual elements determines the overall story coherence and the mood of the comic. It can thus even direct how we might categorize a comic book—as more pedagogical than pleasurable, or as a combination of both. The way, for instance, that Gaudiano renders the verbal and visual elements in *Azteca: The Story of a Jaguar Warrior* swings more toward the verbal. Its long descriptions of Aztec legend and the history of genocide in the conquest of the Americas lean us toward considering it serious and pedagogical. In *Cihualyaomiquiz, the Jaguar*, Laura Molina foregrounds Latino resistance within an oppressive and bigoted Anglo-dominated America, but its balance between the verbal and the visual gives it a less heavily didactic feel.

In Jaime Hernandez's *La Maggie La Loca*, we see how a Latino author-artist balances the visual narrator and the verbal narrator: its heavy inked lines, its solid yet subdued palette (brown, yellows, blues), share page space with an interior monologue in a subpanel caption box; we overhear Maggie's flashes of thought about herself, her friends, and her surroundings. Part I opens, "I woke up in the morning" (April 23, 2006, 35). As the serialized story of La

"La Maggie La Loca," Part 1

"La Maggie La Loca," Part 2

Maggie unfolds, our brain has already mapped the verbal narrator's past-tense first-person voice to the visual narrator's focus on the character Maggie. And here things begin to get interesting. The visual narrator can describe Maggie—facial expression, gesture, behavior—in ways that emphasize or conflict with the textual—the verbal narrator's voice. One can depict happiness while the other describes frustration; one comfort, and the other paranoia. In such cases, Hernandez challenges—and even plays havoc with—the reader's cognitive schemas that work to infer interior state from outward gesture, that allow one to determine a state of pleasure or contentment from a smile.

So the force of the double narrator's pendular swings affects the feel and the kinetic quality of the story. As each story unfolds, it acquires its own unique pendular rhythm, swinging between the visual narrator and the verbal narrator in ways that lull and surprise. Within this rhythm, we are constantly registering minute shifts in the degree of presence of either verbal or visual narrative configurations.

Palomar: The Heartbreak Soup Stories

We derive a certain pleasure in figuring out how Hernandez uses the verbal and visual elements of the narration to create certain tensions. We can begin to read—and even delight in—the unreliability of Maggie's voice. In spite of the primacy given to Maggie's interior thoughts and impressions, such cognitive movement between the verbal and visual narrators creates certain tensions that allow us to step outside of her positionality—for example, to perhaps not use her as the standard for judging a character like Rena—and there is pleasure in this recognition.

All Latino comic book author-artists choose how they want to configure the verbal narrator and the visual narrator. The degree of presence of either can vary from panel to panel and also from comic to comic; the author-artist has total artistic control in the way he or she chooses to vary the pendular swings. However, it would appear from the interviews, that this artistic control diminishes when they begin to work for mainstream comic conglomerates. The types of narration can exist in harmony or in tension. One may barely be present; Frank Espinosa's extended wordless sequences in *Rocketo* are a case in point. A heavier or lighter presence of either will affect not only the pacing and rhythm of the story, but the feeling we have when encountering individual panels: for example, too much of the verbal narrative element within a panel can create a sense of claustrophobia; little to none, a sense of expansiveness.

In the case of Wilfred Santiago's *In My Darkest Hour*, we see how the visual and verbal narration works to project the story as if it were a lucid dream. Not only does the story begin with Omar waking up—does he ever wake up, or is this a dream of him waking up?—but this is also emphasized by the light yellow and gray color wash over the panels, along with the juxtaposition of disparate images in a rather haphazard-seeming montage: a small-panel subjective filter of a street scene, then a jump to a splash page with a stylized Captain America dropping bombs on Iraq, then a panel just with an eyeball. Movement in the comic book seemingly defies the laws that govern time-and-space relations in our everyday waking life. The narrative can show a bird's-eye view of a city one instant, then a close-up of someone walking naked in the street. To step into the shoes of Santiago's ideal reader, we have to apply the logic of dreams to how we read the plot as well as the visuals and the verbal text. If we don't follow the logic of dreams, then the story won't work for us. This verbal and visual narration determines how we are to cluster together elements for scenes, characters, events—that is, determines the contract we are to sign when entering into any given Latino comic book storyworld. With Santiago, we must sign on to read and view a story told in the mode of a dreamlike subjective realism.

 ## LATINOS CONJURED UP

All these elements give shape also to our sense of a persona creating the storyworld; not necessarily, say, the flesh-and-blood Jaime Hernandez who exists as more than the author of *La Maggie La Loca*, but that sense of a master of control who orchestrates how the visual and verbal elements balletically pull together, who determines the particular patterning of visual and verbal elements that creates in the mind of the reader-viewer an image of a supra-entity giving the comic book its own sense of style. It is this "will to style" that gives *La Maggie La Loca* its distinctive feel and look. It is Hernandez's particular style that leads readers to return time and time again. And if the style of *La Maggie La Loca* appeals, then we become invested in the characters like Maggie, wondering why she is so paranoid, suspicious, and apathetic. The will to style works to draw us in, then the story signed "Xaime" pulls us back every time it is published to learn more.

It is this will to style that moves readers; it is why a critic like Jared Gardner would refer to the unique style of Gilbert Hernandez as "folk sculpture" and that of brother Jaime as "pop culture collage"—and even how the work of one in "juxtaposition with the work of the other" strengthens both ("Borders and Moments," 119–120). It is this will to style that allows a reader to read certain stylistic juxtapositions (hand-drawn lines alongside digitized pixels) in Rob Cabrera's strip *Silo Roberts* as references to influences from Japanese anime to *Peanuts*. It is why we might recognize in Bobby Rubio's *Alcatraz High* a heavy brushstroke style we identify with animation. It is why critic Chris Arrant identifies Frank Espinosa's style in *Rocketo* as "one part Yves Chaland and one part Flash Gordon, without losing any originality in his vital work" (www.forum.newsrama.com/showthread.php?threadid=38937).

And, it is this recognition of an author-artist's will to style that allows one to notice subtle but important shifts between different narratives. Lalo Alcaraz has a trademark style that allows us to identify him as the master of controls of both *Migra Mouse* and *La Cucaracha*; it is the reason why Robert Harvey can note in his blurb for *La Cucaracha* that Alcaraz "spots blacks nicely, and the strip has a crisp attractive clarity" and that his style is "simple and somewhat angular with an unvarying line, is entirely competent" (*La Cucaracha*, 6). But, of course, while there is a unifying style, each strip can and does deploy variations on that style: one is more macabre and less playful than the other, for example.

It is this element of the will to style that either sends us back for more or stops us dead in our tracks. I didn't like the post–issue 28 style of *Blood Syndicate*, so I stopped following it as judiciously. I am particularly drawn to the

Alcatraz High, Issue 1

YOUR BRAIN ON LATINO COMICS

will to style of Risso and Trillo in their *Chicanos*, but less so Risso's style in *100 Bullets*. It is what sends me back for more of *Rocketo* but not *Outsiders*. The presence of this will to style can have material consequence. I think here of Los Bros Hernandez's work on Dean Motter and Paul Rivoche's *Mister X* in 1984; after four issues, Motter and Rivoche decided that Los Bros Hernandez's style didn't match up with their sense of a Bauhaus–Fritz Lang–art deco vision for this other world—they were "too cartoony." (See Arlen Schumer's introduction to *Mister X*, in which he also discusses how Los Bros missed the mark because they gave Radiant City too much of a "barrio feel" [Motter and Rivoche, *Mister X*, 13]).

Each Latino comic book and comic strip has a greater or lesser degree of presence of this will to style. This is why we reread some comic books but only read and throw away others. It is also why we might evaluate them not as inherently good or bad, but rather according to how they register the presence of the will to style. When critics make distinctions between those cranked out for easy consumption and those that are "alternative" and complex, they are distinguishing between those comic books and comic strips that employ only one or two storytelling ingredients (suspense, say) and those that include many more elements (temporal play, embedded intentional states, unconventional panel layout, and so on).

21 REREADING RACE AND ETHNICITY

Latino comic book and comic strip author-artists organize the visual and verbal elements in ways to guide and even educate readers in how to engage with their storyworlds. As I mentioned before, not all readers will pick up on these signposts; nor will all comic books or comic strips appeal to all readers. This is to say, Latino author-artists always have in mind when creating their stories a flesh-and-blood reader-viewer, even if it is only himself or herself. And it is here that we begin to see how their comic book worlds might appeal more to one audience than another: a Latino more than an Anglo, a female more than a male. Many of the author-artists interviewed here speak about trying out their scenes on an audience. Some, like Gilbert Hernandez, have internalized this audience and so don't tend to literally act the scenes out. It is why many of the authors interviewed here speak of how they will storyboard, then take a step back to see how a particular visual moves them, revising as they see fit.

It is this dimension of the reader being moved cognitively and emotionally that allows us to understand how Gilbert Hernandez can create a scene in which the character Carl isn't visually depicted as violently stomping an African American woman—we simply see his shoe—but earlier panels and stored characteristics (he is a racist) imply that this is what is happening off-panel. Hernandez gives us just enough detail to fill in the visual blank—our cognitive frames and schemas supply the defaults for the gaps. Our minds do the work, and therefore our bodies feel more viscerally Carl's foot violently stomping.

It is also this cognitive gap filling and schematization that allows us to understand how Gilbert can use simple marks on the page to upend deep misconceptions about speech (language) and thought—that, for example, the way we speak reflects directly on the quality of our mind. Gilbert powerfully drives home how this misconception can reinforce racism and bigotry. In *Love and Rockets X*, the verbal and visual narration presents Maricela (Luba's daughter from Palomar) as speaking in a truncated, broken English while cleaning the house of a white character, who reads her broken English as evidence of her being illiterate and a dullard. However, a few pages later, we see her speaking very well and conveying her ideas in nonbroken English. The difference: Hernandez uses angle brackets to indicate to the reader-viewer that we are actually listening to her speak Spanish (in English translation). It is not that the quality of her mind changed from one day to the next, but rather that in English she had difficulty in expressing her thoughts.

Other Latino comic book and strip author-artists use various configurations of visual narrator and verbal narrator to prime fragments of memories and emotion (our own and those of others) that direct us to respond in specific ways to predetermined racialized, sexualized, and gendered scripts. While there are cultural particulars in Hector Cantú and Carlos Castellanos's *Baldo*—El Cucuy (a Tejano-styled bogeyman), guayaberas, and *curanderisma* cure-alls—they playfully rescript essentialist cultural-identity categories. For example, they introduce the Anglo character Britney "Smiley" Rogers, who first visits Baldo's house and asks, "Where's the tortilla maker? Don't you decorate with piñatas? I don't see any Ricky Martin posters!" (115). In *Raising Hector*, Peter Ramirez turns traditional gender schemas (men work, women cook) upside down. He also complicates certain expectations of Latino-ness: not all Latinos speak Spanish, as the grandfather informs PJ, but this doesn't make them less Latino. We all "have something to contribute," his abuelo informs him (www.raisinghector.com). In *Pablo's Inferno*, Rhode Montijo takes his readers into a world filled with pre-Columbian imagery and figures, but sidesteps presenting this as somehow untouched by other cultural influences. When Pablo encounters the Spiderwoman, the reader learns of her pan-indigenous (Caribbean, Arawak, and North American) mythical identity. By focusing on a panoply of contradictory and complex ethnic- and Anglo-identified characters in the *Love and Rockets* series, Los Bros Hernandez don't play into a United Colors of Benetton, easily consumable multiculturalism.

When studying Latino comics, we must keep centrally in mind the dimension of the author and reader. Not by looking to biographies or interviews for those nuggets that point to a one-to-one correspondence between fiction and biographical fact, but by noting how certain visual and verbal techniques move authors (as readers) and readers cognitively and emotionally. Indeed, that we can imaginatively enter into and be moved by the worlds of Latino comics is a result of our evolved capacity to distinguish from an early age the difference between fiction (make-believe) and reality. It is the result of our evolutionary capacity to enjoy indulging in all sorts of narrative fictions—comic books included—not only because they are safe places to practice virtual survival strategies, as some would argue, but also because we enjoy the formal aspects of the way in which the storytelling is done.

Our ability to inhabit multiple pasts and futures via storytelling in the present has given rise to the evolution of new temporal and spatial modes of meta-awareness. With storytelling, we began to develop the ability to distinguish between a past, a present, and a future tense. This unique capacity for multitemporality marks the evolutionary moment when we became aware through storytelling of our reality in ways that distinguished us from (as far as we know today) other animals. H. Porter Abbott proposes that "narrative time is constructed time according to creatural priorities" ("The Evolutionary Origins of the Storied Mind," 250). His hypothesis gets us closer to understanding how tense is central to Latino comic book narrative. The visual and verbal telling of a comic book story in the present can recall a past (from the present moment of telling) or predict a future; such telling involves centrally readers capable of imagining a present, past, and future different from their present. Indeed, the evolved capacity to employ increasingly more sophisticated symbolic modes of representation in narrative allowed for more complex orchestrations of temporality and eventually led to the splitting of narrative into a double chronologic: the way the story is told (third person, say) and the content of the story (the events and characters, say). This helps us understand better why a Latino comic book author-artist can manipulate narrative point of view, lighting, panel layout, and so on not only to tell a story, but also to engage audiences and readers on a number of different levels.

In reading the signposts laid out by Latino comic book and comic strip author-artists, we are cued to reexperience or reconstruct our core selves in complex and specifically directed ways: ways that direct us to realize a fuller experience of U.S. ethnicity—specifically, Latino and Latina identity. All this while constantly reminding us of the difference between self and life, and life and fiction.

22 IT'S A BURRITO WRAP

This is but a first baby step in the study of Latino comic books and comic strips. More needs to be done on specific author-artists, on the recovery of lost or marginalized texts, and on understanding more deeply how we are moved by their storyworlds.

Nothing is hands-off to these Latino author-artists. Both in form and in content, their comic book narrative fictions can be about everything and anything and can be materialized or expressed in the most surprising and unexpected ways. They can playfully riff on and more seriously refer to one another's work, comic books generally, and universal narratives from the world over. They can use the techniques and combinations of visual and verbal narration to convey particular moods and to move readers and audiences to imagine holographically other worlds in specific ways. And the cultural particulars of one comic book narrative might trigger a specific response in one reader and not another. And yet it is possible for the author-artist to transcend the particular and to transport a reader-viewer from Columbus, Ohio, to the streets of East LA.

In continuing to develop a method and approach to Latino comic books, we need to consider the specific devices available and used by the comic book medium—the verbal and visual double narrator, for instance—as well as how these devices move reader-viewers. Therefore, we need to consider how an author-artist distills and distorts various elements in order to engage our cognitive faculties (language, memory, emotion, and so on). This means that we consider not only how the will to style creates a gestalt image of an authorial-artistic persona (or an ideal author-artist), but also how flesh-and-blood author-artists transform the everyday activities and events of the world into objects that engage us in new and interesting ways.

Keeping in mind always that the particular (Latino), general (U.S. society), and universal (neurobiological capacity for language, memory, emotion, and the like) are at once separable and inseparable, I have begun to show how rich and complex Latino comic book and comic strip storytelling can be. I have begun to show how the author-artists can playfully riff on and more seriously refer to one another's work, comic books generally, and universal narratives from the world over. I have begun to explore how different techniques and different combinations of visual and verbal elements convey particular moods and move readers and audiences to imagine holographically other worlds as well as to read complex interior states of mind. I have begun to show how cultural particulars might trigger a specific response in one reader and not another; for example, the mention of "El Cucuy" in *Baldo* will have a specific resonance for Latino reader-viewers from Texas, but not for Chicanos from Sacramento. I have also begun to show how it is possible for a reader like me, who is not, say, a Chicana who grew up in Los Angeles, to holographically imagine such a world in the particular verbal and visual panel compositions of Laura Molina's *Cihualyaomiquiz, the Jaguar*. I have begun to show that the capacity to be able to read minds—to infer from gesture and behavior the interiority of a character—can cause reader-viewers to be moved to feel the pain, happiness, anger, and sadness of a character. It is the cross-culturally shared ability to read minds, empathize, communicate, imagine a past and a future in our present, and so on that allows a San Diego–born, Filipino author-artist like Bobby Rubio to give life to a Chicano protagonist in *Alcatraz High*. It is why the Argentinean writer-artist team behind *Chicanos* can vitally imagine and vibrantly create a Chicana character who inhabits a North American metropolitan space.

This isn't an attempt to wash out difference. Of course, my experiences and memories will resonate differently from those of a Chicana from East LA, but only by degree. This is to say, for the study of Latino comic books and comic strips, we must at some point account for the interconnectedness of the particular (growing up Chicano in places like Sacramento), the general (living in contemporary U.S. society), and the universal (the emotional and cognitive faculties I share with all others). Indeed, as the section that follows confirms, we need to keep in mind always the worldly dimension of Latino culture: that the reader and author share common faculties (language, memory, emotion, and so on). As the authors themselves forcefully attest, we need to keep in mind that nothing in the world is alien to Latino comic books and comic strips.

PART III

CONVERSATIONS
WITH THE CREATORS

David Alvarez

David Alvarez was born in 1972 in San Juan, Puerto Rico, then grew up in the town of Manatí. It was here that he began to develop his passion for drawing at age five. His early training: to spend hours drawing the expressions and faces of Disney cartoon characters. He continued to develop his craft in high school and college; he studied graphic arts at Manatí's Vocational and Technical College, then telecommunications at the University of Puerto Rico, Arecibo. Alvarez's talent was quickly recognized by Warner Bros., which hired him to work as a freelance artist on a variety of projects, including the Sylvester the cat stories.

While in college, Alvarez created his popular comic strip *Zacha and Anyelín*. He returned to the strip while freelancing for Warner Brothers, transforming it into what is now known as *Yenny*.

He continues to live with his family in San Juan, Puerto Rico, where he continues to create *Yenny* and other comic strips, such as *Changuy* and *Kii-Kii Kokí*—both published in Puerto Rico's first island-wide newspaper, *El Nuevo Día*. Alias distributes *Yenny*, which is widely available. You can visit his website at http://www.yennycomics.com. And daily and Sunday strips of *Yenny* can be read at www.ucomics.com.

FREDERICK LUIS ALDAMA: Does this give you a particular angle from which to see mainland U.S. Latino identity/experience?

DAVID ALVAREZ: Definitely. I've been always surrounded by average pueblo people.

FLA: You mention drawing Disney characters at age five. When was your first encounter with comic strips, comic books generally?

DA: Yeah, I used to have a wall in my room full of Disney characters. All in different expressions.

I had a first encounter with comic strips. I was a fan of Guy Gilchrist's Muppet comic strip and *Garfield*. We weren't so wealthy, so comic books appeared later in my life. I used to read *Woody Woodpecker*, Bugs Bunny adventures, even *Blondie* comic books. All in Spanish from Editorial Novaro.

Eventually I became a fan of the Smurfs comic books, which also were published in Spanish.

FLA: How about in your later years?

DA: Later on I got hooked up with *Condorito*. I became a quick fan of Pepo's humor. *Memín* was also very good, and I learned storytelling from those particular comics.

FLA: When did you begin to draw Puerto Rican culturally specific characters/cartoons?

DA: I did that when I created *Zacha and Anyelín*. Before that I tried to mimic the American-ness of the other comics with other characters of my own.

FLA: Why choose to work within this storytelling art form?

DA: I wanted to do animation, but, like I said before, we weren't very wealthy, so animation studies and materials were too expensive for my parents to buy, so eventually I had to settle for comics.

FLA: Why Yenny as a character?

DA: I remember watching Roger Rabbit in theaters, and like everyone else, I fell in love with Jessica Rabbit. But like *every* other female character, she was just the male main character's love interest.

That's when I took the decision of taking Anyelín, (from *Zacha and Anyelín*) to the leading role. I also sent her to the "Toon Gym," so she could acquire more curves and look more Latina.

FLA: Can you talk a little about *Changuy*?

DA: *Changuy* was my first official comic book. I created *Changuy* with David Martinez. We published it in Puerto Rico, and it became very successful back in 1991. It was a Disney-like funny-animal comic book. *DuckTales* and *TaleSpin* were hit shows by then. I think that helped a lot for the sales of the book.

FLA: Why tell stories in comic strip form?

DA: It was the fastest way to get my characters published. Comic books were too saturated, and it would've taken me decades for *Yenny* to be noticed.

FLA: Why not short story, novel, etc., or even the longer comic book form?

DA: I've always wanted to do that. But sadly, I've to do everything that brings meat on the table first. That's also why I chose comic strips. They only took half of the time to do. Actually, animation had always been my goal, but it was unreachable at the early stages of cartooning.

FLA: The art of cartooning differs from the comic book?

DA: Definitely. Storytelling through art is quite different.

FLA: How do the elements of the visual and textual interact to make it a comic strip instead of a comic book?

DA: It's rather difficult. What I could tell in a comic book I have to condense in three panels. I got used to it, though.

FLA: Why humor? Is it more conducive to satirizing society?

DA: Yeah. People like to laugh, and I've used comedy as a way of telling "serious" stories without being tragic at all.

FLA: What is the essence of the comic strip, in your opinion?

DA: Daily gags.

FLA: Does warmth and humor have to be an element?

DA: Absolutely. If your characters are not loved by the reader, there's no future for them.

FLA: Is there a place for political critique in *Yenny*?

DA: I've tried. Especially for local politics, but I was censored by my newspaper. The editor didn't want *Yenny* to touch those lands. I try to stay away from it, anyway.

FLA: Do you continue to work as an illustrator storyboard artist for DC Comics, Looney Tunes, Disney? Can you make a living off *Yenny* alone?

DA: Yes I am and . . .well . . . I'm coming close to that.

FLA: Has your style changed since 1988, when you first drew *Zacha and Anyelín* for a local newspaper, and today's *Yenny*?

DA: Yeah. Those were individual gags, à la Garfield. They didn't have a storyline at all. Yenny has *much* more personality now.

FLA: Was it difficult breaking into Puerto Rican, then U.S. publishing media markets?

DA: No one's a prophet in his own land, so breaking into the PR market was very tough. There were two little local comic strips and comic books, and the idea of a new comic was rather "childish" to many editors and publishers. So ironically, the U.S. market treated me better.

After a few years of Looney Tunes comic books, some people knew my name, so I used it to publish the first restored *Zacha and Anyelín* comic strips, named now *Yenny*, on the Toonzone forums. Eventually I moved over to Ucomics' recently created *Comics Sherpa*. *Comics Sherpa* was a very big window of exposure. That led me to DrunckDuck.com and eventually Moderntales.com. It was Moderntales who made Yenny an official comic book girl. Readers were asking more about the rest of the characters and how Yenny grew up and all that. She became a rounded character in there.

I was the black sheep of comic strips. A girl with short shorts just entered the sacred world of cats, dogs, and family jokes. Many people thought I'd never make it with a bare-thighed girl as a main character, but after a few years—three, to be exact—Ucomics approached me with an offer to join their lineup.

God is good.

FLA: Perhaps this has something to do with an increased Latino readership? The Latino population in the U.S. now stands at about 31-plus million . . .

DA: Really? We reproduce faster than guinea pigs!

FLA: Will *Yenny* be published in book form?

DA: This is still in the talks. Sadly, most of these comic book deals are just done because you really want to do it, but no serious money comes from them. It takes years to establish a comic book, and it already took me years to establish *Yenny*.

So, I'll keep everyone posted if something happens.

FLA: Can you speak to collaboration with other artists?

DA: Rangely Garcia, Richard Cruz, and Ivy Beth Gladstone are excellent artists! They've done *incredible* interpretations of Yenny, and their original material is worth millions. Eventually we'd create more stuff outside of *Yenny*.

FLA: Any conflicts working with others?

DA: Richard sometimes helps me with the Sundays, but we don't have any creative conflicts, because we make a lot of teamwork.

FLA: Can you speak to the creating, coloring, and inking process?

DA: I still draw, ink, and color every single panel in *Yenny*. Almost everything is done by hand, and the rest is done in computer.

FLA: I read somewhere that cartoon strips can avoid stereotyping if they do not demean the person or group depicted. Any thoughts?

DA: Cartoons are all about visual stereotyping. There's no way you can draw a Chinese character if you don't draw the long eyes, or draw a black character if you don't darken his or her skin. However, you don't have to demean them to make a humorous point.

My characters are all Latinos, and they don't go around screaming, "Arriba, andale!"

FLA: You mention elsewhere that you grew up surrounded by every Latino stereotype imaginable. You also mention that Yenny was inspired by the physical type of the Puerto Rican *caserío* [hometown] girl: she eats and dresses freely and is always in good shape.

DA: That's true. I grew up studying in public schools, and my friends were all barrio people. Many girls in Puerto Rico are like Yenny. Big thighs and all that. They ate fast food and fried food, but their stomachs were always flat!

FLA: How do you complicate Latina/o types when the cartoon has to employ certain recognizable types?

DA: There's nothing much to complicate once you know the characters.

FLA: Can a character like Yenny complicate Latino stereotypes? I think of some of the early cartoons like Speedy and his lazy, lusting mice gang . . .

DA: I don't know. Maybe we'll start seeing girls in shorts and colored hair in future comics and movies. [laughs]

FLA: She is shapely and beautiful but not a runway model?

DA: For everyone's personal horror, I used to model for a short time. Yeah, male model. And catwalk models have to be incredibly skinny, and no physical exaggerations should be shown because the spectator should only concentrate on the clothes they are wearing—something a little difficult for a curvy, big-footed Yenny.

FLA: Her big feet shake up the concept of what is beautiful. Is the idea that beauty is not perfection?

DA: You said it. Beauty is not perfection. No one's perfect. And those who look perfect from the outside are totally not perfect in the inside.

The big-feet thing is a minor issue in the storyline, but it gives Yenny a reason to fight.

FLA: You have your animals interact with humans very normally.

DA: At least in Yenny's world. Yeah.

FLA: Why the pet iguana, Zacha?

DA: I didn't want a dog or a cat. There are no iguanas in the comic strip world, so it looked good to me at the time. I'm very influenced by Disney's talking cartoon animals. I always liked the way they look beside human characters.

FLA: How about the way you conceive of the character?

DA: I always think about the characters. Everything is about the characters and what can happen to them that particular week.

FLA: Already back in 1988 you mentioned how you wanted to create a female protagonist in a comic strip world dominated by male characters. Is this still the case?

DA: Yes, it is. Yenny's world is a female world after all.

FLA: Why set the story in an imaginary place called Villa Los Kubos but that's in an identifiable Puerto Rico?

DA: I wanted everything to take place in an imaginary place in my island. It's easier for me to write. Being in an imaginary place gives me the freedom of creating places for them to be.

Yet the language and food—*quenepa* [Spanish lime] or a *mofongo* [mashed plantains, garlic, and pork cracklings] and so on—give it a uniquely Puerto Rican cultural quality.

Readers like the fact that Yenny lives in a hot, warm place. I think, deep inside of us, we love to hang out in those places.

FLA: You also poke fun at representing an essential Latino identity and experience.

DA: It's part of my daily life.

FLA: You turn the tables on generational expectation. It's the younger generation that is concerned about the older. Yenny's concerned about the mother's singlehood and dating.

DA: Young ones, especially those who come from divorced parents, are always concerned if a new daddy or mommy will appear on the scene—especially if the mom dates an ex-boyfriend.

I did it to create a little chaos among readers; the feedback was pretty strong. I got a reaction from a mother who used to date a younger guy just to feel young again. That's how I came up with the end of this saga.

FLA: With the comic strip, it's difficult to have multiple storylines, which are one of the main ingredients for creating suspense in comic books. How do you create suspense?

DA: I got used to the single-storyline structure. I try to let the characters tell the story. Eventually, their personalities will clash and the suspense will be created.

FLA: What type of audience do you envision reading your comics?

DA: Teens usually read my comics and identify with them—they love the way the characters look. The older ones like the stories and the continuity of it.

FLA: You publish *Yenny* in Spanish and English?

DA: Yes. In English and in Spanish for Puerto Rico!

FLA: How do you find that balance between telling a story for a Puerto Rican audience and one aimed at a more mainland mainstream?

DA: I include Puerto Rican personalities or situations from time to time, but the gag is universal. Everyone can get it, even if you don't know the person I'm mocking. The warm Latina has life experiences we can all relate to.

FLA: *Yenny* is both sexy and family friendly?

DA: One of the advantages of living in a hot place is that you get used to seeing girls in shorts or with belly-revealing attire; it's pretty normal. So I translate that to my strips.

Having Yenny and her friends running around in short clothes is more than enough to make the comic strip sexy. I don't have to emphasize that. Otherwise it'll become tasteless.

FLA: How do you conceive of the visuals and the textual elements working together?

DA: I'm more visual than textual, but I've learned to balance them.

FLA: Occasionally, you omit a frame around your panels?

DA: Sometimes I do it because I find it visually attractive.

FLA: As one reads more and more of *Yenny*, the more we become invested in the character's struggles, reactions, emotions.

DA: I try to make my characters as clear as possible. New readers appear every day, and I want them to grab their personalities quick.

FLA: Has your work in animation influenced your comic strip style?

DA: Not much, really. My Looney Tunes work can influence Zacha's behavior and look, but not Yenny's. I've got to disconnect from everything Looney before starting work with Yenny.

FLA: You vary the pace and rhythm of the strip. Occasionally, you interrupt the flow with the introduction of the sea turtle character, Buke.

DA: Sometimes I do it because the newspaper in which *Yenny* appears is only published six days instead of seven. So if I see that the storyline is about to get to a high point, I add a Buke strip to accomplish my Ucomics quota, and on Monday I get back to the storyline. Some people hate me because of that, I know!

FLA: Do your shifts in perspective from close-ups to long views, and so on, have a similar effect?

DA: Yeah. Just for it not to get boring.

FLA: You tend to use the same colors from the many that you might choose from the artist's palette.

DA: Latino readers are attracted to high-toned colors. That's something the newspaper in which *Yenny* gets published told me about. So I use those colors intentionally. So the characters are always portrayed in warm colors.

FLA: You choose to draw in a more cartoon rather than realistic way.

DA: It's easier for me to handle.

FLA: Yenny is a twenty-two-year-old woman, with big feet and an absent father, who aspires to be a model. Any significance here—maybe her big feet rooting her more in her Puerto Rican identity, for example?

DA: She met her father, but he's not mature enough to maintain a family. Yenny's mother, Yunissa, was a model too. So she unconsciously passed the seed to her. Stories go easier with an all-female cast, after all. As far as her feet, she was born that way and had to deal with it over time. She became a model to hide her big feet from everyone else's sight. It doesn't have anything to do with her ethnicity.

FLA: Yunissa travels and dates but is very supportive of Yenny.

DA: She's young, so she totally understands Yenny's desires and thoughts. She acts like her friend.

FLA: Significance of names like Yenny, Yunissa, Zacha, etc.?

DA: I liked "Yenny" because it sounds very girly. More generally, I wanted names that could be mentioned in English and Spanish with no trouble at all. So every time a new character appears I look for a universal name for him or her.

FLA: Do you see any of the characters experiencing deep transformations?

DA: Eventually it will happen. One character will start living a totally different life.

FLA: Is *Yenny* a place to suggest values of good and bad?

DA: The characters always learn their lessons in my stories. No matter how many times Yenny wants to do wrong, something will bring her back to her usual self.

FLA: Future projects?

DA: New-new comics. Sooner than you think. Moo-ah-ha-haaa!

Gus Arriola

Born in 1917 in Florence, Arizona, Gus Arriola moved at a young age with what remained of his family to Los Angeles; his mother died of influenza when he was six months old.

Arriola showed a gift for drawing as early as the sixth grade—and a love of the Sunday color comics like *The Katzenjammer Kids*, *Happy Hooligan*, and *Krazy Kat*. By the time he attended Manual Arts High School, he was set to study design, commercial art, and life drawing. In high school he began drawing the weekly cartoon *As Seen Around Campus*. He had his eyes firmly set on a career as a professional cartoonist. While working in an orange-juice processing plant in downtown LA, he answered an ad about courses in animation offered in Hollywood. His skill landed him a sixteen-dollar-a-week job as an in-betweener (an artist who makes the intermediate drawings between the key poses drawn by the animators) at the Mintz Studio (which later became Screen Gems), where he would also sharpen his drawing skills. Lured away by a better salary, Arriola moved to MGM in 1937. It was at an MGM Christmas party that he met his future wife, inker and artist Mary Frances Sevier.

A little disturbed by the racial prejudice at MGM—he was asked to create Mexican characters as only dirty banditos—in the evenings he would work on his own characters and stories, which would positively portray Mexican culture and people.

In November 1941, *Gordo* was syndicated nationally, appearing in the *Denver Post*, *Chicago Sun*, *Los Angeles Daily News*, *San Francisco Chronicle*, and *San Diego Union*, among others. The strip followed the adventures of a fat Mexican bean farmer. Arriola's content and style were bold, and aimed to move and culturally educate his readers. *Gordo* appeared in nearly three hundred newspapers, and had a forty-plus-year run before Arriola ended the story in 1985. Arriola died February 2, 2008, in Carmel, California.

FREDERICK LUIS ALDAMA: What were some of your first experiences with cartoons, comic strips, and the like?

GUS ARRIOLA: Like most children, I was fascinated by the color Sunday comics. My family said that as a six-year-old I would lie on the floor on my belly and read the comics. When I was eight years old, we moved to Los Angeles from Florence, Arizona . . . This was the height of the Hollywood era—the golden years, when talkies had just arrived and animated cartoons were beginning to develop. In 1928, Disney came to California, and with it Mickey Mouse—a cartoon that fascinated me.

FLA: When did you first begin to draw cartoons?

GA: I used to sit down and copy the Mickey Mouse cartoons. But I really didn't know I could draw until one day at school my sixth-grade teacher asked if anybody could copy a picture of the U.S. Capitol on the blackboard. Not knowing if I could or not, I volunteered. I went up and I copied the thing out of the book. The teacher was very impressed; it was her encouragement that sort of got me started with drawing. I continued to study art at Manual Arts High School, a wonderful high school established in the early 1900s that offered courses in commercial art, design, theater arts, all sorts. I took them all. I especially liked the freehand and design drawing classes.

FLA: Did you know at this point that you wanted to pursue a career in cartoon/animation arts?

GA: After high school, the animation business was really booming. When I graduated high school in 1935—the height of the Depression—there were no jobs; my family couldn't afford further education. At the time, the animation studio in Hollywood, Columbia's Screen Gems, was doing a series of *Krazy Kat* and other eight-minute theatrical cartoons. I decided to take a chance and show them some samples of my work. It paid off. I was hired as an in-betweener—the fellow who, after the assistant animator has cleaned up the animator's rough drawings, puts in the in-between drawings on a light board. The experience really helped me to develop my graphic skills.

After a year and a half at Screen Gems, MGM decided they wanted their own cartoon department. So they organized a group of people from other studios; people from New York came out. The news traveled to us at Screen Gems, and about six of us in-betweeners left to work in MGM's new cartoon department. We were making sixteen-fifty a week at Columbia, and at MGM we went up to twenty-six dollars a week, which was quite a raise in those days. At MGM, I wasn't too fond of the animation part. I liked the idea of material writing, so I applied to go up to the story department. I made a couple of trips up there and sat in on some story sessions, adding gags. They liked them, so I moved up from in-betweener to the story department. This was a time when Bill Hanna and Joe Barbera (creators of *Tom and Jerry*) were directors working at MGM, so I first worked with them, then with Rudolph Ising (of Harmonizing Pictures).

FLA: How did your strip *Gordo* come about?

GA: In the late 1930s, while I was working at MGM, I was working at home on my own comic strip—something I had always wanted to do.

MGM wanted me to create a couple of Mexican bandit characters for a terrible cartoon called *The Lonesome Stranger*. Well, I was a victim of stereotyping as much as anybody else in early Hollywood, so I designed these dirty-looking Mexican bandits. The cartoon itself was nothing to brag about, but it gave me an idea to do a strip on Mexico. My dad had grown up on his father's hacienda in Sonora, Mexico. He used to tell me tales about his early life there. I was fascinated with the whole Mexican-history bit, so I turned one of my Mexican characters that I had designed for them into a fat bean farmer.

In the early part of 1941, I decided to take a leave of absence from MGM so I could take the strip to New York. I left some samples there, and in a month they called me back to ask if I would be able to do it, because they were interested in producing it. I said I certainly would, so the president, George Carlin, of the syndicate United Features in New York came out to Los Angeles. I signed a contract with them.

There was something about *Gordo* that Carlin liked. Unfortunately, he died early; the new director wasn't too gung-ho about it. And the salesman who sold strips to the newspapers didn't quite know how to sell *Gordo*. It never really did get the push that *Li'l Abner* and *Peanuts* got.

FLA: Working on your own strip must have been quite a change for you.

GA: I had to quit my job at MGM. I couldn't write and draw six dailies and a Sunday page by myself every week and work for MGM.

The change was scary. Unlike working at MGM, where we'd work as a group, sitting around a table and throwing story and gag ideas back and forth, I was suddenly all alone. I didn't realize how much work the strip was going to be. But I did it.

They decided to release *Gordo* in October of 1941. Well, you know what happened in December of 1941: Pearl Harbor! The event crippled my coming into the business. I was A-1 on the draft. I was able to work on *Gordo* for a year; it appeared in about thirty-five papers from October '41 to October '42. Then Frances, my wife, who was working as a painter and inker at MGM in the cartoon department, heard that my former director and boss, Rudy Ising, had received a commission with the United States Army Air Force as a major to start the Air Force's own training-film outfit. General Hap Arnold wanted his own unit. Up until then, the government had been contracting with the existing animating studios for training films. A lot of secret work. And the navy did work. But Hap Arnold wanted his own. So he formed the first motion-picture unit of the army air force, based in Culver City, where we were living at the old Hal Roach Studios.

The army borrowed all the best directors, writers, artists, animators, cartoonists. As artists, we didn't have to take basic training; this would have fixed us forever at not being able to draw. We were there for three and a half years, creating animation as well as stop-action-camera-based training films. For about a year and a half, Ronald Reagan was our captain.

We had an apartment on the army base in Culver City, right near the studio. When we first started, Hal Roach Studios had three big sound stages. One of the big sound stages they fixed up as a barracks; for the first six months, we slept there in the sound stages.

Thank goodness during the war the Special Services in Washington gave me permission to continue drawing the Sunday page. We were able to live off the post, so I had all day Sunday to develop the strip.

FLA: Was it difficult to switch gears from animation to comic strip?

GA: Animation was fun. It's just it wasn't my thing. It was too exact. I mean, you had to work according to the speed of twenty-four frames a second. And it was too confining. I like the freedom of design. But I ended up using a lot of what I had learned from animation in drawing the strip. It gave me a freedom of action and expression with my characters. If you flip through some of my strips, you'll see that there's a lot of exaggeration in the expressions. All of that came from the animation.

FLA: Did Frances continue working as a painter-inker?

GA: No, she worked for a while, and then she quit helping me. She used to do a lot of the footwork, taking the Sunday pages into town to be photostatted; I had to color the photostat copy and send it in with the black-and-white original. She used to do some of the filling in of blacks and touch up here and there. She was mostly busy raising our child.

FLA: What happened to the strip once World War II was over?

GA: In 1946, I restarted the daily. At first, we had it in maybe forty to fifty papers. But through the years, it grew. Not as fast as I would have liked, but because of the nature of the strip, many editors resisted it. They thought that it was too foreign. This sort of held it back, but also made it distinctive.

It was unusual in its day because it wasn't set in this country. In a way, that was kind of a handicap, because it limited me to what I could do. But to remedy that, I did a lot of animal gags. In the animation business, I had worked with animals, so I had the dog and the pig, and I had an owl, and they all talked, but not to the humans, just amongst themselves. They never did relate with the humans. They were kind of a Greek chorus, making comments. On days [when] I couldn't think of human things to do, I would do animal things, talking about the humans.

I was still feeling my way with the strip, not knowing exactly where I wanted to take it. Gordo spoke broken English and was a lazy farmer, which were not good. But as I say, I was stereotyped myself. So little by little, the more I learned about Mexico, the more fascinated I was with its history. I cleaned Gordo up and made him a tourist guide, which was a good image for him, and easy for me to get material.

FLA: You moved to Arizona at one point?

GA: In 1951 we went to Arizona. We met a lot of people, like Mr. Frank Lloyd Wright and his students—a lot of whom became good friends of ours. The weather was just too hot for me to work in the summers, so after five years we decided to move to Carmel. All along the way I met people who influenced my work. Al Parker, one of the most famous magazine illustrators, for example, got me started on doing a lot of illustrative-type artwork.

FLA: You mention elsewhere the influence of authors like Steinbeck. Were there other influences?

GA: I like fiction generally because I like to get away from things. And I used to read some Mexican comic books that a friend would send to me from Mexico, called *La Familia Buron*. They were funny, and I liked their approach. Nothing holds them back.

There was also our son, who was a great source of inspiration for *Gordo*. All through high school, he came home with ideas. He didn't know he was giving me ideas, but he was. Unfortunately, we lost him to an automobile accident. A lot of the fun went out of creating the strip when we lost him.

FLA: There's a noticeable shift in the 1960s in your characterization of Gordo and your story lines.

GA: Yes, Gordo becomes a tour guide; up until then, he was just whatever I needed. In the later strips, Gordo is a bachelor—a ladies' man. I got into all sorts of narratives, including science fiction: a flying saucer appears, and the widow Gonzalez travels into space. I also introduced a little rich Texas girl who would introduce Gordo to a lot of things that he otherwise wouldn't have known.

FLA: *Gordo* went through many different changes of style?

GA: As time went on, the strip couldn't help but change. I got better at drawing. I found it easier to create a situation graphically as the years went by. When you do something every day, which I did, you set your standards pretty high, and you just go until you reach that level that you're looking for. You can't help but improve. As I grew up and learned myself, I applied it to *Gordo*. *Gordo* became more sophisticated.

FLA: Did you have a routine that you followed every day?

GA: There were four days: one of thinking, three of drawing. Monday was usually the "thinking day"; I would spend the day sitting here with my feet up, looking out at the trees, just kind of reflecting on things, writing down ideas for a sequence or a story on a yellow pad. Then I would break it down to the moving of the story along in daily episodes and end each strip with a laugh. It was hard work breaking down a continuity into six daily strips, each strip carrying the plot, and then providing a laugh at the end. Once I had that written out, the actual drawing would follow. Depending on how involved the scenes were would determine how long it would take to draw—maybe two to three days to draw. To save myself trouble, I kept a lot of that stuff to a minimum and just focused on the characters. Then there was the bigger Sunday page—three strips—it would take a day and a half.

It was a seven-day-a-week job. The only way I could get ahead of my deadline was to simplify it and maybe do two strips instead of one in a day. This would give me one or two days off a week.

I never could get away to travel. We finally got to go to Mexico quite often, but we never got a chance to go to Europe. I was strapped down to that bloody drawing board.

FLA: Where do you get your ideas for the characters?

GA: Any acting that is done on a comic strip is the artist himself. There's a large part of me and my life in the characters. When I created the little Texas girl, I had my wife Frances (from Louisiana) say what I wanted my little Texas girl to say. Then I'd spell it phonetically.

But I also draw from other sources. When I created a *curandera* in Mexico, I practically stole her visually from John Steinbeck's *The Forgotten Village*.

FLA: Why did you choose to keep Gordo in Mexico?

GA: People at the syndicate wanted to bring him up here to make it more popular. I couldn't do that. Up here, he would have been a second-class citizen. In Mexico, he was in his home ground. He could be anything, do anything. But up here he would be restricted. So I never did.

FLA: Can you talk about your panel layout?

GA: In the Sunday pages, I did more design work than in the dailies. I wanted to catch the reader's eye, so I did it with broad blacks, or broad colors in the Sunday. But once I caught the reader's eye, I knew that I had to give the reader some meat, something to read and hang onto. For example, in a strip done during the LSD hippie period in San Francisco, Gordo wants to know what "psychedelic" means. When Pepito, his nephew, tries to explain to him what it meant, I tried to convey the meaning with the visual layout and design. In another instance, when Gordo tells the tourists about the early Aztecs, I use the visuals to depict the pleasure of Montezuma's fabulous aviaries.

FLA: How about humor?

GA: All my life I've been a smart-ass gag man. In any crowd, I would wait until somebody had said something, and then I would move in with a little top to it. I came from a family of six brothers and two sisters, and I was the baby of the family. And I was always popping off at the dinner table, much to the annoyance of my older brothers.

FLA: Do you know why its syndication peaked at around 275 newspapers?

GA: It was a mystery to me that we couldn't get over 250–275 papers. The thing is, you need a lot of papers to make a living. A lot of big papers will pay maybe a hundred dollars a week for it, but a local paper like the *Monterey Herald* would only pay about ten dollars a week.

Not only did I lose papers, the papers themselves went out of business. San Francisco had five or six papers, now there's only two. LA had seven papers, now there's just two. Most of *Gordo*'s papers were liberal papers, and they all failed.

Simpler strips, less papers. It's very competitive. Papers would drop *Gordo*, but the public would react and the paper would reinstate it. The *Denver Post* got such a reaction that they had to print it on the front page: "*Gordo*'s back." I think the competition drove it out. Now there are just a handful of popular strips.

FLA: Who read *Gordo*?

GA: I never got the mass audience of *Peanuts* and *Li'l Abner*, but the audience I did get was very nice. I got wonderful mail. Art teachers and history teachers used to write me. They liked the fact that I would use Spanish words now and then. With the little Texas girl, people would write to her; they thought of her as a real person.

FLA: Were there any tricks up your sleeve that you used to increase readership?

GA: I used cliffhangers so that you would buy tomorrow's paper to see what was going to happen. All those early strips that I grew up with—*Andy Gump*, and *Li'l Orphan Annie*, and Milt Caniff with *Terry and the Pirates*—all told stories that had you waiting eagerly to get the paper the next day.

FLA: In the forty-four years that you published *Gordo*, had your audience also grown and become more culturally sensitive?

GA: I was reaching a different American audience out here. At first, I had to sneak up with this Mexican-history stuff and customs. In the late '40s there was nothing like this in the papers. I introduced piñatas, Cinco de Mayo, Day of the Dead, and all kinds of Mexican customs. I knew that to reach people I couldn't hit them over the head with it. I sneaked Mexico in on them with a little love and a little humor and a lot of art. And it worked. Now this Mexican cultural stuff is commonplace.

FLA: Why end *Gordo*?

GA: For forty-four years I did *Gordo*: I can show you thousands of strips. While it never reached beyond 250–275-newspaper syndication, it was enough to make a living. I was happy with it. It was a nice life.

But forty-four years of deadlines almost did me in. It's a good thing I quit when I did. My wife made me. She said, "You've got to stop. You're killing yourself."

FLA: Other Latino comic book and comic strip authors have remarked on how important your work has been for them.

GA: I just opened the door.

FLA: *Gordo* as a film adaptation?

GA: There was somebody in town here who was a movie producer, and he wanted to do a *Gordo* movie, so we went to talk to Luis Valdez about it. He read and liked *Gordo*, but never quite saw it as a movie. In the mid-1970s there were several attempts in Mexico City, but they couldn't get the money. Nobody found *Gordo* bankable.

It wouldn't have been a good movie anyway. It's an entirely different medium.

FLA: How might today's comic strips compare with earlier ones?

GA: Today's crop of funnies are all stand-up-comic talking heads. There's very little art in them. You don't see the art in modern comics that you did when I was young. Milt Caniff's *Terry and the Pirates* and Alexander Raymond's *Flash Gordon* both had marvelous artwork—big influences on my own work.

FLA: Was there room for political satire in your comic strips?

GA: I didn't want to get involved in conflict. I've done it. It led nowhere. I tried a nice approach. It worked. A more conflicting approach only meant trouble.

FLA: Do you follow the Latino comic strips of today, like Lalo Alcaraz's *La Cucaracha* or Hector Cantú and Carlos Castellanos's *Baldo*?

GA: Not as closely as I should. I'm almost ninety, and my time is limited. I try to do the things that just please me.

FLA: Any final words?

GA: The strip is a unique American art form. It covers both literary and artistic efforts. It isn't just looking at a landscape or an ocean scene, it's an art that takes in literary material.

This said, I can't recommend anybody going into it today. It's kind of a losing battle. Television has really crippled news readership. And I don't know what the future of newspapers is, but I wouldn't try a comic strip at all today. I think I just would learn to talk dirty and be a stand-up comic.

Hector Cantú

Cocreator and cowriter of the comic strip *Baldo*, Hector Cantú was born in 1961 in the Rio Grande Valley of South Texas, where his family had lived since before the mid-nineteenth-century annexation of the northern Mexican territories by the United States. When Cantú was in the third grade, about the time he saw Walter Cronkite present  the space walk on television, he and his family moved to the birthplace of La Raza Unida political party, Crystal City, Texas. His parents were school administrators and moved for a job. Cantú's formative years were spent growing up in Crystal City in the 1970s, surrounded by Chicano activism, protests, and rallies. At about age ten, he attended La Raza Unida's first national convention in El Paso, Texas, seeing and meeting legendary activists such as Reyes Lopez Tijerina and Rodolfo "Corky" Gonzales. Cesar Chavez even slept in his family's house in Crystal City—instead of putting Cantú and his brothers out of their beds, Chavez asked to sleep modestly with a blanket on the floor.

During this "early baptism" into politics, as Cantú says, he began drawing cartoons. His older brother began a community newspaper called the *Key*, and the paper soon featured a political cartoon by the twelve-year-old Cantú.

The family later moved to Dallas, where Cantú went to high school, and he then earned a degree in journalism at the University of Texas at Austin. After working at newspapers, he became managing editor of *Hispanic Business Magazine* in Santa Barbara, California. This is where he was first introduced to Carlos Castellanos's graphic artwork. A few years later, the two created *Baldo*—now a nationally syndicated comic strip.

Today, you can read *Baldo* in papers such as the *Washington Post*, *Philadelphia Inquirer*, *Miami Herald*, *Dallas Morning News*, and *Los Angeles Daily News*, and also buy it in collected book form in *Night of the Bilingual Telemarketers* (2002) and *The Lower You Ride, the Cooler You Are: A Baldo Collection* (2001).

FREDERICK LUIS ALDAMA: Can you speak to your first experience authoring a Latino cartoon?

HECTOR CANTÚ: When I was a twelve-year-old, and it was in the early '70s, when the Vietnam War was coming to an end, and many Vietnamese immigrants were coming to the U.S. So the political cartoon I drew for my brother's newspaper touched on that. I drew a map of the United States, and I drew an arms-out, smiling Border Patrol agent welcoming a line of Vietnamese people to the United States. On the Mexican border, I drew another Border Patrol agent holding a gun and motioning to people from Mexico that they couldn't come in. There were no words involved, but the meaning was clear: "No Mexicans allowed," and then on the other side, "Come on in, everybody." Now, looking back, it was a little naïve. The Vietnamese were political refugees—different than economic refugees. But that's how I felt at the time, like there was a double standard.

FLA: In *Baldo* you contribute the verbal narrative element. When did you begin working with words?

HC: Maybe my brother's newspaper had a big influence and eventually pushed me into journalism. I was always fascinated by words. When I got to high school, I wanted to write, so I started writing for, and became the editor in chief of, my high school newspaper. I also did a couple of cartoons for the newspaper, though I knew I wasn't really that great of an artist. I really got more into the writing part. After high school, I went to UT-Austin and studied journalism there. I got on the *Daily Texan* staff. UT has a great tradition of turning out cartoonists. Berkeley Breathed, who did *Bloom County*, was there and so was Michael Fry, who created the *Over the Hedge* comic and movie.

FLA: Why the comic strip and not continue with journalism, or even pursue other forms of storytelling, like the short story or novel?

HC: For the longest time, I think writing newspaper stories and features took care of that desire to write and tell stories. I mean, you're out there talking to real people, talking to real characters, real personalities, real events, death, tragedy, happiness, triumph, fame, success. You're dealing with all of this when you're a journalist. I've covered the king of Spain. I covered the pope. I've written about mass murderers. I've covered just about everything that you could want to write about. So in that way, it was kind of satisfying my need to publish stories.

I've always thought about writing nonfiction, and I have tons of notes and tons of ideas that I've collected over the years for nonfiction, but I've never really put anything together until *Baldo* came into my head.

FLA: Let's talk about *Baldo*, from creating to getting it up and running.

HC: As managing editor at *Hispanic Business Magazine*, I was in charge of free-lancers—photographers, writers, and illustrators. I had seen Carlos's work in one of those illustrator catalogues, and I liked it, and I had given him a call. He did a cover or two for us, and other work. He was very professional, very fast, and we got along great over the phone. We must have worked over the phone on and off for two or three years, just with magazine assignments. So when the idea for *Baldo* came, it was natural to call him up and say, "Hey, are you interested in illustrating, drawing this comic strip submission for me, this idea that I have?" Carlos had faith in me. He wanted to try it. We did it.

Now, in 1998 or '99, or whenever we came up with the idea, it's not like we were the first people to come up with a Latino comic strip. *Gordo* by Gus Arriola had launched in the 1940s and was probably the most well known. Well, syndicates get tons of submissions, and there have been tons of Latino comic strips sent to the syndicates. But for various reasons, they didn't launch any Latino comic strips. It could have been the strips—the quality just wasn't there. It could have been there was a hesitation about the market. It could have been that the creator drew thirty really damned good ones, and when they asked him to draw the thirty-first one, he couldn't do it.

When we sent out our package of our cartoon family, there was an appealing authenticity and a quality. The art was good. The writing was good. Everything came together for the syndicates to say, "OK, this is the one that we're going to take the chance on."

We put together thirty strips. We sent them out and we got two offers. I'm not going to say it was easy, because we had a lot of experience between us. We were a safe bet for the syndicates. I'd been a writer for all these years, had a wire column going out on Knight Ridder–Tribune, and worked for *Hispanic Business Magazine*; Carlos had been working as a professional illustrator for ten years. It's typical of Latino stuff. You have to be over-qualified to get the job. Even though you're as qualified as the next guy, something's going to hold you back. I think we know what that is.

Now that the door is open and *Baldo* is out there, maybe we might see other comic strips. I'm waiting for the day when some kick-ass Latino cartoonist who's in high school or college can come out and give us a kick-ass comic strip that's totally different, totally cutting edge, totally wild, and totally cool. It'll be a really great day for me when we have two, three, four Latino comic strips in the paper.

FLA: *Baldo* is less in-your-face about political and social issues than say Lalo Alcaraz's *La Cucaracha*. Might this also have had something to do with production and reception?

HC: Daily newspaper comic strips are not traditionally political. You go pick up any newspaper, and it's not twenty-five political, in-your-face comic strips. From *Peanuts* to *Luann* to *Dilbert* to whoever you want to name, it's not in-your-face politics. So, yeah, *Baldo* fits into the more traditional format of daily newspaper comic strips. If we do politics, it's done in a subtle, sneaky way.

FLA: Is there room for political commentary?

HC: Sure. Aaron McGruder has done it wonderfully. McGruder's in about three hundred newspapers, and now he's got a TV show. *Doonesbury*, of course, is the other classic, using traditional comic storytelling with political commentary. Garry Trudeau's been a pioneer with that, and he's in hundreds and hundreds of newspapers. There are others, like *La Cucaracha* and *Mallard Fillmore*. But most newspaper comics are about universal stories, with universal appeal, bringing everyday experiences to everybody and having everybody relate to fun kids, to crazy adults, to loony aunts and tíos.

FLA: You allude directly to Gus Arriola's *Gordo* in *Baldo*. Can you speak about some inspirations?

HC: We did a week in December 2005, right before Christmas, when I challenged myself to do six strips with no words. Just pure movement, miming the situation with no words at all. This was very much inspired by Sergio Aragonés, the *Mad Magazine* artist. I grew up with *Mad*, loving his comics. I remember seeing his name when I was a kid and thinking, "He must be Latino." Now, I don't think anyone told Sergio, "You've got to do political Latino cartoons because you're from Mexico or Spain." He did mainstream *Mad Magazine* cartoons. And he's a legend. And there's Cuban exile Antonio Prohias, and his *Spy vs. Spy*, also in *Mad*. These guys did mainstream American pop art, and they were great at what they did. Sergio and Antonio are considered greats of American cartooning.

Carlos and I see *Baldo* as part of American pop art. But you know what? We're still talking about Latinos. Our characters do talk Spanish. And they do deal with issues that Latinos deal with. But we still consider *Baldo* part of mainstream American cartooning art. Don't tell me we can't be part of American pop culture.

FLA: Can you speak about your approach and technique?

HC: We generally follow the classic cartoon gag-writing rules: always shoot for a surprise, a play on words, or some emotion in the last panel. The more you can outwit and throw a curveball the reader doesn't see coming, the more people appreciate you. Getting something you weren't expecting, being outwitted, is the cornerstone of comedy: "You got me! Man, that was good." I think that's what comedy and comic strip writing is about. If the reader sees something coming, something's taken away. If you don't understand what just happened, it takes something away. If there's no smile delivered, the reader moves on. If there's no emotion delivered, you move on. When I sit down, I have these tools, this cast of characters—Baldo and Tia Carmen and Gracie and Dad—and then the secondary cast of Cruz, Smiley, Billy, and Che. And these guys are our tools to build the surprise at the end of each strip. Can we deliver something—an emotion, a laugh, something that's going to get the reader engaged? That, generally, for me is my daily challenge in writing a comic.

FLA: How do the visuals and the text work together to lead to that moment of surprise?

HC: The perfect comic strip to me is when I use words and images together to deliver a gag or make a point. When Michael Jantze of *The Norm* comic strip lived here in Dallas for a couple of months, we sat down for coffee one day and talked about comics. He said, "You know, the perfect comic strip is one where, by itself, the art makes no sense, and by themselves, the words make no sense. It's when you see them together in your panels that it all comes together." That, to me, is what I strive for. It doesn't happen all the time, but it's an ideal.

FLA: There are certain character types, certain features, used in comic strip art that readers recognize and that imply meaning. Do you think that it's possible to use types to undo stereotypes?

HC: Humor generally is based on stereotypes. Whether it's the crazy caveman, whether it's the silly Viking, whether it's the crazy nurse, they wouldn't have a comic strip if they were normal. If you're a normal, everyday person, you're not going to have a comic strip. What makes you special is wit or something that sets you apart from people, a stereotype of a characteristic, an extreme element of your characteristic that makes you comic-worthy. And not only comic-worthy, but story-worthy. Most characters in books, in movies, in plays, in comics—there's something special about them that makes them worth writing about.

OK, but now you're dealing with the element of presenting Latino characters. On a national level, we're seeing this with the George Lopez TV show. I mean you're saying, "OK, you're going to have an audience of 15 million people every week, looking at your Latino family. How are you going to present these characters?" You're George Lopez. What do you say? We face this dilemma of representation as Latino creators working on a pop-culture stage. Sure, we have responsibilities to not present stereotypes. My characters don't go around riding burros and wearing sombreros and eating tacos. As an artist, that's my responsibility, to move the Latino character, the state of Latino characters, beyond that. So when we created this family, we weren't going to go for the cheap, easy stereotypes that are involved with humor. Pick up all those humor tools that you have in your humor toolbox, that are the easy ones used all the time, and throw them out. They're gone, man. So now we're left with other tools. We've gotten rid of the sledgehammers, and now we have the little screwdrivers left to do our humor. We have paper clips left to do our humor.

It's very challenging to say, "Let's get rid of the sledgehammers, the big, easy stereotypes for humor, and let's use the smaller, little, tiny chisels to build our comedy." It's hard. Our *Baldo* characters are not easy stereotypes. But they do have characteristics of normal people, characteristics that everybody can relate to. Baldo's a teenager and wants to be cool. Every kid wants to be cool in high school, and they usually fail miserably. Is that solely a Latino thing? Well, no. Let's go to characteristic number two: loving cars. Baldo loves lowriders. He wants the coolest ride in town. To me, these are not negative stereotypes. And then you move on to Gracie, an eight-year-old kid. Characteristic: she's a strong little girl. She'll kick your ass. Now, where's that coming from? That comes from me growing up in Crystal City, where I saw all these strong Chicanas kicking ass. That's Gracie. That's the characteristic of Latino culture that I saw. It wasn't sitting in the kitchen and making tamales and talking about the telenovelas. Gracie is going to accomplish things. She's going to college, and she's going to kick your butt. That's, to me, the characteristic of Gracie. Where I do get into the kooky stuff is with Tia Carmen. I don't put her in the kitchen cooking all the time, though I don't see that as a negative stereotype. Her characteristics: she watches novelas, plays the lottery, uses yerbas. I think Carmen is our worst stereotype, honestly, but we still treat her with dignity and respect. I think Dad is probably the least defined character. He's basically the patriarch who's just trying to keep traditions alive; he encourages the kids to speak more Spanish and all that stuff.

FLA: On the one hand, *Baldo* speaks to all sorts of readers, and on the other, if you're Latino, it might give you an additional laugh or smile.

HC: Generally, I think newspapers want us to relate to Latino readers. They want a Latino to pick up their paper and read *Baldo* and say, "Hey, I like this. That's me." That's what newspapers want. We're not all Latino all the time. But we do realize that's what sets us apart from other comic strips.

FLA: What about those who don't get it?

HC: With our strip on the immigration walkouts and marches, we got flooded with these immigrant-bashing e-mails: "Draw your cartoon in Mexico," and all this stuff. That's fine if we're pissing off people who hate immigrants. We're not writing for those people. We had Baldo as a reporter talking to teenagers about immigration, how they feel about the walkouts and the demonstrations, right? A lot of the quotes I put in these kids' mouths in the comic were paraphrased from newspaper and TV stories; these were real thoughts that kids were having. And of course some readers thought that was our opinion, but that's fine. I think we got our point across. For a few days at least, there was a voice in the newspaper that reflected the voice of young Latinos.

FLA: Yeah, it's funny how people still read so literally.

HC: I don't mind pissing off people and getting letters sent to the editor. I mean that's perfectly fine. I just hope people can talk about the issue with their family and their kids. If you can send a message through the comics page, I think that's fine. And I think it's more powerful because we don't do it all the time. We're pretty picky about doing political strips. We only do it on big issues like this. So I think it's more powerful.

FLA: You tip the balance toward the issue-related, serious in one issue and not another?

HC: To me, there're several things you can deliver in a comic strip. Obviously, everybody wants to deliver a laugh. Eighty percent of the time you want to deliver a laugh, a smile, a chortle, a *carcajada*, like my mom says. The other times you want to deliver emotions. You want to explore things like sadness and anger. And if you can do that at the end of a strip, that's fine. As a nationally syndicated daily comic strip, I don't want to deliver sadness every day. We've done issues where we talk about Baldo's mom, who's dead. We don't go all crazy about it, milking it. But every now and then I do write strips about Mom, like a few years ago on Mother's Day. And they're sad. I mean, they're sad strips. You'll deliver two days of sadness, and then you do Gracie lightening the mood with something kind of funny or unexpected. Funny and death don't mix so well.

If we're going to do immigration, the purpose is not going to be humor. The purpose is going to be delivering anger or pride—I hope we're getting Latinos reading this who are saying, "Yeah, I'm glad somebody's saying this." With Tia Carmen's lotto-scam story, there was suspense and an element of danger and an element of drama. And, again, we got a lot of e-mails with people saying how they couldn't wait to pick up tomorrow's paper to see what happens to Tia Carmen. There was a sense of "these people are evil, and they're going to hurt Carmen."

The suspense and drama was there. Now, that's what other serial comic strips do, *For Better or For Worse*. That's what they specialize in, and they do it every day. You want to know what happens next. That can be done very successfully. And you can build a pretty big audience by doing that. And many of these strips have a huge audience. *Luann* has continuing story lines. We have Baldo breaking up with Smiley in a couple of weeks. To me, that's a good, strong story, to get people interested in the comic and the characters. It's not all about humor, but it's a good, strong story. People love stories.

FLA: There's obviously meaning in the words that you write. There's also an effect in the style of the lettering that you choose. Right?

HC: You know, the only thing I'll do in my writing is I will indicate to Carlos the words I think are boldfaced. I'll put stars around my boldfaced words. And I do that generally to put an emphasis on the word, like it's a crucial part of the strip. It has to be said in a louder voice. Or the accent has to be on that word to make the story line pop out or the gag pop out. That's the only thing I do. Carlos will choose what to do on other stuff. He interprets it in the artist's chair. Like there was a Sunday strip where Baldo's heading home in the family car, and he's rushing to get home. And I just had Baldo telling Dad, "Floor it." You know? Like step on the gas. "Floor it." And Carlos put it in the—he like used these big, giant [*laughs*], 30-point letters: "Floor it." And I didn't say, "Put it in 30-point bold letters." But I think Carlos gets the feel for it. He gets to interpret how big the words are in a balloon, and he plays that role as well as the artist in making it a complete piece of work.

FLA: Do you read them back to yourself out loud as you're writing?

HC: Sometimes, yeah, sure. They go through my head when I'm reading it, and the natural inclination is to bold-face certain words, and I see them louder. Reading the dialogue out loud helps you see if it flows naturally, like everyday conversation. You don't want stilted or unnatural dialogue. You want your words to express a thought or idea and not necessarily write like an English major.

FLA: We touched on this idea of responsibility as a Latino author-artist. What about comic strips as a place for conveying a sense of values?

HC: I think most comics deal with what's right and wrong. I think it's how you deal with it and how cleverly you deal with it that makes you successful. The best comics do it in a subversive kind of way. They sneak in the message, and you realize a day later, "Hey, that comic just challenged everything I believe in." But it's done in a very subtle, subversive way, like *Pogo*. What makes those strips classic in American cartooning are these cute, cuddly characters making huge commentary on U.S. politics and the U.S. way of life.

Now, as a Latino writer, I don't want people laughing at my culture. At what point do you kind of cross the line into making people laugh at you? We want to deliver laughs, and we want to be in control of the laughter. We want people to laugh for the right reasons. That's our responsibility. We don't want to take the easy road and use easy stereotypes to where people laugh at us. I don't want to do that. Carlos doesn't want to do that. And we've challenged ourselves not to do that.

I think strips can talk about ethics, can talk about what's right, what's wrong. They can talk about real emotions, about real feelings. I think what people relate to universally is, like I said, sadness, anger, happiness. All of those things are very simple messages that I think you'll find pretty much all the time in good comic strips.

FLA: With the larger variety of Latinos being represented in mainstream culture, is there more of a place for subtlety and sophistication?

HC: Absolutely. The more Latino artists we have out there creating messages, the more you can experiment with what your messages are. When there are five Latino comic strips in the newspaper, that fifth one is going to be just wild. The first round of artists does have a responsibility. The producers also have a responsibility. Universal Press was not going to put out as their first Latino family some crazy stereotyped comic strip. They were going to put out a strip that was very traditional, that was classic in its structure. But after you've done that, you can move to the next level, to a different perspective.

I think we're coming around to where society may be a little more comfortable with stereotypes. It seems to me that this whole political correctness thing is kind of deflating a little bit in certain areas. So it's OK, say, for Cartoon Network to bring out this minority superhero called El Jefe with a big sombrero and a weakness for tequila—and he has a superpower, too, using a leaf blower to fly. I'm not going to sit back and go, "Ah, they're representing Latinos all in a bad way, that we all drink tequila and we all wear sombreros." I think we're over that. As a community, we don't really get upset over that anymore. Look at David Gonzales's *The Homies*, and you see all kinds of characters; every single little two-inch Homie is a stereotype of somebody in the neighborhood. Characters like Chango, Huera, Chino Loco. And nobody really cares. They're selling like *churros*. Latinos are eating 'em up.

Carlos Castellanos

Carlos Castellanos was born in Cuba in 1961. Since his parents couldn't get visas to leave Cuba, they sent the eight-month-old Carlos to New York to live with his grandmother; his parents were able to follow him six months later. Speaking Spanish at home and English at school, Castellanos grew up bilingual and bicultural first in the Bronx, then in Latino-populated Bergen County, New Jersey. When he was nine years old, his parents divorced and his father moved to South Florida. Several years later, he and his mother moved to North Miami, Florida, where he lived until 1994.

As an only child, Castellanos would return home from school and watch plenty of cartoons on television. At about age seven, he recalls watching his first episode of *Bewitched*. Watching Darrin Stevens sitting behind a large drawing table inspired Castellanos to do the same. When visiting his father in Florida for the summers, he would watch his father, who worked for a textile company, design textile patterns, draw technical schematics, and draw plenty of cartoons.

By the sixth grade, Castellanos had begun to take a serious interest in comics. On Fridays, he spent every saved penny on items from his wish list at the local comic book store. Today he still has over a thousand comics that he has collected since those early days. He studied the art in these comics—*Fantastic Four*, *X-Men*, *The Savage Sword of Conan*, and so on—learning the styles of the different artists and teaching himself how to draw. This later paid off in high school, where he was recruited into journalism classes as an editorial cartoonist for the high school newspaper. Here, he added the art of the comic strip to his craft.

Castellanos began his college career at Miami Dade Community College with the idea of going into veterinary medicine. But after realizing that his mortuary science drawings were better than his test scores, his science teacher gently persuaded him to pursue art. He began to formally study illustration the next semester. After a year of classes, his instructor recognized Castellanos's gift. He took Castellanos under his wing to help launch his freelance career: he helped him build up a professional portfolio, taught him how to approach clients, and how to price projects. The training paid off. Castellanos began to make money, so he decided to leave college and pursue a freelance career full-time. However, after a year and a half, he knew there was more to learn. In 1981, he packed up his car and moved out to California to attend the Art Center College of Design, where he trained with professional illustrators who were working in the field—movie-poster work, editorial illustration, storyboarding, and so on—until his money ran dry about a year later.

Moving back to Florida, he began freelancing for advertising agencies and graphic-design firms. Instead of having to begin by working on small editorial illustrations for small magazines, he rode his talent on a smooth course straight to the top advertising agencies in South Florida. He later chose to focus his attention exclusively in the area of humorous illustration, working for top advertising agencies and magazines. A contract to do spot illustrations put him in contact with Hector Cantú, who was managing editor of *Hispanic Business Magazine*. Cantú pitched the idea of cocreating a comic strip.

The timing was right. Castellanos had been tinkering with the idea of writing a children's book for the Hispanic American market; he wanted to create something of his own. The idea of creating a comic strip about a Latino family and focused on a teenager was quite appealing. After months of developing the story, Cantú and Castellanos came up with *Baldo*.

Castellanos continues to live and work in South Florida.

FREDERICK LUIS ALDAMA: Given your early interest in comic books, had you considered creating a comic book?

CARLOS CASTELLANOS: No. Throughout high school, I kind of figured I'd like to draw for comic books, but as I got older, I realized it was a lot of work for the money they paid. Doing the humorous work was more fun for me and more profitable.

As far as *Baldo* in terms of a comic book, it was always just a comic strip.

FLA: Can *Baldo* monetarily sustain you guys?

CC: Hector still works, and I still do my freelancing; at this point, however, if I had to, I suppose I could live off of just *Baldo* right now, but I enjoy freelancing for the variety of work and, of course, the extra income.

FLA: You have mentioned elsewhere that it was fairly easy to break into the market. Do you think this has something to do with the mainstream's increased interest in Latino culture?

CC: I'd like to believe that *Baldo*'s out there because it's good; that it's well written, well drawn, and people appreciate it. But at the same time, you can't negate the fact that we came in at the right time. Newspapers are in the business of serving their readers. If a newspaper is in an area where there's a large Latino readership, then they want to address that segment of the population. It's supply and demand. They want to cater to their audience. And newspapers are in that business. So, yeah. Of course, the increased numbers of Latinos in the census didn't hurt, but I think we would have gotten syndicated anyway, because it's a quality strip with a different voice that appeals to the masses.

FLA: Why not create a satirical strip like Lalo Alcaraz's *La Cucaracha*?

CC: I dig Lalo's work. He's very good at what he does, and I enjoy reading it, but I don't think Hector and I are political animals. That's not really where our head is at. We didn't create *Baldo* to make a big controversial splash. We don't want the strip to be a soapbox where we talk politics. Our strip is mostly family-oriented. It focuses on the character Baldo and his everyday struggles; that's why it's not always gag-directed, but driven more by what kinds of insight we have into the character's mind and personality. That's really where we focus the strip.

FLA: Do you see *Baldo* working more within, say, the style of David Alvarez's *Yenny*?

CC: Probably more so, yes. It's not trying to beat you over the head with some kind of message. I think if you can deliver the message without making it so obvious—where you have to read between the lines—then more people will get it and not feel like you're shoving it down their throat.

FLA: There's a trademark visual style that informs *Baldo*, but every once in a while the visual style shifts to that of fantasy and other more experimental modes.

CC: Exercising the different visual styles and imagery helps depict and translate what's going on in Baldo's head, how he sees the world around him, but also plays with the typical comic strip look. We've even done sequences where I've drawn from my influences reading *Conan the Barbarian* [in order] to play with the style of the strip on occasion.

FLA: In *Bilingual Telemarketers*, you include a strip where Gus Arriola's Gordo appears.

CC: It was Hector's idea to do some kind of tribute to Gus. I thought it was a great idea, so we got on the phone with Gus and got some story-line ideas. Then I picked up a copy of *Gordo* to study the art work and to incorporate Gus's style into that of *Baldo*. It worked out well. He was happy with how it turned out, and for me it was a great honor to pay tribute to Gus in this way.

FLA: From references to Jennifer Lopez to El Cucuy to Frida Kahlo, Latino popular culture is everywhere in *Baldo*.

CC: We keep hoping that Jennifer Lopez will pick up the phone and call us, or send us a signed eight-by-ten glossy.

FLA: In *Baldo* there's a sense that the older and younger generations relate to the culture at large differently.

CC: We have conflicts unique to Latino culture—like that of the younger generation not speaking Spanish or not relating to certain cultural tradition. I'm forty-five, and I have aunts who still don't speak a word of English. But if you scratch the surface, you'll see that the generational clashes in *Baldo* are more universal; anybody can relate to it. Regardless of whether you're a Latino or not, your parents grew up in a different era. So misunderstanding goes beyond just culture. We are standing here watching the world go through its motions, but we all see it from a different perspective, depending on how, when, and where we grew up and developed our own philosophy. It's more than cultural difference.

FLA: How do you conceive of developing and drawing the characters?

CC: Many of the characters are people that I've known in my life. At the time when *Baldo* was created, I modeled him after my brother; he had the same haircut, the earring in the left ear, the whole nine yards. Sergio is modeled after an uncle of mine. I haven't really known anybody that looked like Tia Carmen, but she's fun to draw because she's so wacky. I've tried to design the characters in a way that looks natural and endearing, while keeping them simple enough to redraw on an ongoing basis. From a production standpoint, the initial design of the characters is very important: because you have to redraw these characters over and over again daily, you want to create something that's easily reproduced.

FLA: How about the collaborative process?

CC: We discuss story-line ideas over the telephone, fine-tune the rough drafts, rewrite and tweak the writing until we're happy with it. Once the writing is nailed down, I start on the art, and run it by Hector just to be sure we're both happy with the end result.

I love the collaboration process when it involves other creative people that I jell with. You always come up with a much better product when you're able to bounce ideas off of someone else whose talents you admire and respect. You think of something, they think of something else, and that brings it to another level. By the time you're done, you're nowhere near where you started. But you have to be open to other people's ideas and check your ego at the door. A mutual respect is necessary for any successful collaboration and brainstorming session. With the right people, it's always an enjoyable experience for me.

FLA: How do you strike a balance between Hector's text and your visuals?

CC: The writing and the artwork are closely bound together. It's because we hash it out together. A lot of the story lines are discussed beforehand. Sometimes it's a story line based on personal experience—a family reunion, or something. And at other times it's a little harder, and we have to make up the story line from scratch. Then Hector takes it, makes something of the ideas we discussed, then writes it up with clever and significant dialogue—something that's meaningful and that's not just a gag. When I get the strips back from him, if I don't get the sense that there's something meaningful or clever, then we start making changes.

I prefer discussing changes on the phone, since my typing skills really suck. It takes me so long to type that I end up really losing the idea I'm after in my head. But if it's minor stuff, e-mail is fine usually.

FLA: The strip doesn't take place in a specific place or in a specific time.

CC: We don't want to nail the characters down to any specific geographical location. When you think about the strip, you have to remember it's done by two people: one lives in Texas, and the other in Florida; one is Mexican and one is Cuban.

As the creators of the strip, what we try to do is find a way where we can both bring to the table our personal experiences. I didn't grow up in a Mexican home. You know what I mean? I didn't grow up in Texas. Same thing for Hector. He didn't grow up Cuban American. For us both to be able to contribute and personalize the characters and story, it was better not to be specific or to make them only Mexican or only Cuban, but a combination of both.

When *Baldo* first came out, we got a lot of flak from people saying, "Why are you hiding their nationality? Why are you afraid to make them one thing or the other?" It's because they can't be. You've got two different people from two different backgrounds creating the strip. Of course, we've done strips that lean more toward a certain Latino experience than another. And even though there's always that blend, we're not trying to homogenize all Latino culture. What we aim for is to try to find that common denominator that we can both identify with.

FLA: Do you have a sense of your audience?

CC: We get e-mails from fourteen-year-olds to sixty-year-olds. We've had

Puerto Ricans write us and say, "Oh, man, it's about time a Puerto Rican family's in the newspaper." We have people in Miami say, "We're so proud to read about a Cuban family." And Mexicans say, "I love that this Mexican family is being portrayed in a comic strip." This is the big payoff: when a Cuban or a Mexican or a Puerto Rican reads the strip, they see themselves in it. Because they can identify with what they're seeing, they take the family to be their own. Not just the universal perspective of just being a family, but from a Latino viewpoint, they all see themselves in the strip.

We never thought about accomplishing that necessarily, but that's what's happened.

FLA: Is there room for character transformation in *Baldo*?

CC: I think we see growth in the sense that our characters will learn from experiences, but I don't see Baldo becoming as wise as Gracie any time soon. That would change the dynamic in which the characters relate to each other.

The most important part of hashing out the story was getting the right characters developed so they would play off each other. We originally conceived of Gracie as Baldo's older sister, but when we were writing the strips, we realized that the conflicts and story lines we could get out of her being older were either limited or not very interesting. When we made her younger and smarter, it changed the dynamics overnight. She developed this whole life of her own, and it opened up the strip. I think Gracie could have her own strip, even.

The key for me was really developing characters that would in their interactions feed the story line. If you don't have that right mix, it becomes really difficult to create the dynamic conflicts necessary for daily story lines.

FLA: Future projects?

CC: I think we'd like to do a guest artist-writer kind of thing once or twice a year if we see somebody out there that we'd like to give some exposure to and whose work would fit into the strip. We have other projects in the pipeline in different phases of development.

FLA: Might there be a Gracie spin-off?

CC: We've discussed it, you never know. Anything is possible.

Richard Dominguez

Richard Dominguez was born in 1960 in Dallas, Texas. One of seven siblings, he grew up in the area of west Dallas known as the "Devil's Back Porch"—a term coined during the Depression—that was predominantly African American and Latino. While his jack-of-all-trades father made sure to provide for the family, life was pretty rough for young Dominguez. During visits to his grandparent's house, he would find solace in the world of comic books. He would spread out his favorites on his uncle's bed and enter into all those storyworlds otherwise kept in a cardboard box. And if Dominguez was lucky, his uncle would lend him a few to take home or take him down to the local bodega, where Richard could pick from the spin-rack fresh-off-the-press favorites like *Spider-Man*, *Superman*, *Batman*, and *Captain America*. Thus began his passion for reading, drawing comics, and creating comic book stories.

Dominguez fine-tuned his drawing skills while attending Skyline High School, where he took three years of commercial art. He learned the craft of animation under the tutelage of Bud Norton—a one-time student of Burne Hogarth of the '30s–'40s *Tarzan* comics. Norton introduced Dominguez to a series of Hogarth's books, which taught him about comic techniques, shadows, line art, basic physics, and the anatomy of the comic book. He considers these books the bible of basic comic-book drawing, and still owns them today. In the early 1980s, Dominguez's passion for life drawing led him to junior college, where he spent another two years studying the arts. He was more teacher than student, assisting the instructor in teaching anatomy drawing.

The experience landed him a job in the art department of a local supermarket chain. His promotional art and designs won several awards. While in college and during this period of working for the supermarket's art department, Dominguez began conceiving of and fine-tuning his Latino superhero. After years of sketching, note taking, and ComiCon visits to get advice from the pros, Dominguez eventually realized his creation by publishing *El Gato Negro* in 1993.

Dominguez continues to live with his family in Dallas, where he continues to create his series *El Gato Negro* and *Team Tejas*. You can visit his website at www.dominguezillustrations.com

FREDERICK LUIS ALDAMA: What were some of the comics that made the biggest impression on you as a kid?

RICHARD DOMINGUEZ: I was amazed by Jack Kirby's *Hulk*, *X-Men*, and *Fantastic Four*. I couldn't wait for the next episode of *Spider-Man*. When I would read them, I would completely enter their worlds—the world around me would completely shut off. I was fascinated by the artwork; this is when I began to develop my drawing skills. I've been basically teaching myself ever since.

FLA: During the mid- to late 1980s, you had already conceived of a Latino superhero?

RD: I started doing my own Latino comic book because there weren't any fully dimensioned ones in the comic book industry. At that time there were a lot of Caucasians, blacks, and even Asians, but no Latinos. Even the black and Asian characters, however, lacked a depth and authenticity. You see this with the 1980s *Black Lightning*, who was created by a Jewish guy in Ohio; it never lasted that long. And when they did create a Latino character, El Diablo, the non-Latino creative team couldn't capture the complex essence of the Latino community. It, too, had a short run, not even making the twentieth-issue mark.

But when I would show up at comic book conventions and show my portfolio, none of the mainstream companies showed any interest. They'd just give me their business cards. I'd call them, but they'd never return my calls.

The popularity of the independent comic books—especially the *Ninja Turtles*—helped to change the perception of independent comic-book authors like myself. So I rode this wave and created *El Gato Negro*.

FLA: Can you speak more specifically to your conception and creating of the character El Gato Negro?

RD: I originally had him as a member of a government-sponsored antiterrorist superhero team based in Texas and known as Team Tejas. But I grew fond of this particular character, so I put the others on the back burner and concentrated on developing El Gato Negro.

At first, he didn't have catlike ears. He just had a mask and wasn't very

El Gato Negro, Issue 2

appealing, so I drew from one of my favorite characters as a kid, Batman, and I flared him up a bit.

I was always fascinated by superheroes who didn't have superpowers like Batman, Nightwing, and Daredevil, who relied on their smarts and martial arts skills to get the bad guys. Superman was less interesting mostly because how can you create an interesting nemesis to someone who has powers far beyond those of mortal men? I was more into those characters who did their best and took chances in their protecting of the community and loved ones. To me, that's a real superhero. This is what I wanted to capture with El Gato Negro.

FLA: How about the story?

RD: An old mentor of mine, the late Tex Henson, who was a former Disney animator, told me that when creating a character, you are the storyteller first—and the artist second. Good art alone will not sell a product. It has to have a good story to back it up. But I was a stronger artist than writer, so I had to study a lot of comic books in order to truly get the lowdown on good story writing.

FLA: What was the process of producing and getting out to readers your first issue of *El Gato Negro*?

RD: When issue 1 of *El Gato Negro* debuted, I sold a lot of books. Somehow the media found out about it, I did an interview, and this acted like free advertising. I did a print of 5,000, and within that month it was gone. I heard from comic book retailers that it sold faster than any *X-Men* title in the area.

FLA: Did the demand continue with the following issues of *El Gato Negro*?

RD: I released issue 1 of *El Gato Negro* just before the comic book industry took a dive into turmoil in the mid- to late 1990s. With issue 1, the distributor, Heroes World, out of New Jersey, really promoted it to a lot of retailers nationwide. And I thought issue 2 would sell even better. Unfortunately, this was the time that Marvel and DC decided to play vultures and buy out the distributors to use them exclusively to promote their comics. Diamond went with DC, and Heroes World went with Marvel. This was the beginning of the downfall of a lot of independent publishers; many went bellyup before their first issue ever hit the stands.

Needless to say, issue 2 didn't do as well as number 1. By the time I was working on issue 3, I decided to fold my arms and wait for the dust to settle. I advised a lot of independent publishers to wait it out, but they were pretty impatient to make their mark in the comic book business, and I never heard from them again.

FLA: You also published *Team Tejas* during this period.

RD: In 1997, with issues 1–3 of *El Gato Negro* out, I was receiving a whole lot of submissions of artists who wanted to work with me on *El Gato Negro*. With the exception of one submission, one way or another they all got *El Gato Negro* wrong. This exception turned out to be Michael Moore, who actually had a real handle on the story of *El Gato Negro* and the character; he'd actually read my book carefully. I took a real liking to the story he wrote, so I gave him the opportunity to write the story of *Team Tejas*. To this day, we've been working together. He's taken over the story line for the new *El Gato Negro* series and the revamped *Team Tejas*.

FLA: Do you think that Michael Moore's being Latin American (half African American and half Brazilian) might have something to do with why he captured the essence of your Latino character best?

RD: Absolutely.

FLA: You published one issue of *Team Tejas*?

RD: We only did one issue of *Team Tejas*, and then we decided to wait till the comic book industry might turn around. But this was also the period when I was devoting a lot of my time to helping my wife raise our daughter, who is autistic.

When we did return to the comic-book-publishing scene, we decided to focus our energies first on *El Gato Negro*, and then once this was up and running again, go back and revamp *Team Tejas*.

FLA: When's the next issue of *El Gato Negro* coming out?

RD: I'm working on issue 2 right now, but it's been slowed down because I'm trying to create enough revenue from my work as a freelance illustrator to finance the publishing of this issue by myself—this, and support a family.

FLA: Has the process for creating *El Gato Negro* changed over time?

RD: Doing the artwork for the original *El Gato Negro* issue 1 was pretty straightforward: sending the original artwork to the printers, then having them scan it and create plates for it right there. Nowadays, they don't want you to send the original artwork, but send a burned CD. This means scanning each panel and each comic page yourself. They say it cuts costs. But for who? It costs me more when I do that. I'm still in the process of learning about how to use the new technology out there. I've been such a traditionalist, doing everything the old-fashioned way for so long, that I'm having to learn all the new processes that are out there. So I'm attending school to learn more of certain techniques and programs like PhotoShop and Illustrator CS. Hopefully, once I've mastered everything, I'll be able to make more comics with greater ease.

FLA: Were there big differences between your 2004 published *El Gato Negro* and the 1993 original?

RD: Mostly, I wanted there to be more behind-the-camera scenes. While I would continue to have sole control over the character and concept, Michael would write the story, and Efren Molina would do the pencil work. Efren's heavily influenced by Mike Mignola's *Hellboy*, so he gave the character El Gato a darker, grittier look. I continue to do the inking.

El Gato Negro: Nocturnal Warrior, Issue 1

FLA: Who are your readers today?

RD: Mostly Latinos from the South Texas region as well as from the Bronx area and the West Coast. I even have some from Japan, England, and Mexico. And you'd be surprised at how many girl fans are out there. A lot say they'd love to have a Francisco Guerrero as their boyfriend.

FLA: How do you decide the general layout of an issue?

RD: We do the storyboard panels and layouts according to the stories that Michael has dished out, and then Efren takes over and executes it with the penciling. I do all the finals, as far as the inks and the lettering, as well as ad placement and cover design.

FLA: How do you envision the panel layout—even the angle and distance of the shots?

RD: Since I'm the only one that has the eye for that, I make the decisions as far as laying out everything. I try to make it appealing for the reader's eye as much as I can. Because I myself am an avid comic book reader, I like to create layouts that are amusing for my eye and that make the story engaging.

FLA: Do you also read it out loud to yourself?

RD: Yes, I do. I even act it out to get a feel for what Francisco or his grandfather would say or do. It's like script reading. I act it out to give it some flare. And if a scene doesn't work, I just change it.

FLA: You play with different size panels as well as include more or less panels on a given page to vary the rhythm and convey a mood?

RD: We make sure that all of our stories flow. Like water. We work together to make sure the layouts flow, to make sure it appeals to the eye.

FLA: Working with black-and-white as opposed to color?

RD: It boils down to a money thing. But the way I do my black-and-whites is like putting color in it. I do this process called Zipatone—patterned dots of different shadings. They're hard to find, but I can purchase them in bulk at a discount at my local art store. Some call this the lost art, because this was the way they used to do it with their black-and-white newspaper ads and old comics. This is my way of coloring a black-and-white; it truly captures the shadows and sets the mood for each panel. I wouldn't change it in any other way.

FLA: You talked about acting out some of the scenes. Do you do this also to get a feel for how you are conveying the character's moods?

RD: You know, we use a mirror process: I make expressions on the face, capture it with pencil, then try to relate the expression to the character we're portraying in the story. This process can really capture the true essence of that particular emotion flowing in a particular part of the story.

FLA: How did you conceive of Francisco Guerrero as El Gato Negro?

RD: First, I named him after the Mexican revolutionary in the early 1900s, Pancho Villa. Second, I gave him the last name "Guerrero" because he was a warrior, fighting for what he believed was right. Orphaned as an infant, Francisco doesn't know who his parents were; he's raised by his grandfather—a retired Mexican wrestler turned adventurer from the '50s and '60s. So Francisco is raised by his grandfather and the community at large. That's why by day I made him a social worker, so he can give back to the community by helping others who cannot help themselves. His upbringing teaches him to know right from wrong. And I made him psychologically complicated in that he asks questions: he wants to know where he came from, what his purpose in life is, why he's here.

FLA: Your characters often have to overcome individual obstacles before they can work—often with others—to vanquish the villains.

RD: For instance, in *Team Tejas* each of the characters has their own issues to deal with, and then at the same time to learn to work together as a team. It's like a multicultural *Fantastic Four*. By giving them psychological problems they have to work on, it gives the characters a more down-home feel. For example, the Native American superhero, the Plainsman, who's the chief of his tribe and who has trouble deciding whether he should work for a government that had his nation and his people reduced down to a reservation. The Jonathan Gonzalez character is mixed Latino and Anglo and raised as a Tejano who knows well where he came from. He struggles to come to terms with his father, a well-respected bureaucrat in Texas politics who leads the team. The siblings Calibre and Reata are Latinos born as metahumans and whose powers are assigned by the government for special use.

FLA: Villains like the rebel in Bosnia that confronts the Plainsman are also complicated.

RD: Michael Moore was trying to make the readers aware of current events and that land could still be taken away from people—as happened with the Native Americans like the Plainsman.

The true villain of *Team Tejas* was Dexxis, a former Team Tejas member who wants to use this darkness that comes out of the earth as his ally. He's the original Lone Star turned evil. In *El Gato Negro* there's the villain El Graduado, the graduate, who's the spoiled, rich brat of a son to Boss Ochoa—the drug lord in that region. He went to the best schools all over the world, including Harvard and the University of Bogotá, where he studied the environment, but rather than use his knowledge for good, he uses it for evil and destruction.

FLA: As a Latino comic book artist-author, do you have a sense of responsibility to your stories and audience?

RD: My responsibility is making sure that all the artwork, characters, and stories are worth talking about—and for a very long time. To create interesting characters. I myself learned recently from a blog that *El Gato Negro* was the first comic book to introduce non-Anglo villains.

FLA: What might the ingredients be that make Latino comic books *Latino*, that make the difference between an *El Diablo* and an *El Gato Negro*?

RD: What we Latino comic book authors do is put a lot of ourselves into the story and character. I see myself a lot in El Gato Negro because there's a lot that I need to tell, a lot that I want to do, a lot that I can't do. But I do have the ability to strike it with a pen. So it boils down to being able to put a lot of yourself into the Latino character. That's the real chemical makeup of the Latino comic.

FLA: Today it would seem that more Latino characters are getting play in the mainstream. I think of the *Blue Beetle* and *Araña* series. Yet there are still a lot of creators like yourself, Fernando Rodriguez, Carlos Saldaña, Laura Molina, and many others who aren't making the big bucks.

RD: I cannot speak for all of them, but I feel like they wouldn't have it any other way: to have that freedom to do what you want to do with your characters, not what the company wants you to do with them. Who knows? Araña has her own title today, but for how long? How long will *The Blue Beetle* be around? Will the creative team change for the better or worse?

FLA: You're working on *El Gato Negro: Nocturnal Warrior* issue 2 and you're going to return to *Team Tejas*. Are there other projects in the pipeline?

RD: There's been a lot of demand for the *El Gato Negro: Nocturnal Warrior* series, so I'll continue with that. Michael and I are working on a graphic-novel concept for *Team Tejas*. Efren is going to be penciling a one-shot comic book story, *Relampago*, that I'll write as a way to pay my respects to Judge Margarito Garza, the man who introduced me to comic book making as far as Latino characters are concerned.

FLA: Any last words?

RD: *¡Con todo ganas si se puede!* [We can do it if we really want to!]

Frank Espinosa

In 1962, Frank Espinosa was born in Havana, Cuba. When Espinosa was seven, his family moved to New York City. While comic books were around in Cuba, it was after he moved to New York that he began to immerse himself in their worlds. To pass the hours as a young boy, he would often spend time reading Superman and Batman comics—as well as the newspaper characters that his father introduced him to.

Espinosa had a passion and talent for drawing from a young age. He would later more formally hone his skills by studying animation and cartooning. After graduating from the High School of Art and Design and the School of Visual Arts, Espinosa was first hired to work at Walt Disney Studios. He was then hired by the consumer products division of Warner Bros. as art director.

In his triple-Eisner-nominated comic book *Rocketo*, we see autobiographical experience mix with an expansive imaginative vision that gestures to expressionist art, Homeric epics, and postcolonial literature. Espinosa's creative work gives testament to his remark: "Yes, we're Hispanic, but we can imagine, just like anybody else, other worlds."

Espinosa taught a character-design, mythology, and world-making course at MIT in 2006, but he lives most of the year in California, where he continues to create *Rocketo*. Image Comics publishes *Rocketo* and Espinosa's *Killing Girl* (volume 1). His website is www.frankespinosa.com.

FREDERICK LUIS ALDAMA: Do you remember any particular experience reading comics as a young Latino?

FRANK ESPINOSA: Comics were just a wonder. They opened up a whole new world. In Cuba there were no comics that I knew of; everything was the comic strip. I read *The Phantom*, *Mandrake the Magician*, and *Popeye*—the classics. When I got to New York, I discovered that *Superman* was in the comics—a whole fifty-two large-sized issues! This was a giant sized Superman with Batman! I was in heaven. Then came *Spider-Man*, *The Hulk*, *Captain America*—each one with its own history, its own myth.

That is what I love: the history behind the heroes. It wasn't that Spider-Man fought crime, or Superman fought crime—that was a given. It was the fact that Superman was from another planet and was a stranger, and that Spider-Man couldn't pay his rent. This is what made them unique—and attractive to me.

FLA: Do you recall any comic books that you may have read as a young boy in Cuba?

FE: I don't remember reading *Batman* and *Superman* in comic form, but I had seen the newspaper strips and baseball cards and other paraphernalia around. I especially knew the image of Superman. When I arrived in the States, I recall being surprised to see Superman comics. I thought we had invented him in Cuba.

FLA: You trained in animation and comics. Can you speak to this experience?

FE: I attended the High School of Art and Design in New York City. I went there as an animation-cartooning major. It was expected that you go into one or you go into the other. To me, however, animation and comics were like two cousins. They both require the same type of skills. It's not because I would train in animation that I would be able to draw better or worse. They were interchangeable. In fact, when I looked at a Wayne Boring drawing of *Superman* or the classic Bob Kane *Batman*, I would want to animate it.

FLA: Can you speak a little about Rescue Comics and your early storytelling projects?

FE: Rescue Comics started with a friend of mine, Juan Ortiz. We had met in high school, then years later decided to come up with a little comic book that we would put out ourselves. And we did. We put out, I think, three or four issues, and then we just said, "OK, that's it." Funny enough, the first version of *Rocketo*, titled *Major Rocket*, appeared in a very comedic sense in Rescue Comics.

We were two New York City kids, and we were doing city stories. I wasn't deliberately trying to give a unique Latino cultural perspective, but they were stories that had to do with the inner city. Rescue Comics had a short life span, but I think that if we had gone further into it, ten or eleven books, all the issues of living in the inner city would have come out normally—and in a fun, larger-than-life way.

FLA: You mention elsewhere a Japanese influence?

FE: Well I love manga. In fact, I discovered Japanese animation in the late

'70s. I was watching *Future Boy Conan* and all these other little things that played on TV. Curiously enough, *Future Boy Conan* was aired on a Spanish TV station in New York. I have yet to see it in English. And I knew right away that whoever was behind this was a genius. So I became a big follower of Hayao Miyazaki. I still think that he's probably one of the greatest animation directors that has ever graced the earth.

I learned a lot about timing and sequencing—actually having some quiet moments—from watching his movies. During this time in America, you didn't have these quiet sequences. You punch a guy through a wall in the first frame of the film.

FLA: *Rocketo* is very literary and artistic. Can you talk about some of your other influences?

FE: Homer's *Odyssey*, Joseph Conrad's *Heart of Darkness*, and the myth of Orpheus were big influences. Visually, I was moved heavily by the German expressionists. I love the power of their drawings; they were *pure* emotion. I try to look at everything. I don't think a day goes by when I don't pick up a book, movie, discover an artist, or look at something that I haven't seen before. The other day I was looking at ancient Chinese designs. They in turn influenced a sequence where petals were patterns in a background for *Rocketo*. I love that part of the process: the study and the research.

FLA: Can you speak to the process when you made the transition to the crafting of *Rocketo*?

FE: Comics are not as financially rewarding as, say, animation. So comics are really a labor of love. It's a lot of hard work; in some ways, it's harder than animating a cartoon. I thought it would be the other way around! Of course, with comics, you don't have to go through endless meetings in order to approve, say, a character's color.

Naturally, I am speaking of the world of commercial animation. If one does animated films on a personal level, then the choices are all yours. In comics, independent comics, you have the ability to make all the decisions yourself, so you have a lot of freedom, a lot of control, in the way you tell and pace the story. But the work itself, the actual labor, is really hard because you're telling the story without motion, you're telling a story without sound.

Yesterday I was watching Charlie Chaplin's *City Lights*, which is one of my favorite comedies. I was learning from it by sketching Chaplin's movement. I was amazed at how Chaplin gracefully sets up his scene, the gag, and the transition to the next scene. I was amazed at how his body language, the music, the timing could convey an idea. But as comic book storytellers, we don't have real movement. So somehow we have to try to get this idea into your subconscious in between the panels.

FLA: Who do you write *Rocketo* for? Do you have an ideal audience in mind?

FE: I started writing *Rocketo* for the kid in me. But when I get my fan mail and go to comic conventions, I see that the actual audience is really broad: all sorts of ages and with no real set ethnic demographic.

FLA: How have your experiences as a Cuban émigré influenced your work?

FE: *Rocketo* is the story of a Mapper—an explorer. Explorers like Marco Polo and others are really in some way temporary immigrants; they're always the stranger wherever they travel. So Columbus comes to the New World. He discovers that he is not the first. He is the stranger. He has to learn the ways of the indigenous peoples.

Coming here from Cuba, I was the stranger. I felt like I had to learn a new language: the culture, food, dress were all different. It was quite a shock. When I left Cuba in 1970, it was frozen in the 1950s: the cars, the styles, and so on. Arriving in America in the '70s was a gigantic leap forward in time.

With *Rocketo*, I'm trying to tap into that experience—especially in the next story, "Journey to the New World," when he starts going off to all these different countries where he's trying to figure out what the hell everyone is saying. That to me is the adventure of the explorer and immigrant.

After going to school during the day to learn English, I would work with my dad in his shoe store. I would see him struggle with the customers. They would say something in English, and he'd look at me in confusion. I would help him understand with whatever little I knew at the time. In that sense, too, I put a little bit of myself and experience into *Rocketo*.

FLA: Why tell stories in the comic book form and not, say, the memoir or short story or novel?

FE: I love to draw. It's the best way I can communicate my ideas and my feelings very quickly. It was Marie Taylor who brought out the writer in me. So the memoir would be out, and the short story would not be short as I explain all these images that fall into my brain. So comics were a natural extension.

No matter your age, you can open up a comic book and you become a kid again. It's an art form where you can describe visually, but still leave a lot to the imagination. Like Japanese prints that imply more than they show. So I purposely leave a lot of details out in my drawings—like Rocketo's floating observatory—because I want you to make up the rest. I want you to use some of your imagination. I draw just enough, and I let you fill in the blanks because you're a much better artist than I am in that respect.

I chose the comic medium because I love it. That's the medium that taught me an appreciation for literature. As a kid coming here from Cuba, I learned to read from comics. It was *Superman* and *Batman* and *Spider-Man* that taught me to read English. Marvel Comics gave me a great introduction to literature. At the time, Jack Kirby—a genius in graphic design and storytelling—was drawing *The Hulk*. In his own way, he's Dr. Jekyll and Mr. Hyde. In the rest of the Marvel and DC lineup, there were references to *Treasure Island*, to the *Three Musketeers*, Norse mythology—as well as to all sorts of weird, esoteric stuff like Armageddon.

I always say that *Rocketo* is a tribute to all the things that I loved when I was a kid: *Flash Gordon, Buck Rogers, Zorro, Popeye the Sailor, The Arabian Nights*, and so on.

FLA: *Rocketo* feels as if it is in motion, like an animation.

FE: As an animator, I will tell you—and I think this is true of all animators in some form or another—I was fascinated by movement when I was a kid. There's something about movement—how and why things react when in motion—that really gives me a thrill. Literally, my mind and imagination explode.

While working on the first version of the *Rocketo* comic, I drew a couple of pages more like a traditional comic: Rocketo's pants and shirt drawn at the same height and always the same length, and the whole bit. And that was really getting to be no fun at all. So I went back and I said, "I've got to have fun doing this." I started looking at my roughs before I would clean them up, and I found out that the roughs had much more energy than the very finished drawings. So I took the rough drawings, cleaned them up a little bit here and there to give you a little bit more information, then I started to develop this, and I said, "Oh, this really keeps what I felt. This doesn't slow my drawings down." Again, the movement was dictating the drawing.

The question I kept asking myself was how do I get that sense that Rocketo has turned his head or is about to reach for something. I act everything out before I draw it. I try to see how the anatomy of a gesture is working. I would struggle with getting that feeling of that push—the arm flexing, the slight movement of the fingers after an action, and so on, to give the audience the feeling that this character is in motion. To me, if I draw too much, my eye stops taking in the details; it doesn't pick up the movement.

In animation there's a bag of tricks. Sometimes in animation you do one drawing that has five or six hands in it. So, for instance, if a character is reaching for a glass of water, and he's reaching for it real quick, in the first drawing you're going to see a hand stretching. Then in the second drawing there will be a drawing of three hands on one drawing. Then in the third drawing you'll see him grabbing the cup. So that little in-between drawing is going to have three hands in it, and when you see it projected, you don't actually even see it. It's not even a blur—it's a feeling that the hand is moving. It's a weird illusion. If you have the ability to freeze a single frame of an old classic cartoon, you will see, say, Bugs Bunny grow eight different heads, or eight arms in different lengths.

I wanted to bring some of that magic back to cartooning.

FLA: What's your storytelling process?

FE: It's like the chicken and the egg. Sometimes the visuals come first, but there has to be a reason for the visuals to be there. I can't just think about a great visual and try to hang a story around it. I always try to ask what am I going to try to say here? For instance, I'm working on a sequence now, Rocketo fighting a war, and I know what happens here in this setting, and so the visuals start to come.

It goes back and forth. Sometimes when I'm drawing it, the words start pouring into my head because I am so focused on this new reality that I've already created with little thumbnails. Then on other occasions, I don't hear a single thing. That's when I know its not working. I try to storyboard different versions of the same sequence. But when you're working on a deadline the way I am, you don't really have that much time . . . Then I talk the final version through with Marie [Taylor, a writer]; she keeps me on track. Then I go for it. I have the big picture in my head, and then I lay those Caribbean colors on.

FLA: You've worked with other people when doing animation, and you work solo as a comic book author-artist. Can you talk about both processes?

FE: Working in animation is more of a group project. Everything works when the team is great together. The creative team really becomes one big human being. That in itself is a great feeling, that sense of a team and a goal to reach. And while I love to collaborate with other great artists or writers, at the same time I also like to explore what I can bring to a single project by myself—or with just one more person.

One of my biggest influences is *Astro Boy* creator Tezuka. He works on his comics by himself or with a small team, producing these wonderful personal stories. I love that feeling that you can be an auteur with comics. While Orson Welles may have been one of the last of the auteurs in cinema, you can still be an auteur of comic books. You can still write it, draw it, ink it, color it, and do it all by yourself. I think that's beautiful. It makes it more of an art form for me; it makes it more personal. I think the best comics are the real ones that resonate with personal issues, that you can feel and where there's a distinctive voice coming through.

FLA: When you're doing your storyboards, making choices about the visuals and the text, are you making choices that move you to feel pleasure, pain, happiness, and so on?

FE: Yes, to me it's all about the emotion. The text gives me one emotion, the visuals have to give another emotion, and so on. They must work together and not mirror each other at the same time. Every choice in the planning stage is about the emotion that is being felt. There's a new biography on Gustave Flaubert that talks about how long he worked, just trying to painstakingly get every sentence laid out right—twenty pages in six weeks, or something like that. He would get this thrill out of it. That's just like doing a comic book. Animation works with one frame next to the other frame next to the other frame. Comics work the same way. But now you've got sentences and you've got frames, panels. And they work together to give you this feeling.

I'm my own best and worst audience. Once in print, I can tell where I overindulged or where I should have taken something out. But what am I going to do. At the time, this is what I was feeling. I can't go back now. At the time when I was doing the book, I always say, "This is my best book." I'm doing it now. I'm going, "This is my best book," because I felt like this is where I really was in touch with whatever emotion I was trying to convey at the moment. Two months from now, I'm going to read it and go, "No, this is my best book."

FLA: The long-page format of *Rocketo* is a little unusual.

FE: I love this format because it gives me the chance to make-believe that I'm working on my 150 million dollar film. I can make these very long—Sergio Leone's, or David Lean's *Lawrence of Arabia*—cinematic shots, something that's normally hard to do with comics. I love doing those single panels that I begin on the left page and stretch across over onto the right page. It also brings me back to the adventure comic strip that newspapers have dropped for some crazy reason.

I was trying to break it up a little. *Rocketo* was an attempt to grow out of this comic book format constraint. It was an experiment to offer readers another way of engaging with the story. It has been done before, and it's not very new, but it's a format that needs exploration.

I think comics are an art form just as novels and all the other books that fill up the Barnes and Noble shelves. You're not going to require that every single book in Barnes and Noble will be fifty-six pages long and an identical certain height and format. But for some reason, in comics, experimentation with different formats, page texture, design, is something that some people do not like.

FLA: Why the particular stories that make up *Rocketo*?

FE: Originally, these stories were all going to take place on different planets. Rocketo was going to be jumping from one planet to the other. It was going to be a space adventure, like *Flash Gordon*. But that's been done a hundred times. That was the original idea; it was the idea presented in Rescue Comics in my early twenties. When I came back to the world of comics in my late thirties, I looked at this character, and I asked what if I created this character now. What can I bring to it with my life experience?

So I started from scratch. The idea came to me that we've been exploring this world ever since we walked out of the cave—almost 10–12 thousand years ago. We've got satellites flying around, and we still find new species. We still have yet to explore the ocean's depths. I wanted to capture that feeling I get when looking at old maps of Africa from the 1800s, where there are still big giant parts in the maps missing information. The dark continent. The unknown lands. Those old, ancient maps before Columbus when the world was flat, when you would sail to this point and then drop off the face of the earth where the monsters rise from the depths.

I started thinking, wouldn't it be great if I could do a story that captures that old sense of the unknown? But how do I work with and then develop it into a story? Then it came to me. I realized that I had to destroy the world! Because that was the only way I could give it that feeling that you're eight years old and you're going off to this adventure. Remember, I'm from Cuba, and America was the New World. From Cuba to America was like coming to Mars. How do I project that feeling for the readers? I had to figure out a way of breaking it up, changing it, making it into a big puzzle, smashing continents into tiny little islands, and then saying, "OK, now we're going to start from zero."

Now going to South America's interesting. It became larger than life. Now that South America is a bunch of shattered islands, what type of civilization would be there? Would it be more or less advanced than the rest of the world? What type of technology would they have? How would that affect the rest of the world politically or economically? And so like Sinbad the Sailor and the seven voyages, Rocketo would go forth and would have four journeys. Seven is too long, and I need a life.

FLA: Not only do maps, but memory plays a vital role in the world of *Rocketo*.

FE: Yes, the maps, the Mappers, and memory are all connected. Each Mapper downloads his life and his thoughts into a map for another to follow and learn. Mappers like Rocketo are the ones that unite the world. The emotions, knowledge, cultures, and wisdom that are handed down through generations of Mappers are really what will unify the world.

I love the world's tapestry of cultures: its songs, art, myths from the Middle East, Europe, North and South America. It all comes into play in *Rocketo* at some point.

When I came to America, it was supposed to be the great melting pot. This is what we were led to believe. And as you grow up, you start going, "Well, where is it?" I grew up on 181st Street and saw many different cultures that got along and that didn't. There wasn't this fusion that I thought would happen in my tiny, kid brain. So I thought, okay, here's my chance to create a fusion—a celebration of world culture. I know that sounds quaint, but I want people to read *Rocketo*, visit what India has become in the New World, and respond: "Look how beautiful that is." It's the mythology of India that has become the way that India (now known as "Lunaripal") has shaped its culture. The same with the mythology of Russia and of Italy. I just find it very exciting.

FLA: The Asian princess Tien tells Rocketo that believing in stories can make some things true, especially if you believe it when everyone else says otherwise. Is this what you mean about myth keeping memory alive?

FE: Myth is a form of memory—an ancient subconscious memory that flows from one land to the next. This is very Joseph Campbell. I was also trying to lay in there the groundwork for the last book, *Journey to Ultamo*. The first book and the last book are united, and I already had worked on my ending. So these words will come back. In Rocketo's memory, it's about believing in self, coming back to life.

FLA: Volteo tells young Rocketo that if he wants to be a Mapper, he must

THIS WORLD AND ITS PEOPLE HAVE BEEN **SHATTERED** AND SEPARATED FOR TOO LONG. IF YOU WANT TO BE A **MAPPER**, YOU MUST **LEARN** HOW TO USE MORE THAN JUST YOUR EYES.

Rocketo Vol. 1: The Journey to the Hidden Sea

learn to see with more than just his eyes. Does this allude to issues of race and racial prejudice?

FB: There's the character Saturn Ivanoff, who is black but has a Russian name. And Rocketo's brother; they grew up together.

The world of *Rocketo* isn't filled with the same prejudice that we see today. It's not so much racial prejudice, but prejudice on a different level, a genetic prejudice. What makes us human? Rocketo looks human, at least. If you're a Dogman, what problems do you face? In the early part of the story, Rocketo is just modeling off the prejudice that he's picking up. But later, because he's learned to look at the Tigermen differently, he fights alongside them against the bad guys.

Rocketo Vol. 1: The Journey to the Hidden Sea

FLA: I've noticed in comic books there's actually in a way two narrators working: a visual narrator that's telling us the story through the visuals, and a text narrator.

FB: As for other comics, I'm from the school that both of them should be working together, but the text should never explain what you're seeing. A character who flies through a window and yells out, "I've been knocked through a window," is a bit old now.

FLA: You employ multiple narrators: Rocketo, Spiro, and a third, objective narrator.

Rocketo Vol. 1: The Journey to the Hidden Sea

FE: Spiro's narrative is his version—his journey. He is as big a part of the story as Rocketo. In a way, Spiro's journey is more interesting because he is not born into a legacy of right and wrong. Spiro's narrative adds to the mystery of what happened to Rocketo at the end of the journeys.

Then there is Rocketo's narrative, the heart of the story. They both come together near the end of the journeys.

FLA: You stretch your panels to provide these great panoramas and also break them up into smaller panels. Can you talk a little bit about this process?

FE: It's an intuitive feeling that guides the decision when I need to suddenly change from a long shot to a close-up to trigger an emotion. All of it is an emotional metronome. Emotion is going to dictate long shot, medium shot, and close-up. I'm from the older schools of comic art: Will Eisner, Milton Caniff, Roy Crane, E. C. Segar, and so on.

My guide is the emotional metronome. I look at this as a film. I run it through my head, and I say to myself, how can I convey the emotion of this shot the best? Should I pull back or move forward? I try not to have extreme close-ups, if you notice. I try to keep the close-ups old-school style, where it's still a little bit of a shoulder shot. If I pull back the camera, I want you to see what's going on. Alex Raymond's original *Flash Gordon* comic strip did that beautifully: he pulls back the camera, and one could see how that beautiful pose of Flash Gordon could tell you a whole story.

FLA: What about your use of gutters?

FE: I took the black border around them out because the only black I want is on the characters. I don't want the reader to think about the black border. I even took the black borders around the balloons out. It looks great in other comics, but for me I wanted all the reader's attention to be on the black and grays on those characters.

FLA: The way you mix your palette is very interesting too.

FE: I wish I could tell you that I have a formula for bringing out all those colors, but I don't. I look at everything from the German expressionists to the French impressionists as a guide. In the process of creating *Rocketo*, everything else is very controlled: my pencil, my inking, where I'm going to put my shadows, where I'm going to put my blacks. But when it comes to the color, that's the part where I just say I'm just going to sit here, have some coffee or cocoa, whatever, and I'm just going to play. And I don't even try to give you continuity from one page to the other. I have a certain palette that I will always use—I don't want your brain to go all over the place. I know that my shadows will be blue; my lights, yellow. Everything in the middle

 YOUR BRAIN ON LATINO COMICS

is up for grabs. Those are the only two rules. Shadows are always blue. And yellow and white highlights. That's it.

Color for me is also ruled by emotion and movement. Sometimes it takes a few days to color a whole book, and other times a week or so. I have no idea how long a book will take. I've talked to other people who color comic books, and there're some fantastic colorists out there. But I just feel that now I have to set the stage for *Rocketo*.

FLA: Your characters are otherworldly and at the same time recognizably human. How did you conceive of the stylizing of your characters?

FE: Well, they're cartoons. I don't try and draw anything realistically. Again, artists like Wayne Boring (one of the early *Superman* artists), Frank Robbins, Roy Crane, and others from the 1920s through the 1950s had a big influence. People are caricatures. Everything feels larger than life.

FLA: Can you talk about how you conceived your characters' actions and personalities in *Rocketo*?

FE: At the beginning of the series, it was difficult to trust that the characters would speak for themselves and attain a life of their own. Like the character Spiro, who has that grand swag and '30s talk of Humphrey Bogart in *Treasure of the Sierra Madre*. Sometimes I would finish a penciled page only to erase it and start again because Spiro's emotions were wrong. Then I work with the pencils, then the inks and color to convey the right emotion.

FLA: Do you think the comic book author-artist has a certain responsibility to convey certain values?

FE: Yes, all art, music, film, and the like is a representation of the artist's emotions and values. We would like to think that in some ways it does not have an influence, but it does—especially on the younger generation. For example, there was a sequence that I had drawn for issue 2 where they torture Rocketo. They rip his skin and they peel it back. It's really hard-core stuff.

I remember sitting at the Comic Convention in San Diego, signing cop-

Rocketo Vol. 1: The Journey to the Hidden Sea

ies of the first Rocketo story, *Siren's Call*, and this young woman with a baby in her arms and her husband come to the booth. She says, "Oh, this is *Rocketo*! When he grows up, I'm going to read him *Rocketo* because I heard so much about it." I signed the book to the kid, then broke into a cold sweat because I suddenly started thinking that at home, at my drawing board, there is a future sequence where Rocketo is getting his skin ripped apart. When I went back home, I reworked the sequence, used only a drawing of Rocketo strapped to this giant chair. I said to myself, "This kid doesn't need to read this. He doesn't need to see this. There's enough of this stuff going around." It changed my whole view on how I should write and put together this book. There's enough of that stuff going around: fighting and war with people dying every day.

I don't want to edit comics, just my comics. Comics are an art form. They're for everybody. But I don't know, there has to be a little bit of light now and then.

FLA: Your sense of responsibility as a Latino or Hispanic comic book author?

FE: We're Hispanic. There's this image of the Hispanic male and the African American male as the gangbanger or the wild guy. As a Hispanic writer and cartoonist, why would I want to show that when I'm working long hours a day on my book? Why should I draw a story about a kid who's blowing up other kids in the head? Why would I want to do that?

When people see my last name, Espinosa, they can assume that because I'm Latino, that's all I can know. No, we're Latinos and we read literature. We know Homer.

So that is my responsibility. It's not just writing about our people and saying this is what I grew up in. It's also about writing about us as people. When my family came to the U.S., we first lived near 145th Street in New York. It was a very rough neighborhood back then. As a kid, I did not want to pick up a comic book that had Harlem in it. I wanted to read *The Three Musketeers*, *The Arabian Nights*. I wanted to get as far away from the hood as I could.

Years ago, before *Rocketo*, when I was trying to break into children's books, I went to a couple of publishers with this idea for a line of children's books based on a little African American girl who has all these fantastic adventures. They didn't want it. They said, "No, no, no. This kid doesn't look like an African American character." And I said, "What are you talking about?" And they said, "Well her father is an airplane pilot. And her mother is a graphic designer." And I said, "Yeah?" And they were like, "No, no. You want to write it so the people can relate to this. How about if her

 YOUR BRAIN ON LATINO COMICS

mother lives in the ghetto." So I responded, "Have you ever lived in the ghetto? Because if you lived on 145th Street, that's the last place you want to think about when you're there."

Some assume that because we're Hispanics, and because we're African American, that's all we can write about. I took a trip to the bookstore when I was doing research for my children's books, and I was amazed to see that almost all books with African American children were colored in sepia tones. We are some of the brightest, most colorful people, and we've been reduced to sepia tones.

We as Hispanics, as African Americans, as any minority, can write the new *Lord of the Rings*, the new *Star Wars*, the new Harry Potters, but if all we do is just talk about one experience in our lives, we will remain trapped.

Roberta Gregory

Born in Wilmington, California, in 1953, Roberta Gregory grew up there in the '50s and '60s. Her mother's side of the family was, as she says in conversation, "almost a caricature of a big Mexican family . . . we would all get together to help Grandma make tamales . . . Uncle Dickie was a real car fiend and had a souped-up lowrider-looking '59 Chevy." Her father's side seemed "very, very Anglo"; she recalls hearing "rather racist things being spoken, especially about black people."

For Roberta, life in Wilmington "was kind of a schizy." She remarks how "from the culture at large in Los Angeles, I got the idea that 'Mexican' was not the best thing in the world to be, but then here was half of my family. . . . Very strange."

Comic book art ran in the family. Her father wrote stories for Disney, so she always had *Donald Duck* and *Uncle Scrooge* comics around. Children's comics like *Dennis the Menace*, *Little Lulu*, and *Sugar and Spike* were especial favorites. Her father even knew some of the comic book creators, like Carl Barks and Al Wiseman, whom she met as well. At an early age, she began to draw animals with dialogue balloons; she would collect the pages and then staple the books together to sell to members of her family. She did not really care for romance comics, developed a slight penchant for *Archie*, but had a real enthusiasm for DC comics; *Superman*, *Superboy*, and *Supergirl* were her favorites because they included a whole family of heroes, and even a cat, a dog, and a horse. As she remarks, "This was the 1960s, after all. Later, adolescent girls my age would be reading *Love and Rockets*. Quite a contrast!"

In 1971, she attended California State University–Long Beach, where she experimented with different cartooning styles in the college paper. In 1974, she created the *Feminist Funnies* and also sold her first story to Last Gasp's *Wimmin's Comix*. This story was later published as a regulation-size comic book, *Dynamite Damsels*; she was the first woman to publish in this format. She continued to contribute stories to *Wimmin's Comix* as well as to *Tits and Clits* and *Gay Comix*. In the late 1980s, she began working on the ambitious, mythically inspired graphic novel *Winging It*. In 1991, *Naughty Bits* appeared, and that eventually gave rise to the *Bitchy Bitch* series.

Roberta Gregory lives in Seattle, Washington, where she continues to work on her novel, *Mother Mountain*, as well as other comic book stories.

FREDERICK LUIS ALDAMA: Do you consider yourself of a certain school of the comic book art form?

ROBERTA GREGORY: Oh, no . . . I would just write and draw the comics I wanted to see but which nobody else ever did. My comics have always been rather strange and out in left field. *Bitchy* is the most mainstream thing I have done up to this point, and that is too weird for a lot of people.

FLA: Why choose to tell stories in the comic book form?

RG: I always liked to write and draw. Actually, now I have been doing more writing in prose, I guess you call it. Words only. I tried drawing *Mother Mountain* as a graphic novel, and I realized it would just take too long. I have just started the third book of a trilogy. It would take me several lifetimes to draw this much story as a graphic novel. There are ways that comics art and words work best. I can't imagine *Bitchy* being anything but a cartoon. My *Winging It* story played a lot with people's expectations. Some of the characters were of very indeterminate gender, either hermaphrodites or sexless, and it was very hard for the reader to make a quick decision about what someone was, like we do so much in real life. This seems like something that would work best with words and pictures on the printed page. *Winging It* seemed to be too far out in left field for most readers, but it is so far the favorite work of mine, as badly drawn as it is—at least until *Mother Mountain* gets finished. I think of myself as a writer first and an artist second.

FLA: Can you support yourself as an independent?

RG: Oh, I wish. I have always tried to make it financially. About the only time was when these animators were developing *Bitchy* into an animated cartoon, but that did not last long. At the moment, I am getting by as best I can: the occasional paying comics job, teaching, typing, doing janitor work on-call. I have hopes of some projects in the near future that may bring in some more cash. I am so tired of being poor! It was kind of fun when I was twenty, but at fifty it really is starting to suck!

FLA: Did you face any major obstacles breaking into the comic book marketplace?

RG: I never really had too many difficulties breaking in. There was *Wimmin's Comix* and similar titles early on when I was just getting started in the 1970s, and they went out of their way to publish women. Plus, there were not as many comics back then, so more people would read them. Some men joked that it was easier to get published as a woman than as a man. But so many women have not stayed with it. I can see why they haven't. The pay is really not so good. Nobody has ever been around to pay my way and let me just work on all the projects I want to do. I find it so sad to think that so many of the comics and stories and art I want to do will never get done, but when you are over fifty, that is the reality. Still, I have gone through stages where I have done more day jobs than trying to survive on the comics, as when I had the regular title *Naughty Bits* and I was still struggling financially but had no creations to show for my work besides repetitive stress injuries and such. I have learned my lesson, and hope to get more projects done.

FLA: Can you speak to your different experiences with self-publishing and that of working with independents?

RG: I have mostly worked with Fantagraphics and self-published. It is hard to say which is better. Fantagraphics seem to try to promote my work somewhat, but I don't think it is really their line when you see what else they publish. I find it so stressful to try to switch from being creative to trying to be a marketer, so I hesitate to do more self-publishing, though it could be easier these days with the Internet. I would love to have a small publisher that would share the wealth and be very much behind my work. I have so many good projects in mind that I would love to take off on.

FLA: You're known as a feminist alternative comic book author mostly, but there is a Latino dimension in some of your work.

RG: Well, in *Winging It*, the one main human protagonist is a young Latina woman, Lupe Contreras. But that book is so obscure, although you can buy it on my Web site, most people who know my other comics have not seen it. Lupe is struggling with deep spiritual issues and trying to survive and retain her integrity and is *not* too overtly Latina, as there is really nothing specifically cultural about her story beyond the fact that as a child she was traumatized by seeing the gory, crucified Jesus on the cross so typical of Mexican churches, and has rejected Jesus, who is a minor character in the book, as a result. Although it is not a Christian story either. She is single and suicidal and trying to be an artist and was once a prostitute, so it is far from what one thinks of as a "typical" Latina role, which always to me seems to carry a cultural context. She is almost an allegorical character that can serve as a stand-in for nearly anyone's spirit.

I really have no idea why I made Lupe a Latina woman. The whole story line is full of things I had no idea why I did what I did. Many of my comics and other creative works do not seem all that deliberate to me. Why do the people of *Mother Mountain* have wings? I just start working, and the story evolves into what it seems to have to be. Bitchy started out as a bit of a joke, and she just turned into a more "real" person as I wrote about her.

FLA: Can you speak about some of your influences or inspirations?

RG: I am not sure if anything really inspires me in that sense. I tend to do the sorts of stories I want to do, that nobody else is doing, because that is what I want to read, myself. I do read my own works a lot and really enjoy them. I am very inspired by Donna Barr's energy and drive and fantastic imagination and superb drawing, but I do not think I am doing anything that remotely resembles hers. Except I did draw little cartoon stories of horses as German soldiers back when I was maybe twelve or so. And got rid of them all when I learned that Germans were "bad" people. I wouldn't know Donna until decades later, and this Swiss gal, Diana Sasse, who was also drawing like Donna before she ever knew Donna. Very mysterious, though we have our own theories, that we could be reincarnated German soldiers. Perhaps we were very cruel in the past life and had to come back as women to overcome hardship in some karmic sense.

FLA: How about Latino inspirations?

RG: The only folks I know there are the Bros. I always thought of *Love and Rockets* as sort of a Latina *Archie Comics* for more grown-up and open-minded readers. The art seems a lot like *Archie* art to me, especially Jaime's. I rather preferred Gilbert's work, since it has mystical elements of magical realism, such as in *Blood of Palomar*.

FLA: In the recent collection with Fantagraphics, *Bitchy Bitch*, you insert panels that portray yourself in between the issues. Is this a way to draw the reader's attention to the artifice of the story?

RG: Honestly, most of the time I have no idea whatsoever why I do what I do. I usually start writing a story with a rather vague idea of the story line and some graphic sequences and some wild inspiration, and I can be very surprised by the outcome, usually in a positive way.

I just always stuck myself in as a character. In my very first comic book, *Dynamite Damsels*, in 1976, I draw myself in the inside front cover chatting away with the reader, accompanied by my cat, Pumpkin. I put a lot of cats in my work, too. That would just set a theme.

FLA: Given your own mixed-race identity, what are we to make of those moments in *Bitchy Bitch* that highlight issues of race, like the moment when her classmate talks about Jews smelling, Mexicans are considered nothing but trouble, or when she's an adult on holiday in "in some . . . Third World hell hole . . . Shit!!!"?

RG: Well, that's the way people are, particularly people who are not very self-aware, like Bitchy. I suppose it seems comforting, in a way, to have others around who we can feel better than, or people to blame for always being predictable in a negative way, etc. She has a rather bitter, frustrated nature, so she must get some sort of grim satisfaction from being "right" about her lowered expectations. I know people like that and try to avoid them as much as possible. There are times I catch myself really expecting the worst, so I think this must be common to most people.

FLA: Do you have an ideal audience in mind when creating your stories?

RG: Wow, I don't know. Whoever would enjoy reading my comics. As I said, I write what I would like to read but isn't out there, so maybe my reader looks a bit like me!

FLA: How about the interplay of visuals with the text as ways to engage an audience?

RG: I clearly do not think about these factors as much as other people do.

FLA: Why black-and-white and not color?

RG: Well, if someone would pay to publish my work in color, I would do it in color. Color printing is a lot more expensive than black-and-white. I am trying to learn to use Photoshop so I can do some work in color. I just have a very small work area now and don't have a lot of room for paints and messier media.

Gilbert Hernandez
of Los Bros Hernandez

Gilbert Hernandez was born in 1957 and raised in the racially mixed farming community of Oxnard, California. He and his sister and four brothers, including comic book author-artists Jaime and Mario, grew up surrounded by comics. Their mother, a hard-working single parent, harbored a great love of them, passing this legacy first down to the older brother, Mario, then down to Gilbert and Jaime. Gilbert read every comic book he could get his hands on except romance comics.

While Hernandez's passion for drawing, writing, and reading comics began at an early age, he would more carefully hone his storytelling craft as he grew older. Without much formal training—in high school he took life-drawing electives, but quit night-school classes because of the teacher's apathy—he was driven by his own passion to become a comic book storyteller, and taught himself by constantly studying the visual and verbal aspects of comic book storytelling. This would eventually lead to the development of his own trademark style, which we see in his series *Palomar: Heartbreak Soup* and its various spin-offs, like the *Ofelia* and the *Luba* series.

Hernandez has been telling stories in the comic book mode for two and a half decades, bringing a vivid and rich array of stories that follow a panoply of Latino, Anglo, African American and other characters to readers worldwide. In several cases, the stories crisscross the fictional Latino border town of Palomar as he textures vividly the lives of characters like Chelo, the puritanical town sheriff; the political idealist Tonantzin; and the hedonistic entrepreneur Pipo.

Investing his graphic stories with the density and visual sophistication of novels—flashbacks and flash-forwards, for example—and with an ear for the rhythms of all varieties of speech, Hernandez has cultivated a worldwide readership and won numerous awards. His stories at once complicate and normalize the everyday experiences of Latinos. His work has influenced a generation of Latino comic book author-artists.

He lives in Las Vegas, Nevada, where he continues to create new stories for his *Palomar* series. He has published several graphic novels, including *Sloth* (DC Vertigo, 2006) and *Chance in Hell* (Fantagraphics, 2007) and *Troublemakers* (Fantagraphics, 2008).

FREDERICK LUIS ALDAMA: What is your training in the art of comic book storytelling?

GILBERT HERNANDEZ: Most of my training is self-taught, from reading comic books mostly. Not necessarily copying, but absorbing and studying artists that I liked. Eventually, I developed my own style that accommodated my limits.

FLA: What were some of those comic books that were particularly interesting for you?

GH: There were so many, but mostly it was superhero comics like Jack Kirby's *Fantastic Four*. Kirby's fertile imagination and his subtle, naturalistic capturing of body gestures make him one of the greatest mainstream-comic adventure-story artists ever. His art was hugely influential. I learned a lot from other artists, like the couple of better artists that did the *Archie* comics. The better *Archie* comics were drawn by Harry Lucey, Dan Decarlo, and Bob Bolling with a real naturalism and a little bit of humorous exaggeration. This suited my drawing style.

FLA: At what point did you know that you wanted to become a comic book storyteller?

GH: I took the art of comics relatively seriously once I entered high school. I wanted to draw and tell stories better. I knew that I wanted to get to a point where I could draw a professional-looking comic book. This developed more when I got out of high school, when I didn't really have much to do, so I worked on sharpening my drawing and storytelling skills.

FLA: You're also a musician. So why go into comics and not music, or the writing of novels?

GH: I dreamed of telling a story like a novel, but I knew I couldn't master or muster the energy to learn how to do that. While I had this strong urge to tell stories, I was also really into drawing; comics are the perfect mix of words and pictures that I can use to tell a story. I learned how to control every aspect of the story. With comic books, I could work by myself, but with music I was dealing with a lot of people's personalities. We could never agree on where we wanted to go with our music. I just didn't know how to get my 100 percent in it, so it didn't go anywhere.

FLA: At what point did you know that you could make a living as a comic book author-artist?

GH: It wasn't right away. When we started doing *Love and Rockets*, I was hoping that this would be it—my professional job. At first, we didn't make much money, because it was new to readers and the print runs were real low. So I thought I'd have to find another job to survive while creating my part of the *Love and Rockets* series. Luckily, another publisher from Canada came around and asked Jaime, Mario, and I if we would like to do this book, *Mr. X*, as a work-for-hire project. So we worked on *Mr. X* for money and *Love and Rockets* for fun. But *Mr. X* didn't pan out; it took a lot of our time and didn't end up paying very well. It took the wind out of our sails as far as wanting to work with somebody else for money. Fortunately, during this same time, *Love and Rockets* started making money—enough to make a meager living for the needs of this twenty-five-year-old.

FLA: Did you do any more freelance work after *Mr. X*?

GH: Any time we tried to get work with a company or a person willing to hire us, they wanted *Love and Rockets*. *Love and Rockets* became so prestigious at the time that they didn't even want us, just the name. To this day, it's bigger than I am as an individual artist. When we started to do comics that weren't called *Love and Rockets*, we weren't selling.

FLA: Was this that period in the late 1990s when you took a break from *Love and Rockets*?

GH: Yes, but then we started doing *Love and Rockets* again. During that time between the two versions of *Love and Rockets*, we actually did more comics than we ever have, but they went almost unnoticed. It's not the old days, when *Love and Rockets* was hugely popular, but it's still doing well and definitely worth continuing.

FLA: Recently, you wrote your first graphic novel.

GH: I just finished this major project for DC/Vertigo, titled *Sloth*. It's a break from my other work and a completely original piece. You'll never see the characters again, except in this book.

It's about youth culture and boredom in small, out-of-the-way towns where young people know what's going on out in the world because of the Internet and cable TV, but they're trapped where they are. To create their own diversions and stimulations, they go into dark territories, like drugs and violence. A teenage boy can't stand where he lives and who he is, so he wills himself into a coma for a year. Then he wakes up, and we follow his adventures with the people around him and how he's able to cope. Because of his slow movements, he's called Sloth. He becomes an urban legend. It's very surreal.

FLA: Was there pressure from DC to change your story?

GH: I worked very closely with my editor, who was gung-ho into making this a really great novel and making it very clear to the potential readers as to what's going on story-wise. That's my weakness in my *Palomar* work: the reader doesn't always know what's going on. That's the one big complaint I get. That, and that there's too much sex in it. Because I'm normally not that closely edited, working with an editor who does want to make sure my vision becomes a cohesive piece for a general audience taught me how to make compromises within myself for the sake of clarity and coherence. It was a different experience. It took a long time to readjust to this way of working.

FLA: Your *Palomar* series was both published issue by issue and also as a weighty collected-book volume. Is there a different process in creating, say, a story issue by issue versus a story that you know is going to be collected and sold as a book?

GH: I've always thought of the *Palomar* stories as pieces of a large work. I wasn't necessarily thinking of one big, giant book, the way the stories were collected and published by Fantagraphics. I was thinking more in terms of how I would follow the lives of those living in this little town as they grew from children to adults to elderly people. I didn't want to follow things in chronological order, so I'd start when the characters are in their twenties, then mix in stories when they're very young, and then when they're old—and move back and forth in time. I get so wrapped up in continuity and developing interaction between the characters that I've always got a sense of the whole picture.

While I always conceived of the stories of *Palomar* as making up a larger work, I did want some stories to stand on their own. They're shorter stories that the reader can pull out from the rest and not be confused.

FLA: In a way, then, you've always been on the same track as the graphic novel—it's just that the *Palomar* series was cut up.

GH: I've always been impressed by the publication of single-issue comics. I liked those books in the 1960s like *Charleton Premiere Comics*, issue 2, that published a single epic comic-book story in one issue. Each issue had different and complete stories. I·also like to read *Classics Illustrated* comics—butchered versions of classic novels funneled into forty pages. Even

YOUR BRAIN ON LATINO COMICS

though I didn't know much about the novels, I was impressed by having this epic story in one book. I also liked those comic-book adaptations of movies where the artists never saw the film and worked only from stills. So they had to make up their own story that sometimes went other places than the original movies.

FLA: From idea to storyboard to inking, what's your nuts-and-bolts process?

GH: What I used to do when I first started was probably a better process. Now I have to work so fast, it's different.

I originally used to make notes all the time because I had these fantasy projects in mind—projects I hoped might see print, but that might not actually make it. I would spend all my time preparing for these projects instead of finishing them. I always made a lot of notes about character development and story ideas to create these worlds, but they stayed as notes. I had lots of notes, for instance, on science fiction epics, but always concerned with the humanity of the characters. So when I put pen to paper, I already had a lot of characters that I had created. Because this process was so involved and had so much planning, I never finished the stories. I got so burnt-out on planning it. A lot of this ended up in sketchbooks.

In the early *Palomar* stories, I followed this same process. I had to because there were issues of *Love and Rockets* that needed to be filled. I spent a lot of time doing character sketches, developing what the town would look like (in these early versions, it was a shanty village). Then I would add dialogue to these sketches.

Because I already had the characters developed, I would write out pages and pages of people talking, but without any drawing. This is how I learned to write.

Now I have to work so quickly, and I know my characters so well, I'll just write and pencil characters directly on the paper. As I'm doing this, I'm thinking of what they're saying and what they're doing. It depends on the story, but sometimes I don't even do preparation sketches. I just get right to it.

I think I do my best stuff in my sketches. If I have to redraw it, it's not as good; it lacks the vitality of the original sketch. Since I do it old-fashioned—I don't use a computer—I just drop pencil to paper and draw it right then and there.

FLA: Why south of the border as the setting for your *Palomar* stories?

GH: My family tree starts in Mexico, so why not start this story from the egg. Dad's from Mexico, Mom's from that part of Texas that used to be Mexico, and I'm born here, so I'll start with a little village, and then one day have the characters cross the border. Then I'll tell stories about their experiences on the U.S. side of the border. While I projected that far ahead in the story, I knew that I would need to create in the original south-of-the-border stories a solid foundation so all these future stories, like those that make up *Luba in America*, would stand strong.

FLA: In the *Palomar* stories, there are everyday romances and tragedies as well as exaggerated melodrama (Tonantzin lighting herself on fire), the appearance of aliens, and monolithic rocks that smile?

GH: I just wanted it to be a fun world that I could control. If I felt like making it deadly serious or mundane in one story, I would. But if I felt like telling a story with flights of fancy or working in surreal elements to the nth degree, I would.

I never worried about being criticized for doing fantasy or for being too serious in this series. The most important thing was to communicate with the reader that this is a surreal world, and everything that happens in it belongs in it. So while I did what I wanted, I tried not to throw in something that just did not belong.

FLA: Does it work because you maintain a certain logic in the story?

GH: Somebody pointed out recently that most of the stories, even if a child isn't present, are told from a child's point of view. So when we read the stories, it's as if we're experiencing them as children. That's why sex is confusing in some stories. Things happen and nobody knows why. And sometimes nobody questions it.

FLA: Sometimes when reading the *Palomar* stories, the reader steps into a flashback sequence without knowing it.

GH: I ran into trouble with that a lot. When I first started, I used the old comic-book cliché of writing the word "flashback" just to make it clear for the reader. As my editor suggested, the strip was starting to develop in such a way that it didn't really need this nudge. So I started presenting a flashback more like in a film. But I wasn't so good at it. What I thought was a natural, smooth transition from modern times to a flashback wasn't always identifiable by the reader. In a lot of reprints, I rework transitions to make a flashback clearer.

FLA: How do you imagine balancing the visual elements with the textual elements?

GH: On a technical level, I don't know what makes it work. It's completely organic and comes from my overloaded, fevered mind.

I learned early on to trust my instincts. You have to toot your own horn while you're working, and say, "You are an intelligent person. Your intelligence will come through if you're honest." You have to trust yourself that it will happen. It doesn't always work—as with the transitions of flash-backs—but if you keep in mind that there is a reader that you're communicating with, then you'll soon learn what does work.

FLA: Do you have a sense of your actual audience?

GH: I would say it's about 60 percent white college kids and 40 percent minority: Latinos, a smaller percentage of blacks and Asians, and then the remainder would be superhero fans just trying it out. In its prime, *Love and Rockets* had about 40 percent women readers; now it's down to about 20.

FLA: When you're done with a story or a panel or a series of panels, do you read them out loud to see if the text is working with the visuals to convey the intended effect?

GH: No, I just write it down. I'll rewrite it if it isn't clear or I feel that a character wouldn't say this or that, but usually I go with the first thing I wrote.

FLA: Is there an intended rhythm with the particular sequencing and layout of the panels and gutters?

GH: It depends on what I'm trying to tell the audience. If I want a story to be kinetic, I'll do more panels on fewer pages. If I want it to breathe more, I'll do a longer story with larger panels with the characters talking less.

Lately I've been doing classic *Palomar* stories that I never told before for a magazine-size book. I have so much room now to tell stories, I'm opening up visually like I never have before. I'll create one-page scenes with no words, then cut into only two panels on the next page, then three on the next, for instance.

I have this habit of severely editing down my work, say, taking a twenty-four-page story down to fourteen pages. Sometimes I'll end up with twenty-six characters in an eight-page story when it should be a fifty-pager. I don't like doing this. I've always liked the type of comics that breathed. I'm able to do that now, so I'm happy.

FLA: You've worked mostly in black-and-white, but also with color. Do you prefer one over the other?

GH: I like color because I grew up with it. I worked with it on *Sloth*. But it's such a pain in the ass to get it right. It's a much longer process. Once you're done, then you have to have it checked. I still have a lot to learn with using color. Black-and-white's easier. I can start a page, and in two hours it's done.

FLA: How about the facial expressions and emotions of characters? Does this change depending on whether you're working in black-and-white or color?

GH: It might make a difference if you're somebody who's very good at shading. I envy artists who can do shading and back lighting. Even though I've never been good at it, it's a technique I've always admired—even as a kid. If you look at the old EC comics, the artists do a lot of heavy shading. They have that great film noirish look; the shading gave a lot of mood and a sense of atmosphere to the stories.

I have a more coloring-book style. I do a lot of cross-hatching and stark, black-and-white contrasts.

FLA: How about your sense of perspective?

GH: Like back lighting, perspective is faked. A noir film on Turner Classic Movies will give you all the art direction you need to create a forced perspective in a scene. It wouldn't really look like this in real life, so you fake it to make it feel real and believable. I've had horizon lines and vertical lines that wouldn't match with a ruler, but they work.

FLA: The way one draws characters is also a kind of illusion-making process that creates a sense of the believable and real.

GH: That's what's great about cartooning. You can exaggerate the character's body language in ways that the reader knows what the character is feeling or doing without having to spell it out. Instead of having the character say, "Woe is me," you can have him slumping in an exaggerated pose. In real life, a person's neck would be breaking if they were in this position. Or when drawing someone running very fast, you have them pitched forward like they're falling on their face. That's not how people run. They run with their head back and chest out. But if you draw it this way in a comic, you won't convey that sense of speed. So it's cheating, but it gets the effect across to the reader.

FLA: Your characters are culturally Latino, but they're also much more. Is this a way to convey to your readers a more complete—and normal—picture of Latino life north and south of the border?

GH: It's me projecting all over the paper. Whether it's conscious or unconscious, the stories just develop out of what I know. I grew up in a big close-knit family of four brothers and a sister and lots of cousins, aunts, and uncles—too much family sometimes. This is the real world for me. So it was normal in creating *Palomar* to have all these characters interacting. It's the way of life I grew up with.

I've been asked before, how come the Catholic Church isn't more involved in your story? How come the government's not involved? How come the men aren't as macho as they should be? Well, I say, if you already know that, why are you asking me? If you already know that the Catholic Church is this, that Latino men are like this, why do you need to see it on paper? Why do you need to know what you already know? My goal is always to show the reader that Latinos are people. That's my job.

FLA: Is there a place in your comic book worlds for addressing issues of, say, racism, sexism, and the like?

GH: There are artists that do hit hard with issues, and that's why they're who they are and respected for their work. I also touch on these kinds of issues—in a natural way. It's just not my focus because it's not where my storytelling strengths lie.

FLA: The role of history or myth in your stories?

GH: As with the character Tonantzin, when I use such a name, I research it, but just enough to fit it in a comic. You don't want to funnel the Atlantic Ocean into a bottle. You want enough of the basics to engage and amuse the reader. My goal is not to teach, but to amuse the intelligent mind. I expect the reader to be smart already. It's the intelligent mind—and libido—that I try to stimulate and entertain.

FLA: Speaking of libido, tell me about *Birdland*?

GH: I wanted to create an action comic that wasn't superheroes, an action comic that was just sex and no violence. It was as wild as I could make it at the time, holding little back in terms of sex and making sure not to have any cruelty or violence.

FLA: Did you alienate some of the *Love and Rockets* audience when you published *Birdland*?

GH: The readers who spoke up that didn't like it were women. There was a woman who liked the way I handled sex in my serious work, but she thought *Birdland* was just typical male stuff.

FLA: Are there particular ingredients that make a comic book Latino?

GH: I like to draw Latinos looking like Latinos, to name them like Latinos are named, and to put myself in their story. I'm not just talking about superficial things like the kind of car you drive or music you listen to. I'm talking about who you are. And if there are guys out there embarrassed about being Latinos—I've met plenty—then they need to read my comics.

FLA: Does *Sloth* have Latino characters?

GH: They're all Latino characters. But because the *Palomar* characters are so ethnic-looking, in *Sloth* I drew more international-looking Latinos: blond characters with freckles and that kind of thing. But they're still Latinos. People still see a blonde woman who's a Latina and say she's not a Latina because they think Latinas can't be blonde. As if half of white girls are naturally blonde.

FLA: DC/Vertigo contracted you to do *Sloth*, and your brother Jaime writes the Sunday strips for the *New York Times*. Is this an indication of a turn for the better for Latino comic book authors?

GH: I think so. But stepping up to the plate is still the most important thing. If there is a Latino artist who can draw and write and has a story to tell, then it's certainly easier today than when I first started, in the early '80s. But the problem is finding these Latino artists and convincing them to do it. Most of the talented, smart Latinos pursue more "respectable" ways of telling stories, like writing novels. Or take more respectable jobs as graphic artists or fine artists. Until recently, the comic book world was seen as a ghetto.

FLA: Do you think the improved image of comics as a profession has to do with you and your brother's work—and the alternative-comic-book scene generally?

GH: It started slowly with the underground comics, but that was a bumpy road, and then once alternative comics came, they have more say in the way a story could be told, and a character is handled as a real person.

FLA: Current and future projects?

GH: I'll continue to focus on my half of *Love and Rockets* as well as a magazine series, called *New Tales of Old Palomar*, that follows the classic stories of *Palomar* that I've never told before. The challenge will be to try to sell it as a new book. I think a lot of readers will take a first look and think that it's reprints because it looks like the old *Palomar* stories and has some of the same characters. But it's not. This was all due to the success of the *Palomar* collection. People just wanted more. So I jumped right back on it, like riding a bike.

FLA: Speaking of the *Palomar* collection. Sold as a collection instead of as individual issues, did you notice more or less attention, more or less money coming in?

GH: It's such a big book that's relatively inexpensive, so it does well. But there are only so many that can be printed because of the bulk of it and the price of production. In the next year, starting in January, they're going to start reprinting in a new format all the *Love and Rockets* collections again. They'll be sold two by two: collections I and II will be together, and III and IV together, etc.

Every three or four years, the packaging and marketing changes for comic books. Right now thicker books are the rage. There's a book called *Blankets*—500 pages of an original graphic novel—that sold phenomenally well. Part of the reason is that readers can fit it in their backpacks and read it on the bus. People are always searching for the next format and package that will sell well, so it'll change again to something else in a few years.

FLA: I noticed that with the series *Araña*, that Marvel moved from selling it issue by issue to selling it as a collected, manga-sized comic book so teens could fit it into backpacks and read it on the bus. Any last words?

GH: I hope to be around another ten or so years—as a cartoonist, I mean. Most cartoonists have twenty years in them at the peak of their powers, then the rest of it is hack work or just not as good. Some guys just flare out after five years, some ten. But they're still regarded as great artists because their best work was that good. There're other guys who just draw like whizzes for years and years and years, but with no interesting story content.

Jaime and I are still in there, so we're lucky.

Jaime Hernandez
of Los Bros Hernandez

Jaime was born in 1959 in the farming community of Oxnard, California, where he, along with his other siblings, including Gilbert (interviewed here), was raised by his single mother. Jaime grew up with comics—their mother harbored a great love of them—as well as in a racially mixed community, a place of both tense racial relations between Anglos and Chicanos especially but also a place of much cultural cross-pollination. Jaime grew up strongly rooted in his Chicano heritage and also punk rock, telenovelas, and lowrider cars. Such a mélange of cultural influences informed directly his story-making and inking of the series *Love and Rockets* (1982).

After three decades of storytelling and inking, Jaime continues to bring a vivid and rich array of stories that follow a panoply of Latino characters to readers across the nation. His strip *La Maggie La Loca* was published every Sunday in the *New York Times* (April–September 2006). While many of the characters are inspired by their Oxnard experiences—punk rock music and everyday Chicano *barrio* culture, for example—one can discern many other creative influences, including those of filmmakers and novelists. In Jaime's ever-popular *Locas* series, he fleshes out the lives and adventures of Southern California Chicanas Hopey (lesbian) and Maggie (bisexual) and their run-ins with various elements of U.S. society, from bigoted police to jealous boyfriends and girlfriends. In another of Jaime's series, *Hoppers 13*, he plunges his readers deep into the lives of working-class Chicanos, Asian immigrants, punk rockers, and gang members who inhabit Barrio Huerta, a place at the outskirts of Los Angeles.

Investing his graphic stories with the density and visual sophistication of novels—flashbacks and flash-forwards, for example—and with an ear for the rhythms of all varieties of speech, Jaime has cultivated a large national readership and won numerous awards. His work continues to be hugely inspirational for Latino comic book author-artists working today.

Jaime lives and works in Los Angeles.

FREDERICK LUIS ALDAMA: Why the comic book for Los Bros instead of other narrative forms, like the short story or novel?

JAIME HERNANDEZ: It's pretty much because we grew up with comics. From early on, I liked drawing; it was my favorite form of art. I wanted to draw comics my whole life, and I wanted to tell stories and make characters. So making comics seemed like the perfect medium to tell what I wanted to tell. It involved drawing and storytelling. It was the perfect means for expressing myself, stories generally, and it was inexpensive.

FLA: When did you realize that it was something you wanted to make a career out of and to make a living?

JH: A couple of years after *Love and Rockets* came out, it started to become something I could support myself with. Of course, I was pretty young then, and I didn't need much to survive. But I was lucky because as my needs changed and I wanted to support myself a little better, so did the comic grow in popularity.

FLA: Did you have to do other jobs to support yourself when you first began publishing *Love and Rockets*?

JH: I was twenty or twenty-one and was still living at home as a bumming punk rocker. I had moved out for a couple of years, but I went back due to lack of funds.

FLA: How did you come into the idea for drawing and writing the stories in *Love and Rockets*?

JH: I liked drawing rocket ships, superheroes, and things like that when I was younger, and that's why you see a lot of this in the early comics. But it also came out of the life I was living growing up in the barrio in Oxnard, California, filled with lowrider and punk culture. It was a fascinating world where punk and cholo came together and that most of the world didn't know about. This was a story that needed to be told, and no one was doing it in comics, so we took the lead.

FLA: Was *Love and Rockets* ever a collaborative process with your brother Gilbert?

JH: We just share the book. We never collaborated, but we inspired each other just by working side by side.

FLA: Chicano barrio and science fiction, lowrider and punk—has it been difficult for you to write stories about Chicanos that don't fit into any one box?

JH: I was always more of a rock 'n roller, whereas my childhood friends were into soul and funk. I listened to this white-boy music and so was kind of an outsider. I always felt like I was somewhere on the outside looking in at my life and my neighborhood. If you're inside it, you kind of don't get to observe it much. If you step back a little bit, you can see how it relates to the rest of the world and how the rest of the world relates to it. I got the best of all worlds.

FLA: In 1981, you submitted your first issue of *Love and Rockets* to be reviewed by *Comics Journal*.

JH: We were looking for cheap publicity because we didn't know how to sell our own little black-and-white comic that we made ourselves. So Gilbert sent it to them to get a review. We thought, even if they didn't like it, it would be free advertising. So we just went for broke, said screw it, and sent it in. They liked it, and because they had been planning to publish their own comic series (Fantagraphics), it was perfect timing. We helped them take off.

We never had time to fail. We were ready with our idea and knew where we wanted to go with it, so when it took off, we were ready to produce.

FLA: Much time has passed from 1981 to today. Have you noticed big changes in readership, distribution, and so on with Chicano- or ethnic-themed comics?

JH: It's a lot better than it was in '81, that's for sure. There're a lot of Latino artists out there doing all kinds of work; it's kind of hard to keep track. It's pretty cool because I feel like we had something to do with that. I'm partially set in my ways, and the world I created has become so vast that I don't look outside that often to see who's coming up, but I do know there are a lot of great upcoming artists. A lot are still toying with this dead superhero thing, though. This doesn't inspire me too much. I prefer a more personal vision.

As for readers, today we have a big Chicano readership. There was a young Chicano who told me that when he saw our comic and read our names, it just blew him away, 'cause he couldn't believe that Chicanos were doing comics. That made me feel really good that I could at least get it out there and spread the word.

FLA: Why black-and-white drawings?

JH: The black-and-white was an economic issue. We couldn't afford to do a color comic because it would have killed us. And we wouldn't sell. That's how it started out. But I've always been a fan of black-and-white things like *Mad Magazine* and all the underground comics that were in black-and-white. So it started out because of economic necessity, then ended up becoming art.

That's kind of the story of comics in the first place. Comics were first created in the '30s as a kind of disposable art. They were reprinted newspaper strips that you read like a newspaper and then threw away. Then they became a collector's thing. That's sort of how we started. We just took what we could afford and turned that into something.

FLA: Can you speak a little about how you conceive of your stories?

JH: Well, since I deal with an ongoing series of characters, the story pretty much evolves as they mature. It's the characters that determine the story's direction. They make the story. This character's going through their thirties, so what can I make them go through? It's only once in a while that I have an actual story idea that I fit the characters into. It's usually the other way around: I fit the story to the characters.

FLA: What's that process between what you imagine and the final inking of the story?

JH: I'm mostly self-taught, so what I do might be considered very primitive. I start off with a loose, partial script. I never script out a whole story at once. Usually the script starts with a basic beginning of a story or middle of a story, and then I fill in the pictures and words that then take on a life of their own. This is what actually ends up giving shape to the whole story. It's very organic.

Most creators start with a script, and then they start doing layouts that they then put on the paper. After I've put something down like a loose dialogue, I draw directly on the paper. I edit it as I'm drawing it on the paper in pencil. And then when I'm finally comfortable with what I see, I start inking. But I try not to jump the gun. I've done stuff that could have been edited down much better, but because I jumped in too fast and finished it, I realized afterwards that it could have been better if I thought about it more.

There's a real art to figuring out how to describe a scene and how you move from one panel to the next. You don't want to give too much or too little detail. As far as characters, I just throw them out there. I don't try to force you to like Hopey. I just give you Hopey, and it's up to you to engage with her. I think that's a big part of the art of crafting comics. That you only give so much, and you trust your readership to do the rest.

FLA: Were underground comics—those that tell stories of America's underbelly—a big influence?

JH: I didn't see a lot of them growing up. I was still a little young, mostly reading superhero and *Archie* comics. The ones that I did notice were the ones my older brothers were reading, like Crumb. What I really liked about the underground comic was the freedom, that the authors were doing exactly what they wanted without any editorial pressure or a big company to tell them yes or no.

They represented the underdog and that was interesting to someone growing up Chicano. You're never in first place. You're always in second or third, so you just fight harder, telling yourself, "I'm going to do this. I've got nothing to lose. I don't have as much to lose as people on top." It's not so much written down. It's in the spirit of the actual work and with the confidence to do this without you telling me whether I can or can't.

FLA: Los Bros have taken risks, like using untranslated Spanish in *Love and Rockets* as well as depicting some erotic, sexual content.

JH: America hates this stuff, so guess what, we're going to do it—because we can. It is easy for us because we really don't have the FBI cracking down on us. We're not really that dangerous. We're not seen as dangerous. Who knows, we may be inspiring something bigger than the comic along the way. Which is not such a bad thing.

FLA: Why the shift, from the early to later *Love and Rockets*, from the use of the fantastical and science-fictional style to a barrio realism?

JH: This was a conscious shift. I wanted to start doing more serious work, so the dinosaurs and robots got in the way. I never hated doing them. I loved drawing all kinds of goofy and weird stuff, but Gilbert and I made a decision that we wanted to take a harder, grittier path. I mean, you don't care if someone's going to get shot when there's a dinosaur outside the door. Its message can't be that serious. I wanted to put reality in front of my readers as best I could.

FLA: *Love and Rockets* is serious. Hopey and Maggie have run-ins with the police, and you depict the violence of La Migra [the Immigration and Naturalization Service], but it's also about family conflict and struggle within the Chicano community.

JH: Our Chicano culture is so rich and has so much to offer that I've barely scratched the surface. I want the whole world to experience it. I've made it my job to make everybody understand it without watering it down and without trying to protect the reader's feelings. Whether they understand it or not, the comics aim to communicate a vision of the Chicano community so readers can see what it's really all about.

FLA: There are aspects of the Chicano community that some would rather not see. For example, your portrayal of the lesbian relationship between Hopey and Maggie. You've received criticism for this?

JH: When they tell me I'm doing it wrong is when I get a little irked. I'm por-

Locas in Love

traying a community that's complicated. That's why I make the characters people first, more than anything. I've become a pretty good observer of people. So that's what I focus on. It's always the characters first. Everything falls into place after that.

I guess the whole mission is just to present the truth of a world that we know or that we've witnessed and that a lot of people try to ignore. I guess the main thing for Los Bros is to try to bring as much truth to our stories as we can. That's the most important, next to entertaining. I mean, even if we're doing serious stuff, we're still entertaining readers.

FLA: Your stories are very melodramatic.

JH: I'm very much a romantic at heart. I'm a very sentimental person, but I know that if I just let the floodgates open, I would be creating the sappiest stuff in the world. To keep a balance, I have to rein in the sentiment. But every once in a while I like to turn on the faucet and blast. Without insulting them, I like to manipulate my audience a little just to draw them in. I'd like to think that I know pretty well how to step in and step out with the melodrama. But I try to keep a balance between the serious and the sentimental because I don't want to cheat the audience.

FLA: Who is your audience?

JH: In the early days, when we first started, our comic was supported by professionals. Comic professionals. They supported and encouraged us. Then we started to build an audience. We had a large female as well as male readership that was mostly white and of college age. I would say that even today mostly white people read it, I guess because mostly white people read comics. Then the Chicanos and other ethnic readers started trickling in.

FLA: You guys took a break from *Love and Rockets*. Why?

JH: Burnout. Our comic worlds had become so big and broad that they were just spilling over the sides, and it started to drive us crazy. We needed a break. Not a break like "I'm not going to draw today," but just a break from what we were writing. The only way we could think of doing that for a while was just doing our own separate comics. We just needed some tiny shift in what we were doing. And it just felt new again.

FLA: You returned with *Penny Century*?

JH: This included the same cast as *Love and Rockets* plus a few new characters. It was the same world, but everyone was older, and some now lived different lives. I also gave it a new format. I went to comic size. In the grand scheme of things, there wasn't much of a change, but it sure felt like it.

I'm wrapping up a Maggie story that I'm going to put in the collection. Everybody's older and has gone different ways. Some characters are reuniting from the early days. They're all supposed to be responsible adults now, but some can't handle it. Some are alienated from their old worlds—kind of like me. I know what growing old is like for me, so I draw on my experiences.

FLA: Reading comics can be a form of escape. Is writing and inking also an escape?

JH: My escape is to be able to sit alone in my studio and create. I'm escaping, but I'm also confronting my world at the same time. Years ago, Gilbert had this great quote where he said, "*Love and Rockets* is our love letter to the world." It's our way of reaching the world. Some people have to stand on a street corner and scream, but this is our way.

FLA: It's pretty rare to make a living as an author, much less as a Chicano comic book artist.

JH: I'm really lucky that I've been able to partially support myself and my family by doing exactly what I want to do. It's never made me a million-aire, but I've never had to interrupt it with something else. I have had to take contract work to help support my family. I can't live on macaroni and cheese, like I used to. I don't need a mansion, but I do want a comfortable enough living where I can be free to do my work.

Javier Hernandez

Javier Hernandez was born April 23, 1966, in East Los Angeles, where he spent the first couple of years of his life. His family then moved to nearby Whittier, where he grew up with his three siblings. It was there he cultivated a love of comic books and drawings, attended Whittier High School, and also Rio Hondo College. His mother was born in Mexico, and his father was born in the United States but was raised on the U.S.-Mexico border in Mexicali, and both parents spoke Spanish at home, so Hernandez's ties to Mexico were strong. A lot of his childhood was divided between watching *Lucha Libre* on the Spanish stations, imported Japanese fare such as *Gigantor* and *Giant Robot*, and such U.S. TV shows as *Get Smart*, *The Addams Family*, and *Chico and the Man*.

His older brother Albert would draw comic characters (baseball and football jocks, mostly), making an impression on young Javier Hernandez. At eight years old he had picked up a knack for it. During this period, he developed a liking for the worlds offered up in his older brother's collection of comics.

His interest in art led to a job as a production artist, then eventually as an art director at the same company. But it was the creation of his own comic book character, El Muerto, that put him where he really wanted to be. He eventually left his position to pursue his comics with more dedication. For the past two years, he has been teaching a comic book workshop at the Pico Rivera Centre for the Arts, a local community center that affords him the opportunity to work with kids and their own comics. Javier often speaks at local schools and libraries, sharing his story with others in hopes of inspiring them to succeed in their dreams.

In 2007, the film adaptation of *El Muerto* was released, winning the award for best feature at the Whittier Film Festival. *El Muerto* can also be found at the website www.elmuerto.com, which features news and information on the character as well as an active message board.

FREDERICK LUIS ALDAMA: When did you realize there weren't any Latinos in comic books?

JAVIER HERNANDEZ: As a young kid, I don't really remember thinking, "Hey there's no Latinos drawing comics! There are no Latino characters!" I don't even think I knew what a Latino was. I do remember tuning in specifically to Ricky Ricardo (*I Love Lucy*) and Gomez Addams (*The Addams Family*) and thinking, these guys sound like my dad. They've got black hair, and they even spoke in Spanish a couple of times. They must be Mexican! In the mid- to late '70s, there were a couple of characters at Marvel that I remember noticing were Latino, or at least similar to me: the White Tiger and one of Spider-Man's enemies, the Tarantula. It was their sporadic use of Spanish as well as their identities that made me notice the similarities between me and them. It wasn't until college that personal cultural identity became something I was aware of as an issue. This is when I started to think about what was, or what wasn't, Latino and reflect on my own Mexican cultural background.

FLA: So this awareness coincided with your more formal study of drawing in junior college?

JH: Yes, I'd say that was a result of growing up and trying to discover what made me or shaped some of my creativity. I started drawing in the second grade, at Ben Franklin Elementary School. One of the first things I remember drawing was Rodan, the flying pterodactyl from the *Godzilla* movies. I had seen a movie featuring him over the weekend, so that Monday at school, I drew him. That's when I was identified as the class artist. Every time we had an art project, all the kids would come to me for help. In junior high school, I would take electives so I could start to take art classes. By high school, it was on full steam. I was taking more art classes and interacting with teachers who I could learn from. It was an awakening at that point. An art teacher paying specific attention to me and my skills was a great reinforcement. In college I was really digging the art classes and being in the same room with other students who were studying art.

FLA: At this point you decided you want to be a professional.

JH: I was in my early twenties, and I knew I wanted to be an "artist," but wasn't really thinking of doing comics at that time. I eventually was hired by my friend at a screen printer's, working in the art department. I wasn't really drawing or creating characters and such, but doing production art. I learned a lot there that would later help me understand the mechanics of putting together my own comics into a comic book—all the design skills and graphic design skills that are required to put the actual book together and ready for the printers.

FLA: Did a light go off: "I need to create a Latino comic book"?

JH: Around the early to mid-'90s, I decided that I wanted to do my own comic book with my own superhero character; I didn't want to go the autobiographical route or do some type of drama. I wanted to do a hero. It was just natural for me to think of my hero as Latino. He was Latino the moment I got it in my head to create a character. So I sketched tons of drawings of different characters, and this one character in a Mariachi outfit with a *calavera* [skull] face kept popping up. This is the character that eventually became El Muerto.

FLA: Why choose the comic book form to tell this story?

JH: It wasn't like I was able to pick up a camera and make my own movie. Or it's not like I sat down and wanted to write a novel. I just started drawing a comic because I could and I was really into it. When I started reading comics as a young kid, I'd sit there and draw my one- or two-page little *Spider-Man* knockoffs.

I had always wanted to do comics. This is how I could tell a story, with words and pictures in my own comic book.

FLA: Do you identify your style with any school? Are there any particularly strong influences you can identify?

JH: Those that influenced me from the get-go were the classic, silver age Marvel artists, particularly Jack Kirby and Steve Ditko. Also John Romita, Sr., who took over the *Amazing Spider-Man* comic books. He had such a flair for the soap-opera aspect of a story. Other artists, like Gene Colan and John Buscema—these guys had such a flair for melodrama and dynamic action. There was a certain visceral quality to all their work, particularly Kirby. He really created the Marvel style. There's just a powerful sense of these characters flying off the page, moving from one panel to another. And yet at the same time, because of the writing, there was a lot of drama—melodrama, even—that I actually liked. Sometimes their personal lives were a mess. Who can't relate to that? Unlike the picture-perfect, one-dimensional DC heroes, these '60s Marvel heroes had feet of clay.

FLA: Did your tastes change?

JH: By the late 1980s, a lot of the art was changing. I just really couldn't handle all of the new type of artwork at the time. But also, to be honest, to be fair to those artists, I was getting just burned out. I had been reading the same characters for fifteen years.

There was some other good stuff, like Alan Moore's *Watchmen* and Frank Miller's *Dark Knight*. They were getting really edgy and sophisticated and deep. But that was like a high point. After that, everyone started going gung-ho with Dark Knight and all these other dark characters. They were overdoing the characters, trying to make them all grim and gritty.

FLA: What took the place, then, of the mainstream comic as far as inspiration?

JH: In the early '90s I had read an article in *Hispanic Magazine* of this artist from Texas, Richard Dominguez, who was doing this comic book called *El Gato Negro*. That he created his own comic with his own Latino character struck a nerve with me. I had also heard of Carlos Saldaña; I saw one of his comics, *Burrito*, at a comic shop in the area. I remember buying the comic and noticing he was from Los Angeles. To me, it was a big inspiration: here's a local guy in LA, a *Mexicano*, self-publishing a comic book called *Burrito*. I found out that Carlos Saldaña was going to be at the Alternative Press Expo in San Jose. My friend Rafael Navarro, who was starting to create his own book also, and I drove all the way up there to meet Carlos. So I was being inspired by the self-publishing work of Richard, Carlos, and Rafael, all with Latino comic book characters. That's when I decided to begin work on something from my sketchbooks. There was that dead mariachi guy again, so I asked, "How could I flesh him out?"

FLA: When did *El Muerto* make its first appearance?

JH: In 1998 at the Alternative Press Expo. I debuted El Muerto in a photocopied comic book. I think I printed about 500 or so copies. It was a real good experience. I knew just by the people's reaction that they were hungry for alternative characters. There was definitely an audience ready for a Latino character, and there was a Latino, as well as a non-Latino, audience for the book. People picking up the comic, asking questions about it was real exciting. As an artist, to be able to create something—draw, paint, or whatever—and get it out there for people to experience is a rush.

FLA: Was there a make-or-break moment?

JH: I realized I had to keep doing this. It was working, and not in terms of sales necessarily, but in the positive response. I knew there was a bigger audience beyond that show in San Jose and that I needed to get the book in front of those readers as well.

FLA: Without a fan base, there's no comic?

JH: It's a big cliché, but it's true. Without the fans, I wouldn't be here. Of course, any artist could decide not to pursue it as a commercial enterprise, as a way to make a living. I've got a friend who is a fantastic comic book artist who puts out 20, 50, 100 copies of a book, drops them off at a couple of stores, and goes on to his next book. But he doesn't look to cultivate a fan base. You can take that approach. There's nothing wrong with that. For me, though, there was a sense of getting it out to readers and growing a fan base, a community of readers. It was just a matter of providing more stories for them to enjoy and meeting them in person via conventions and signings.

FLA: Do you have a sense of your audience today?

JH: Well, I would guess that maybe half is Latino, but it draws in readers of all kinds. And almost half my audience is female. The demographics for comics are similar to that for movies, mostly eighteen-to-thirty-five-year-old white males. *El Muerto* challenges these statistics, though. I think it's the gothic element that intrigues a lot of women: young dead Mexican guy running around in a mariachi suit! I launched my Web site in July 2005, and the message board I have there has given me a great way to interact with the fans directly. I don't know if I could create a story and not want to hear people's reaction. It's not so much that I need to hear how much they loved the story, more so that I like to hear what, and why, they responded. Or what didn't work for them.

FLA: Do you have a day job to help support your comic book craft?

JH: I'm currently working as a production artist. It's a steady income and maintains the health insurance benefits. It's tough because you're working forty hours a week and you're still trying to keep this comic book venture going. And I've been involved with the *Muerto* film from its first days of preproduction to working on various postproduction details.

FLA: Now that *El Muerto*'s been out circulating for some time, has it become a part of a Latino or independent comic book world?

JH: It's definitely part of the Latino comic book world as well as the comic book world generally. But I like to consider it an independent comic first and foremost. To be independent appeals to me as an artist and an individual.

FLA: What about outfits like Diamond?

JH: As far as comics distribution goes, it's the only game in town, and they know it and we know it. They've got guidelines of what they'll carry and if they'll continue to carry it. Although they are there to put the comics in the hands of the retailers, one could argue that they're really there to keep the Big Two's [Marvel's and DC's] dominance on the nationwide comic readership. On a whim from whoever makes their decisions to carry a book, you could be shut out of nationwide comics distribution.

Bottom line: it behooves the independent publisher to really figure out ways to get the book out there. For example, there's the Internet that gives you an outlet to get in front of people. I actually coordinate, as much as I can, ways to move traffic between my Web site, my blog, and even a MySpace page!

I'm in an unusual position. I've got a feature film based on my comic.

And I'm also this independent comic book publisher, fighting, struggling to get my work out there, but I have this 800-pound Hollywood gorilla in my corner! It's about how to maximize the spotlight with what you have. As a self-publisher, while the time eats into my comic-producing time, I really do like the challenge of creating my own promotional opportunities and retailer contacts. You really do become self-made.

FLA: Have you anticipated an increased demand?

JH: I'll put a trade paperback together soon, collecting the first comics. And of course moving the story forward means creating new *El Muerto* comics. Also, I have a few other new comic-book ideas that I want to publish, or maybe partner with comic or book publishers.

FLA: It appears there's a Latino boys' club of comic book author-artists.

JH: We kind of did what the mainstream did, except instead of an all-white guys' club, it's an all-Latino boys' club. But it's not some closed, exclusive entity. This doesn't mean that there aren't Latina artists out there: Pia Guerra is illustrating *Y: The Last Man*, and Lea Hernandez, she's been around for a few years. But at the end of the day, I say, make your own club. I created my own comic and had instant access to the club. I'm ready for more Latina comic creators! When I see photos of the women of comics, I would love to actually see more women of color producing comics.

Maybe it's not really a Latino boys' club, but simply self-published independents. Because of the technology and access to the marketplace via the Internet, anyone can make a comic book. In the old days, you had to fly to New York or whatever, somehow meet an editor at Marvel or D.C., and try to get a job drawing in their style and developing their characters, with no thought of ownership. With the launch of Pacific Comics in the '80s, this changed. Now you've got tons of small publishers, and then there seems to be no shortage of people just creating their own comic books. And you know—what's the old joke in Hollywood? Everybody's got a screenplay— well now it seems like everybody's got a comic book idea.

Again, I say, get up and do it. Create it. Write it and draw it yourself or find a collaborator. The audience is out there; it's a tough market to get into, but the audience is out there for personal, unique ideas.

FLA: Can you talk about your creating of the character El Muerto?

JH: I didn't want to make the book a nonstop, mindless action story. I wanted to create a character that left an impression on people, even after they were done reading the book. Every creator is basically trying to re-create the feeling they had when they were about ten or eleven years old from stuff that really appealed to them as a kid. For me, some of this stuff was *Spi-*

der-Man—especially the Stan Lee–Steve Ditko books. I really loved Spider-Man because he's colorful, witty, and has a cool costume and freaky powers. But I also really cared for the character under the mask, the nerdy Peter Parker: problems getting the girls, a boss that's always chewing him out, he never has money, and the media doesn't like him. That's what I want to do with El Muerto. Visually, he's interesting with this sleek mariachi outfit, but the guy under the costume has got to be interesting and complicated and someone readers care to see develop. It's great to be able to create a character that specifically appeals to other Latinos, but the basic truths about the character should be universal.

FLA: While we're on the topic, were there other early influences?

JH: When I was a kid, I enjoyed Speed Racer—another character that seems very Latino. He had this big, burly wrestler dad with a big mustache who was always yelling; the mom was always in the kitchen cooking up the nice food and cleaning the home; he had the annoying little brother with the dirty little animal sidekick. And Speed Racer and his friend always worked on cars. Also, as a kid I was really into *Lucha Libre*, particularly Mil Mascaras. He was, and is, such an embodiment of what I think a hero should be. Strong, resolute, honorable, and a little mysterious with a cool costume and fanciful name! The *Incredible Hulk* TV show was also something that's always stuck with me. A guy transformed into something not of his choosing, drifting around for answers. The hero-monster was something that Marvel really delivered, the tragic hero trapped in a macabre body.

FLA: In your first issue, "King Size El Muerto," and also in "El Muerto: Mishmash," you mishmash styles, plotlines, and characters.

JH: This comes out of those 1960s Marvel books. They used to put out these big, big sixty-four-page annuals where they have a new story, then throw a couple of reprints in the back, and maybe some behind-the-scenes story of how Stan Lee and one of the artists created the character. I always liked that approach: putting a main story as the lead feature and adding extra things like a pinup gallery and some behind-the-scenes stuff. Also, because I don't publish regularly, when I put a book out, I want to make sure it's got a little extra stuff in there besides the main story.

In "Mishmash," I mix it up with a little manga-styled *El Muerto* done in the vein of those '70s Japanese cartoons and comics with those giant robots. It's also to present El Muerto as a multifaceted creation. You'll read an El Muerto tale in continuity (as we in the comics-geek culture call it), and then he can show up as a manga version, or he'll show up in an autobiographical story with me.

I also put myself in the comics. Not just in an autobiographical story, but in the first issue there's this old guy in there called Adam Gomez. And if you look at him, it's actually me in my fifties or sixties. I've got a weird complex about putting myself in the picture. I think I got that from Diego Rivera. I even scored myself a cameo in the movie!

FLA: By changing the style, even if it's the same character, you drastically alter the mood of the comic.

JH: That's definitely an aesthetic device. The first manga Muerto tale was penciled by me but inked by Rafael Navarro. I penciled it, but his inking gives the comic a totally different look than my own work. And the autobiographical story seen in "Mishmash," "Dos Mil," kind of shows my own personal story. I drew that one, believe it or not, with markers. They were actually Sharpies. I think they'd kill me in art school if I said that I used a Sharpie to draw a comic book! It's a subtle change because I'm not working with color, but I wanted to draw something that would look a little different than my brushwork on the actual *Muerto* comic.

FLA: Sometimes you overhear Diego's thoughts?

JH: It's kind of an interesting way to write a story, so I did that in the story in "Mishmash" where I used first-person narration. Because the origin story in the first book, "Daze of the Dead," is told with a sort of narrator directing you through the story. In the second El Muerto story ("Dead Forever"), I wanted to go inside his head and eavesdrop on his thoughts while he's driving in this van down to Mexico.

FLA: I noticed in "Dead Forever" that some panels have lots of text and at other times you blow out into full-page panels with little or no text?

JH: I wanted to give the effect that you were reading a scrapbook as he narrates his life up to that point. Like looking through someone's scrapbook, you can just run your eyes over small photos or come across an eight-by-ten and just kind of look it over. Because it was a first-person narrative, I had the chance to play with the visuals and the design of each panel.

I just finished the new Muerto comic, "Dead & Confused," and, yeah, it's back to the traditional third-person narrative—there's about five or six, maybe eight panels on a page. But I'd definitely like to play with more stories told in Diego's voice, from his own point of view.

FLA: Do you play with the verbal and visual elements for a certain effect?

JH: That's what I love about the comic book: you can play with the words and pictures. For the most part, I'll always have the standard panels: drawings with word balloons and pointers going to each character. But it's neat to play with this by blowing up the panels or having a free-floating type with no balloon or a caption box to enclose it. It's just there as part of the artwork.

FLA: As our eye moves from static image to static image, we create movement between the panels. How does it differ from the storytelling form of film?

JH: The comic book is its own coherent unit. Each panel has to be composed on its own, but at the same time, it interacts with the panel following it. We can slow down or speed up the reader's eye movement from panel to panel and as it sees the page as a whole, and so have more control over the pacing and tempo. A comic book simply doesn't aspire to the same feeling as film.

FLA: Conventions change, too. I think of some of the recent comics being published that don't use the gutter. How do you conceive of and use something like the gutter?

JH: In these new comics, it's just a sharp line that divides one panel from the other; I think this style crept over from Japanese manga. For me and my aesthetic, the gutter stays, damn it! It's my job as a storyteller to play with the layout and rules. I'll give you all the information in each panel, but in that little gutter between the panels, you're doing the work. Or bringing some of yourself into the story. That's the magic only a comic book can claim.

FLA: English appears along with pepperings of Chicano slang and untranslated Spanish. Can you talk about this mixing-up of language?

JH: That's how it is in my real life. When I'm talking to my parents or family from Mexico, I speak primarily Spanish. I'll throw in some English because I'm short a Spanish word. When speaking in English with Latino friends, I'll throw in a couple of Mexican slang words, as long as they're simpatico to the language of course. While I do include some Spanish slang, the comic book has to be primarily in English because the majority of my readers are going to be English-speaking. And, when I use untranslated Spanish, I'm not trying to exclude the people who don't speak Spanish. The reader-viewer can still look at the drawings and the body language and infer what the characters may be feeling. I'm not going to put whole pieces of dialogue in Spanish; this would lose some of the readers. In the new book, El Muerto ends up in Baja, Mexico, where it's assumed that all the characters speak Spanish. I've got to give the reader some credit and assume they'll know that even though it's written in English, they're actually all speaking in Spanish.

I'll save the all-Spanish books for when I publish trade paperback collections.

FLA: Your bodies, faces, settings all have a distinctive style.

JH: With Diego, I didn't want a big, muscle-bound, six-six, 280-pound, monster wrestler character. I wanted to build a character—five-eight, five-ten, and 160 pounds—based on what personality I wanted to portray: an average guy. If the character's more sedentary, then he's going to appear heavier; if he's hyperactive, then lean; if nasty and ugly as a person, then he'll appear nasty and ugly. The personality defines how they're going to look. This is very consciously done.

FLA: But you complicate these types as well.

JH: Yes, that's true. I'm portraying a superhero, but he's built with a smaller frame. You look at the guy and think, "He can't be much of a hero because he's not a big, hulking brute." So I am playing against type by not making the character bigger.

FLA: Can you speak to your use of humor in the more serious epic story of El Muerto?

JH: To me, it's just like life: we're moving forward, and there's fun, there's tension, there're boring times in life. It's just a way to flavor the books the way my life and everybody else's life is flavored. It's not all just fun and games, but it's not all doom and gloom either. I'm trying to stimulate all these different emotions we all feel in our lives. It's interesting as a writer to bounce back and forth like this. How much is too much humor? Is the story getting too serious?

FLA: Is there a place in your comic book worlds for telling the reader, "This is good, this is bad"?

JH: Like everybody, I've got my strong sense of ethics and morality. So it's not surprising that my character Diego will have a crisis of faith. In "Mishmash," we learn that he was an altar boy, but then is sacrificed by this Aztec god of death, and so he asks if other gods can coexist with the God he's come to know through his Catholicism.

FLA: His various crises lead to transformations?

JH: I would say growth. I like seeing a character in conflict with his own beliefs, to question things that he thought were absolute. Like real life, we question things we do and believe all the time. This is how we learn and grow. Jack Kirby once said of the meaning of life, "I don't know the ultimate answer, but the questions have been terrific." As long as my characters end up with a lot of questions, I think they'll grow and evolve as we do in real life.

FLA: As a Latino comic book author-artist, do you feel a sense of responsibility in the kind of story and character you create?

JH: Generally, I try to keep the Muerto story to the equivalent to a PG-13 rating. All the books I grew up on as a kid didn't have mindless profanity, and I still got a lot out of the stories. I would like to keep *El Muerto* so that it can be read by all age groups, at least teen and up. While I didn't create a character like Diego to be a role model, there are a lot of good, honest values informing his actions and thoughts. I don't want him to be ambiguously moral, but he's not a perfect person either. He has to be fallible, and try to learn from his mistakes. I think most of us have made plenty of mistakes in our lives, so I think it's something to relate to.

FLA: What is a Latino comic book?

JH: Good question, because I ask that myself. What makes an author or a comic book necessarily Latino? Does the person have to be a Spanish-speaking, first-generation Latino? A Latino, Joe Quesada, now sits in that fabled position as editor in chief at Marvel Comics, but does this mean that Marvel comics are now Latino? Marvel Comics isn't a Latino comic company now because he's running it. Does he even consider himself Latino? Or what about George Perez, who has worked on DC and Marvel characters for decades? Do we consider him a Latino creator? My character Diego is definitely Latino; he's tied directly to the Day of the Dead folklore and Aztec mythology. And you look at the comic book worlds that Jaime Hernandez creates, and they're definitely Latino. It seems to me that you would have to intend specifically to create a story that's Latino-themed to be Latino. In this sense, maybe Jessica Abel, a white female cartoonist who tells the story of a mixed Anglo-Mexican character living in Mexico, would be considered a Latina creator. I'm a Mexican American who is also a cartoonist, and *El Muerto*'s definitely a Latino comic book, but it's also an alternative-independent comic book.

FLA: Can you speak to some of your work with aspiring comic book authors?

JH: I teach a comic book workshop locally at the Pico Rivera Centre for the Arts. The community is heavily Latino. Most of the kids are young teenagers, and about half of my students are usually female. Young Latinas are reading comics more than ever nowadays. They read a lot of manga, and I think that's also why most of their drawing is in this style. It's great to see kids creating in the comics medium. It's such a vibrant way to create. And most kids that age seem to be open-minded to drawing a comic even if they aren't highly skilled artists. The desire to tell the story outweighs the need of being a great artist.

FLA: How did *El Muerto* make it into a film?

JH: This tale alone would make a Hollywood movie! I did an interview on NPR a few years ago from the San Diego Comic Con. They were actually interviewing Latino comic artists, and were set up to speak with Carlos Saldaña. He couldn't make the show, so he recommended to the reporter to talk to me, along with Richard Dominguez, Rafael Navarro, and I think Los Bros Hernandez. My one-and-a-half-minute interview aired a week later, and Brian Cox heard it while he was driving in Malibu. He was intrigued by the idea of *El Muerto*. He eventually tracked me down and purchased a copy of the comic, which at the time was still only available as a photocopied zine. He liked the idea enough to pursue it as a film. He contacted independent producer Larry Rattner, who showed some investors the comic. There wasn't a script at the time, but the Leones, the investors, decided to put money up for the film. They came to me with a contract, I signed it, and Brian got to working on the script. They presented the script to Wilmer Valderrama; right off the top he liked it. The film is finishing up it's final bits of postproduction. They actually screened a cut of it at the 2006 Cannes Film Festival and received enthusiastic response.

FLA: Did working with the film adaptation shift at all your comic-book-creating process?

JH: I didn't work on a Muerto comic during production, but I did have a sketchbook on set to keep notes and drawings of the filmmaking process. My plan is to produce an autobiographical comic on the filmmaking process. I worked on the film for six weeks, fulfilling my associate producer status. Which means hanging around the set and telling people I created the comic book. Seriously though, it was really amazing to actually experience and document the filmmaking process from the days before we had even begun preproduction to the actual filming and the hard work involved in postproduction.

The comic book I do on my own. Late nights at the drawing table and computer, my pencil and brush creating the world that's in my head. On the film, you have all these artists and technicians working together to create their own version for the screen. But when the filming was over, it was kind of neat to get back to the drawing board and resume working on the comic. Filmmaking is very exciting and fulfilling as an artist, that's for sure, especially when you're getting a film made of your comic! And watching the collaboration between everyone is really fascinating. But sitting back at my drawing table, once again assuming the omnipotent role of creator and cartoonist, was very satisfying. And there was no way I was scheduling myself to work those twelve-to-sixteen-hour workdays!

Jonathan and Joshua Luna
of The Luna Brothers

Jonathan Luna was born in 1978 and his brother, Joshua, in 1981. With parents in the military, they grew up in a variety of places, including Iceland, Sicily, and Sardinia. These experiences broadened their understanding of people—specifically, how issues of race and ethnicity work within and outside the United States. Such experiences fed into their passion for reading and drawing comics. After years of formal and informal training, including the honing of their craft at the Savannah College of Art and Design, the two brothers created their breakthrough comic books *Girls* (2005) and *Ultra: Seven Days* (2005), both distributed by Image Comics and widely available.

FREDERICK LUIS ALDAMA: First comic books read? First to make an impression?

JONATHAN LUNA: *Uncanny X-Men* ("Inferno"), *Teenage Mutant Ninja Turtles*, *Mad Magazine*, *Cracked Magazine*.

JOSHUA LUNA: *Calvin and Hobbes.*

FLA: What were the first drawings or stories that you both drew and wrote?

JONATHAN: I began officially drawing with *The Forgotten*, issue 4, for Fintan Studios, and didn't officially begin writing until issue 1 of *Ultra*.

JOSHUA: The first thing I wrote that was published was *Ultra*. The first thing I drew that was published was a pinup for the Image Comics title *Invincible*.

FLA: First comic book idea and actual series?

JONATHAN: *Ultra.*

FLA: Your experiences reading comics as Filipinos in America?

JONATHAN: I've never given it much thought. I guess, on a subconscious level, we Filipinos can feel a bit left out, in terms of seeing our culture and characters of the same race in comics. The only time I've seen this is in *Wetworks* (Image Comics), where there was a Filipino character. This was a pretty mainstream comic back in the '90s. I can't remember the name of the character, but he even spoke Tagalog on a few occasions.

FLA: Experiences in the profession as an ethnic-identified author-artist?

JONATHAN: My experiences in the comic book industry seem to be the same as everyone else's. I can't tell if people treat us differently, because I'm inside looking out. We've been fortunate in this field. It's common for interviewers or fans to ask us about our ethnicity, but after that it usually ends there.

FLA: How has your biographical experience influenced your stories and characters?

JONATHAN: Filipino families, or any other minority families, tend to be different than Caucasian families. Through my experience, Filipino and Hispanic families tend to be closer. The dynamics are different. The cultures are simpler. The parents tend to be more overprotective. There's a lot of guilt and shame. Though I hear lately that all parents these days are becoming "helicopter parents."

Our family experiences probably have the biggest effect on us as storytellers, and it shows in *Ultra*, *Girls*, and most likely anything else we will do in the future.

FLA: Can you speak to your formal or informal training? I think of your experiences at the Savannah College of Art and Design, and so on. Would you consider yourselves of a certain school?

JONATHAN: We took art classes in high school, but you don't learn much there. At least we didn't. High school art classes are basically time allotted in one day to concentrate on art. At SCAD [Savannah College of Art and Design] we were broken down and built back up. We learned the basics, and once we figured out what field we were interested in, we took the specific classes. We went to SCAD for comics. At that time, it was the only school to offer a BFA and MFA in comics. It still may be. I didn't plan on going to college, but I got accepted and went at the last minute.

I don't consider myself of a certain school of art. Though I'm sure today's generation of comics influences each other.

FLA: When there are so many different ways to tell stories available out there, why choose to tell stories in comic book form?

JONATHAN: The comic book is such a great medium for telling stories. It's purely visual, and it simulates movement, time, and sound. We love it for its similarities with cinema. Film is also a preference for us, but the process is very elaborate and requires sets, a cast and crew, and equipment. With comics these days, one person, a pencil, and paper are sufficient. A computer is preferable. For us, working in comics means you get control. Others may not have much control if they work for a large publisher. The same applies to film, depending on who's financing the project.

FLA: Difficulties breaking into the market?

JONATHAN: Breaking in is very difficult. There are different ways, and it depends on the publisher. For the most part, people show their portfolios to editors at conventions and get hired that way. Some people get gigs by who they know. With Image, they accept submissions (five pages and synopsis). This is how we published *Ultra*. Not many people get a green light. In *American Idol*, a lot of people think that they can sing. It's the same with drawing comics.

FLA: Monetary considerations?

JONATHAN: It's definitely difficult to make a living doing comics. But it wasn't a worry to me. It's the only thing I know.

FLA: Can you make a living with your comic books alone?

JONATHAN: Generally, many people make a great living doing comics. Some are millionaires. For the most part, it can be tough. For us, we do make a living with comics. That's tough to do with a creator-owned book.

FLA: Can comic book conventions help get a career started—and sustain it?

JONATHAN: Conventions are a good way to get your name out there or see your fans. But they can be expensive—travel, table space—time-consuming—take time out of your schedule—and very tiring. Sometimes the con will fly the creator out to the show and offer a stay at a hotel. We tend to sell sketches as well as sign books.

FLA: How about distributors?

JONATHAN: Image Comics deals with our distributor, Diamond. They're great.

FLA: Experiences working with Image Comics?

JONATHAN: Image Comics is probably the best publisher out there for someone who wants to create their own comics. The creator keeps all rights and pays a minimum for every book put out. Their team is great to work with and very personable.

FLA: Sometimes if there are different people working on a comic book, there can be a split in the author's and artist's vision of the story. Is this an issue for you guys?

JOSHUA: No, it's not really an issue. It just takes a lot of healthy communication. We work very closely in conceiving, developing, and executing our stories together, so we're always on the same page. Of course, we may have a different take on a scene or a specific plot point, but in a collaboration that's expected, if not necessary. As long as we share a common vision and know what the story is about and where it's heading, there's nothing wrong with hearing a different perspective from time to time. It only strengthens the work.

FLA: Do you create the individual issues with the idea that they will be collected into various book volumes? Might this change the idea of the cliff-hanger between individual issues?

JONATHAN: Yes, we keep in mind that the single issues will be combined to form graphic novels. We chose for each *Girls* graphic novel to contain six issues. There should be twenty-four issues—four graphic novels. For each arc or graphic novel, there should be a good ending or cliff-hanger to make the reader want to buy the next graphic novel. The same applies to the single issues. It's very similar to TV shows—episodes and seasons.

FLA: You both mention in another interview various favorites, including *Blade of the Immortal, Alias, 100 Bullets, Preacher*. Other favorites or influences?

JONATHAN: Powers's *Y: The Last Man*.

FLA: What about other media like film, novels, music?

JONATHAN: For film, it's the director M. Night Shyamalan. For novels, it's the author Chuck Palahniuk. For anime, it's *Ghost in the Shell* and *Ninja Scroll*. For music, it's Coldplay, Radiohead, Keane, Portishead. For comedians, it's Patton Oswalt, David Cross, Dane Cook.

FLA: You work within a variety of different story types.

JOSHUA: *Girls* is sci-fi, horror, drama, comedy—but not too much comedy.

JONATHAN: *Ultra* is superhero, romance, comedy, drama, horror.

FLA: How might you be complicating these standard story types?

JOSHUA: We just try to do our own take on the genres we've grown up with. I've always found the private life of a superhero fascinating, so *Ultra* mirrored that sensibility. *Girls* is basically our homage to monster movies, but we wanted to make our monster beautiful.

FLA: How do you conceive of the main story in relation to the subordinate plots?

JONATHAN: With our stories, we use main and subplots, but in the end it should all tie in and feed the same conclusion. It's used to distinguish characters or display different themes. It can generate suspense and affect rhythm for variation.

FLA: What type of audience do you envision reading *Ultra* or *Girls*? Both have two very different moods or visions of the world.

JONATHAN: We want to reach everyone . . .

JOSHUA: Except kids.

FLA: Do you have a sense from fan mail, ComiCons, and the like what type of audience *actually* reads *Ultra* or *Girls*?

JOSHUA: It's a pretty diverse group. Men, women, teenage girls and boys. Our books are fairly accessible and self-contained, so we also tend to hear from people who've never picked up a comic before. Which is great. I think a lot of people out there are unaware of what's being done in comics these days, or maybe they assume the subject matter hasn't evolved beyond kiddie fare. But in order for this industry to survive, I think it's important to make more and more people aware of the good work being done in the medium.

FLA: How do you envision your various narrators in *Ultra*?

JONATHAN: The narrators are the characters themselves. We rarely if ever use classic narrators in our stories. *Ultra* was special in the sense that we wanted to show the world of Spring City through as many media possible.

FLA: How do you decide when to have more visuals than text, and vice versa, and does this pacing work to cast a specified mood?

JONATHAN: Yes, mood and pacing are definitely factors. It just depends on the scene and what serves the story best. There have been instances where I removed long bits of dialogue from a panel just because the art said it all. And for some panels, the image would be absolutely meaningless to the reader if I didn't add words. And that's the beauty of comic books—the synergy of words and pictures. Everything's working together to bring the story to life.

FLA: In your opinion, what do the panels do? I think of *Ultra*, where there seems to be a preference for the horizontal panels.

JONATHAN: The panel is pretty much the only thing that the reader will look at. The design and imagery should be the engaging part. Yes, we tend to use horizontal panels. They're cinematic and better for storytelling.

FLA: Are there certain tensions that you like to create more than others in your choice of panel sequencing?

JONATHAN: To slow down a scene, a comic artist would most likely use more panels, and vice versa.

FLA: How do you decide where to place a gutter to divide one panel from the next? Does the gutter's position move the reader in a certain way?

JONATHAN: We don't really think of it in terms of inserting a gutter. It's more about how many panels or beats we need to tell a scene, and the gutters simply fall into place in between those panels.

Yes, the gutters definitely affect the way a comic is read. In fact, I think the gutter is the magic in sequential art. It's the one thing no other medium has. In that space between two panels, whether the readers are aware of it or not, they are in control. They are using their imaginations, filling in their own blanks between a transition of cause and effect. And by doing this, they become engaged participants of the story.

FLA: *Ultra* has a distinctive style that's made up from the choice of lettering and layout as well as your use of playful mock magazine inserts. Does your style describe a particular worldview?

JONATHAN: *Ultra* pretty much displays our cynicism toward mainstream media. When *Ultra* was first released, audiences grunted because of its superficial nature—but that was intentional. It took some time before the readers got the sarcasm.

Ultra's world, Spring City, is one where everything is exploited. Superheroes are like gods, and they're practically stripped of their amazing nature by the media and the audiences that want to know everything about their favorite heroes. It's a tough position to be a hero in this world, or any world for that matter.

FLA: There's a fine line between pornography and erotica. How do you manage in your aesthetic composition to keep it erotic—playfully erotic? I'm reminded of the opening of *Girls*, where we discover that the guy's masturbating.

JOSHUA: Yes, *Girls* deals with a lot of sexual themes, but the purpose of the book isn't to titillate the reader. Our goal is to tell a story, and I think that's the distinction between pornography and erotica.

FLA: In *Ultra*, you use a variety of different speech registers: the pop journalese of the mock magazine inserts; the way Olivia, Jen, and Pearl speak; pepperings of Spanish, and so on.

JONATHAN: Basically, we use references that make us laugh. In the early stages, we didn't think *Ultra* would be such a hit. So a lot of dialogue has that rawness that a creator has when they don't realize that people are looking at their work. Things have changed for us.

FLA: Both *Ultra* and *Girls* have a distinctive color palette.

JOSHUA: Color is probably one of the strongest storytelling tools in our books. It's the first thing that the readers see when they turn to the pages, and it captures the mood and the atmosphere of each scene instantly.

FLA: You provide maps in both *Girls* and *Ultra*: Spring City is located in the U.S. where Manhattan would be, and Pennystown has a north compass reading and scale to give a sense of realism, yet both are fictional places. One is rural and the other urban?

JONATHAN: Yes, both are fictional. *Girls* is in a rural setting simply because we wanted our cast to be small. It's an analogy of what would happen to the larger part of the world. The urban fits *Ultra* well in terms of being seen by millions, being in the public eye.

FLA: In your stylization of your characters' anatomy, you tend toward the realistic end, versus the cartoon end, of the spectrum.

JOSHUA: I really believe you can capture a broad range of emotions with both realistic and cartoonish styles, but we just felt the stories we've done worked best with a more realistic aesthetic. We're not opposed to experimenting with other styles down the road.

FLA: Ultra self-identifies as a "female, Hispanic Superhero—a triple minority." At one point, too, she falls from saintly, chaste grace, especially in the eyes of her Latino public.

JONATHAN: It's a big goal of ours to tell stories that end. Most don't. With a complete story, you have a beginning, middle, and end. A problem, a realization, and a solution. We feel that a story is much more successful when a character changes. If it's for the better, it makes the reader feel good. If it's for the worse, it's a morality tale.

FLA: In *Ultra*, your characters have superpowers, but they use them like you would if you had good typing ability, as part of a job. Why normalize the comic book superhero?

JONATHAN: Empathy is a huge part of storytelling. The reader must feel some sort of connection with the characters or understand them.

JOSHUA: This treatment of our superheroes was also an extension of how the media and the world as a whole sucks up everything that makes these beings special and unique and turns it into something mundane.

FLA: You normalize what might be considered unusual in terms of the women's sexuality. I think here of Liv, who declares her love of "Drinks, Dancing and Dingalings"; of Jen's expression of love for Pearl, and so on.

JOSHUA: We treated our superheroes like humans. And like humans, our characters are sexual beings. Whether it's intimacy problems, trust issues, promiscuousness, a closeted homosexual lifestyle, these are things that real people go through in their private lives, and that's the kind of angle we wanted to focus on in *Ultra*.

FLA: In a world where good and bad often straddle a blurry line, how do you suggest values of good and bad in your storyworld? I think of your superheroines fighting for justice, but also appearing on billboards that advertise Cool Cola and Llama cigarettes.

JOSHUA: Personally, it's difficult for me to say what's bad or good. As a storyteller, I don't want to get to a point where I'm pushing my views onto the reader. Black and white, good or evil are subjective things to me. What interests me is the gray area. I like to present both sides equally, make an interesting argument, and let the reader draw their own conclusions.

When you look at a character like Liv, who's not only drop-dead gorgeous but superhuman, it's easy to hate her. Especially when she exploits her genetic blessings for selfish purposes at times. But when you look past the exterior of a character and understand their motivations—when you realize that the character is, in fact, just like you—you really see nothing but gray.

FLA: How do you both get a sense that your scene or character is actually triggering the intended emotion in your audience?

JOSHUA: I don't think you'll ever know unless a reader tells you. You just have to trust that if a scene is important to you, then hopefully it will be important to the reader.

FLA: Do you think the state of multicultural comics is becoming more or less diverse in its range of representations today?

JONATHAN: Comics are getting much better. Personally, I predict that comics will become much more diversified, like in Japan. Japan has comics—manga—for everything, even fishing stories!

FLA: Anything in the pipeline?

JOSHUA: Too early to say, but it'll most likely be a creator-owned project.

Laura Molina

Laura Molina was born in 1957 in East Los Angeles. She grew up in the suburbs of Los Angeles near Pasadena. Her mother was born in Los Angeles, and her father was born near San Antonio, Texas, of two families that were made citizens by the Treaty of Guadalupe Hidalgo in 1848.

At six years old she had developed a passion for drawing and painting. By age ten, she knew that she wanted to draw cartoons and become a professional animator. So after graduating early from Arroyo High School in El Monte, California, she entered the character animation program at the California Institute of the Arts on a full scholarship from Walt Disney Studios to train as an animator. She then worked briefly as an in-betweener on Saturday-morning cartoons.

In 1996, she self-published her debut comic book, *Cihualyaomiquiz, the Jaguar*. Molina also appears in the 2001 version of Trina Robbins's *The Great Women Cartoonists*. Molina currently lives in Los Angeles, where she continues to create *The Jaguar* as well as paint, perform, act, and publish.

FREDERICK LUIS ALDAMA: What were your first impressions of cartoons or comic books as a kid?

LAURA MOLINA: Animated cartoons and comic books are related fields, but it was animation that first made the biggest impression. I didn't set out to be a comic illustrator, but when I was a teenager, I developed a real taste for comics. I especially started to pay attention with the arrival in the '70s of the self-published underground comics.

I have a large comic book collection—a huge amount of DC and Marvel as well as all kinds of black-and-white comics—but the majority of the collection is made up of undergrounds. They were more appealing to someone like myself—not male and over the age of thirteen—than superhero comics. Mostly you had to be an adult to buy them, and they were only available in head shops, specialty newsstands, or by mail. Back then, they were hard to get, so I would go on the hunt for them.

FLA: When did it dawn on you that there were few women in the profession of animation and comics and even fewer Latinas—if any?

LM: I realized the disproportionate number of men in the profession when I got to college and began to study character animation. My freshman classes had something like nine women and thirty men; it wasn't as proportionate as the other categories of study for art. In courses on live film or graphic design, there'd be a more equal number of men and women. While it's less so today, animation was a very male-dominated field. Comic books remain very male-dominated.

My awareness of Latina representations didn't really take shape until I came up with *The Jaguar*. All the Latino cartoonists had met each other in the early '90s and started their books, but there weren't really any Latinas. Of course, there were no Latinas working or being represented in the mainstream when I began to create *The Jaguar*. A place like Marvel seemed dead set against representations of Latinos or Latinas.

FLA: *The Jaguar*, then, aimed to change this all-boys, non-Latina comic book landscape?

LM: The [Proposition] 187 immigration debate brought this politics of representation up to the surface. There were hate crimes and discrimination. The country had taken a hard turn to the right, pushing toward something dark and violent. It was a climate similar to today. All of a sudden, positive representations of Latinas and issues concerning Latinos generally mattered a lot. You had to take a political stand because of the overt racism that you faced every day.

Some people chose different ways to take a stand, getting degrees in history and writing academic treatises on Chicano studies and history, or getting the messages out through artwork and through popular cultural media like the comic book. I've always been interested in pop culture, so I decided to go with the comic book. Even today, there might be some Latino comics, mostly teen, but they're pretty lame in their attempt at creating a Latina superhero.

FLA: How were you able to get *The Jaguar* out to readers?

LM: Through the wide network of comic book art. It's a small but very circular world, where the contacts go around very quickly. My friends know all kinds of big shots in comics—people I wouldn't necessarily meet on my own.

FLA: Is this when you formed PACAS [Professional Amigos of Comic Art Society]?

LM: PACAS was founded by Richard Dominguez (*El Gato Negro*) and Carlos Saldaña (*Burrito*). PACAS was a network and support group for minority artists. Some of us were very political, like myself and Lalo Alcaraz, of the daily syndicated strip *La Cucaracha*, and some were doing straight-ahead superhero comics.

FLA: You created one issue of *The Jaguar*, then what happened?

LM: I had wanted to go ahead with it as a series, but self-publishing is a tough business. So I focused more on painting and performance. This took up a lot of my time.

I have been negotiating a contract with Karl Dabney at Workhorse Comics to return to *The Jaguar*. Karl got artists and writers from all kinds of different backgrounds to create a more multicultural team of creators and writers—a silver age of multicultural comics. I'll have to make some creative concessions if my character becomes part of their universe. But because I hold all the rights to it, it should work out well.

FLA: Why the Jaguar?

LM: I was given a couple of Impact Comics' series *The Jaguar*, created in the 1980s. The character, Jaguar, is barefoot and speaks only English; it was poorly written and conceived; jaguars aren't just rain forest animals, they have a desert habitat, too. It was a patronizing piece of junk, so I took the name over and added the unpronounceable Native American name, Cihualyaomiquiz, to the title.

FLA: Each of your creative activities demands something different of you. What about the comic book?

LM: The sequential art of comic books is a tough art form. For some people, it comes as naturally as breathing. Even though I've been trained formally, I still find the storyboarding and layout process—the problem-solving aspect of getting the visuals and the script to work—tedious. I enjoy more the rendering art.

I'm a perfectionist. I can't hack out anything. I figure if I'm going to do any kind of art, whether it's music or painting or comic book, I really want it to be a high-quality product. As a painter, I only finish a couple paintings a year. I'm a quality, not quantity, type of artist.

FLA: Can you make a living as an artist?

LM: With all my creative efforts, I've managed to stay either self-employed or partially employed. I recently lost my former profession as a scenic artist. This had to do with my medical limitations—bronchitis. So I gave myself a new job as a magazine publisher. So I currently have income from the reproductions of my artwork and some acting that keeps me afloat.

FLA: Can you speak to the process of creating *The Jaguar*?

LM: Everybody's got a different inking style, and for some people that goes really quickly, and some slowly, and some use certain felt and ink pens. Carlos Saldaña uses a felt pen, and Rafael Navarro doesn't so much draw as he paints, then digitizes, and then drops in the colors; that's why his style's more abstract. I'm real detailed and more rendered. My pages are very clean; I don't use Wite-Out on any of them. I press out my pencils really carefully, and then I proceed to ink. I do very careful drawings, and I trace those so I never ink on top of my pencils. I'll retrace one panel at a time and ink that. And then when I have the panels scanned together, I just scan them individually and put them on pages. I can move panels from one page to another. If I feel I need to, I can drop a panel into a page. That's the beautiful thing about working with new digital technologies and computers; with the old comic-book method, where everything was mechanical, you just couldn't move things around so easily.

FLA: You use a lot of shading in the 1996 *Jaguar*.

LM: The 1996 *Jaguar* isn't inked. There was a time when I didn't ink anything. I would use an animator's pencil to get the blackest pencil line that I could get. And had it shot. I think it went to a Velox screen. And then it was just set up for Xerox reproduction. If you look at my actual inking style, it's very different.

If you look at *The Jaguar* serigraph that I did for Self Help Graphics, that was an ink drawing done in a fairly large size; then it was done even bigger to become a serigraph silk screen. I also ink on the standard fifteen-by-ten-inch page. I'll try and do drawings in light pencil, and I end up redoing them, like, one panel at a time while inking them.

FLA: In creating the Jaguar character as a Chicana, you must have had an audience in mind.

LM: I wanted to create a strong, nonstereotypical Chicana character who would appeal to girls like myself when I was twelve years old. She wouldn't be subservient or passive, weak, or any other stereotype. She would inspire confidence in young Chicanas.

I want to bust open that stereotype, not just in the comic, but in painting, publishing, and all things that I do. Just being confident in my ability to do these different activities also instills a certain confidence in others—that you can demand respect as a Latina for your work.

FLA: You appear to have an older female audience in mind for the series of images titled *Naked Dave*, which you present on the Internet.

LM: Women tend to love *Naked Dave* and men tend to hate it; the objectification of the man by a woman really pushes their buttons. The male comic-book crowd hates it the most. I get a similar kind of hate mail on *The Jaguar*.

But in the end, this is what good art is supposed to do—get a strong reaction. This is the kind of art that needs guards standing around at the museums because people want to attack it. It's the kind of art that governments try to ban.

FLA: The Jaguar is a Chicana, Linda Rivera, who studies law. Does her character change in the new issues?

LM: She is still studying law, but I'm not sure if she ever gets to be a lawyer. I was going to give her an alcohol problem, but a friend who is a screenwriter said I should keep her pure. I was reminded that when we make art, it circulates out there and belongs to everybody, including young readers. So there's a certain responsibility to those readers that I keep in mind. That's why Linda Rivera remains a positive example for young women, young girls, teenagers, and so on. At the same time, *The Jaguar* definitely differs from young-adult fiction and children's literature. It's not only educating or offering positive images, but there's politics in the way it addresses racism and sexism in everyday life.

In the first two origin issues, she goes through traumatizing personal events. After basically coming back from the dead, she turns into a very intuitive, clever, and strong character.

FLA: Do you see her as a superhero?

LM: She's a superhero, but more like Batman. She's just been traumatized, but uses her own learned skills and resources to carry out her agenda.

FLA: Your narrator's voice at the beginning makes it clear that this is set during a time when California is fast becoming a police state. Is this what you mean by conveying a politics?

LM: Yes, it's like movies that use a voice-over narrator to focus the story through the perspective of a character. It directs us to see the story through a very specific lens.

FLA: How do you balance this type of storytelling voice with the visuals?

LM: When I first put *The Jaguar* together, it flowed in a linear fashion, with the visuals and the text elements finding a natural balance. It was a pretty spontaneous and natural process. I think if you start overplanning a comic book, you can drive yourself nuts. It's like writing a screenplay. You have an allotted amount of time to tell your story, so you storyboard to time out the whole script and concept.

FLA: What about the use of gutters?

LM: I didn't want a straight line, so I use what's called a deckling style. The traditional gutter size is one-quarter of an inch on 150 percent original size of the artist's page. We're not limited by standard gutters anymore. You can lay panels on top of panels. Pages can have black edges, so there's more leeway in the types of layout that can be used. And if using color, you can do the full bleed on the layout. This is all highly influenced by Japanese comics.

FLA: How do you conceive of the panel?

LM: I tend to think of panels as separate little paintings. I lay them out the way I would a single painting, taking into consideration more the composition of each panel rather than the whole. Also, because I can ink one panel at a time and then switch things around on the computer, I tend to look at it panel by panel rather than the whole page. I don't worry about a whole page unless it's a splash page.

FLA: You want to reach all sorts of readers, but at the same time not to wash out the cultural specifics of being Chicana. How do you reconcile the universal appeal with the cultural particularities?

LM: I have standards. That's one of the reasons that I wouldn't go with any publisher that would take away any of the Latino cultural elements. Paul Rodriguez once joked of *Star Trek*, what, are there no Latinos in space? It's our mission to get those Latinos in space.

FLA: So do you think we haven't been making the necessary big strides forward in terms of expanding and complicating Latino representations?

LM: We are moving forward, but not quickly enough. In the all-pervasive television media, we're still pretty invisible. It's better than it was fifteen years ago, but it's still pretty dismal. The acting business still works according to the breakdown of roles for a script by race.

FLA: What's the difference between a Marvel-created Latina superhero like Araña and, say, your Jaguar?

LM: I haven't read *Araña*, but I'd say it's a question of heart. When it comes from Marvel, when they create a Latina character but do so motivated by profits, they don't go for the heart. They just don't get it, because it's all token. If it doesn't have heart, the comic book character won't last.

FLA: Any last words?

LM: Artists have to be artists. An attorney once asked me, "Why do you do this?" In other words, what's the monetary gain? Regardless of monetary gain, art is what artists do. If it were all about the money, you might as well open an advertising firm where there's no real creativity, just slick and trendy style.

Rhode Montijo

The author of the comic book series *Pablo's Inferno* and the children's book *Cloud Boy*, Rhode Montijo was born in El Centro in September 1973, but grew up mostly in Stockton, California. His first experience with comic books was discovering a *Spider-Man* comic on the rack of a dimly lit grocery store his mom would shop at. Sitting on the spin rack in the shadows, it was like a hidden treasure that only he knew existed. While there were other comic books on the rack, it was *Spider-Man* that appealed to Montijo: not only because of his spider-like powers, but also because his full mask reminded him of other heroes, like the luchadores south of the border.

Rhode Montijo lives in Oakland, California, where he continues to write comic books and children's books. *Pablo's Inferno* is published by ABISMO Press, and *Cloud Boy* by Simon & Schuster. His website is www.pablosinferno.com.

FREDERICK LUIS ALDAMA: Can you speak to your experiences in training to become a comic book author-artist?

RHODE MONTIJO: Art school was the best for me. I didn't know what I was going to do with myself after high school until my high school art teacher told me about the California College of Arts and Crafts in Oakland. I couldn't believe there was such a thing as art college. My counselor and art teacher helped me get there with applying and financial aid, and once I was there, I soaked it all in. I just wanted to learn all of it, even if it was something I couldn't see myself doing. I just wanted to learn.

FLA: When there are so many different ways to tell stories available out there, why choose to tell stories in comic book form?

RM: To me, it's one of the best ways to communicate the story exactly how you want, without any outside influence. Also, I always joke that there's no budget for the special effects! Whatever you can think of can be realized.

FLA: Difficulties breaking into the market?

RM: The five single-issue *Pablo's Inferno* comics were made possible thanks to a grant from the Xeric Foundation. It's a foundation that was started by one of the *Teenage Mutant Ninja Turtles* creators, Peter Laird. They give up to $5,000 dollars to around six or so people, two times a year, to help with the costs involved with self-publishing. I couldn't have done it without them. They ask for nothing in return, only six copies of your book when it's printed! You must apply and be in financial need.

FLA: Who's your audience?

RM: The audience was anybody who read it. First and foremost, *Pablo's Inferno* was a story that I had always wanted to read, and that fueled me, but at the same time I hoped that anybody could enjoy it. I definitely wasn't trying to exclude anybody. If anything, I wanted to show a great adventure with a main character of Mexican descent and in a Mexican setting.

FLA: Can you speak to the collaborative process?

RM: It was an organic process with Dan [Chapman] and I. He was working on his own books, but offered to print my book at the printing store where he worked during my last year in college. I asked him to write the first book because I wasn't confident with my writing. At first, we basically did a parody of Dante's *Inferno*, where Pablo travels through the layers of hell as described by Dante. After the first issue, I took a trip deep down into Mexico with my family. Growing up, I mainly would visit the border town of Mexicali, where my mother is from and my dad lived. This time, I visited Mexico City, which I had briefly visited before, but now for a longer period, and got to visit the Aztec temples. I also visited Tepoztlan, Oaxaca, Morelia, Patzquaro, and Janitzio, among other cities. I came back personally inspired, and then later I felt like putting it into the story and taking the book into a different direction. This happened between Book I and Book II. When I returned, I now felt confident in writing the rest of the story.

FLA: When reading *Pablo's Inferno*, I think of Alan Moore and Eddie Campbell (*From Hell*), Mike Mignola (*Hellboy*) and Gaudiano (*Azteca*). Can you speak to some of your influences?

RM: Kelley Jones and the works of Mike Mignola have had a big influence. Mike Mignola went to the same art college I did, but years before.

FLA: Were you inspired by stories you heard growing up?

RM: Definitely. There are lots of things from growing up and hearing stories my mom and grandparents would tell, but more so, it was that fateful trip to Mexico. Everything from the coyote fountain in Coyoacan, Mexico, that fed the idea of coyote-people-infested town, to the underground caverns where Pablo and Quetzal find the lost candle of San Bernardino. That cavernous maze was inspired by underground tunnels in Mexico City that monks would hide in underneath their church to avoid being killed. The mirror stone that Pablo uses to battle the vampires, I learned was used to heat the bathing waters of the Aztecs and as decoration on their temples. Chac Mool, Tlaloc, Huehueteotl were from Tenochtitlan. The church being built on top of the Aztec temple, I witnessed at the *zócalo* [main square] in Mexico City. The prayers in the cracks of the saint container I saw inside that church. So it really was more from what I learned on my trip that fueled the story.

FLA: The character Quetzal is a record keeper. "I am the last link to our past. I am writing so that our history will live on," he says.

RM: Quetzal was meant to be the link to the past that would teach the young

Pablo's Inferno

Pablo about his culture, but also to the reader, who is learning along with Pablo. I wanted to teach, but not in a noticeable or preachy way, but all of it in hopes of aiding and moving the story forward.

FLA: Why the choice of the heroic sacrificial form to tell this story?

RM: Again, it was just a story that I hungered to read.

FLA: But you also complicate these standard genres.

RM: I wanted Pablo to kind of stumble across the adventure at first, but when the story reaches the climax, he now has to make a conscious decision, not by accident, and only then putting into play what was to be resolved.

FLA: [spoiler warning] Pablo has to remain in the land of the dead to help restore balance on earth?

RM: A lot of readers were really wanting to see Pablo come back to life at the end of the story and live happily ever after, but I wanted to show that Pablo and Quetzal's actions, in their deaths, affected the living world.

FLA: In many ways, *Pablo's Inferno* educates readers about Aztec, Toltec, and other ancient Mexica cultures and mythologies.

RM: It was sad learning that most of the original texts by the Aztecs were destroyed by the Spaniards, and as the fates would have it, much of what we know about the native peoples is what was documented by them [the Spanish].

FLA: Do you experiment with lettering and the use of fonts?

RM: I have to admit I got a little carried away with the fonts. I think I would do it differently now. Looking back, some are a bit hard to read, but basically I was trying to have each font relate to the voice. Pablo had a kid-writing type of font, while some of the gods had long, spindly fonts. If the bubbles are done correctly, I think the reader shouldn't notice them. They matter very much, but in a subconscious way.

FLA: How do you conceive of the panel layout and its function to engage readers?

RM: It all comes from reading a lot of comics, and after a while you realize it is a language that is used a certain way to communicate.

FLA: Why not use color?

RM: I couldn't afford it, plain and simple. Knowing that with anything in life, you just work with what you got. I actually enjoyed the black-and-white comics like Jeff Smith's *Bone* and some of the early *Hellboy* stories in *Dark Horse Presents*, which would print the stories in black-and-white. It became a challenge and fun trying to figure how to go about things.

FLA: When using black-and-white, how do you convey, say, the threat of danger that the use of the color red can in a color comic book?

RM: I'm sure there are countless approaches. Offhand, I think one could play with the shadows or maybe even not have shadows if the book is full of them. You can also play with cropping, motion lines for reaction, and even sound effects.

FLA: Does Pablo experience a transformation of character?

RM: I would hope so. Maybe it's not as transparent, but I wanted him to learn about his culture in a way and then use all that knowledge to decide what was the best thing to do when his new friend and mentor, Quetzal, was in the clutches of evil. He has to add up all the small pieces and realizes that the land was dying.

[spoiler warning] From the beginning of his journey, the fire god, Huehueteotl, tells Pablo to retrieve certain objects and that at the end he would find the treasure of life. I wanted Pablo and the reader to think it was the ability to come back to life, but in reality, it was corn, which is the blood of life for so many.

FLA: What is the significance of the introduction of the girl character, Nayelli, who plays games with Pablo?

RM: I wanted to introduce a girl, but one that could see Pablo and Quetzal when others could not. Someone who was tapped in to the supernatural and therefore had extra sight. At the same time, I wanted her to first interact with Pablo as a playful friend, as we had not seen much of Pablo being a kid up to that point. But then later more is revealed about her, and they [readers] second-guess her character. [spoiler warning] Towards the end, I wanted Pablo to be right about Nayelli in trusting all along that she meant well. After he sees her death foretold by the Spiderwomen's textile, Pablo, concerned, runs out of the Spiderwomen's home with a string caught on to his foot, and unravels her tapestry and future. Nayelli is a crucial part of the puzzle and deals the last blow in the final confrontation, too.

FLA: The Spiderwomen?

RM: My mother told me tales of the Spiderwomen, weavers of textiles in Mexico, and I loved the name, and it conjured certain images. To me, they became like the Fates in Greek mythology, who were sisters that could see the future.

FLA: Pablo only speaks a little Spanish. Huehueteotl speaks Nahuatl. Can you speak about the use of Spanish and English in *Pablo's Inferno*?

RM: Yes! Hopefully that wasn't too confusing, that was a challenge. I wanted to show there were different tongues, and even though Quetzal couldn't physically speak, he could communicate with Pablo mentally or telepathically with the aid of the fire god, who spoke the old tongue.

Pablo's Inferno

FLA: Your narrative talks of the Spanish conquest, Aztec myth, and much more. Is there an ethics at work here?

RM: I tried not to tell the reader what's good and bad, just show what happened and let the reader make their own decision.

FLA: Innocence carries a certain power to cut through greed and evil in *Pablo's Inferno*.

RM: I wanted to show that sometimes bad things can be turned to good by how you use them.

FLA: It appears that we're seeing a greater variety of types of stories told by Latino comic book author-artists. Do you think the state of Latino comic-book publishing is improving today?

RM: Yes. The more, the merrier—pretty much of *any* culture. There's so much out there, so many cultures, so many stories!

FLA: What do you have coming out or in the pipeline?

RM: Right now I'm living one of my biggest dreams in doing children's books. My first book is called *Cloud Boy*, a small story about belonging and sharing with art.

FLA: Can you speak to the process of working on *Cloud Boy*?

RM: It was great. I mainly dealt with my editor, who knew where I was coming from with the story and was generally excited about it to help see the book in print.

FLA: *Cloud Boy* is published by the big press Simon & Schuster. How does this differ from your experience publishing *Pablo's Inferno*?

RM: By self-publishing *Pablo's Inferno*, I can finish making the book and send it out to the printers and have the finished product at my doorstep in three weeks. *Cloud Boy* had been finished for close to two years before it came out. On the other hand, *Pablo's Inferno* was picked up by a few stores who saw it in the comic distribution catalogue, while *Cloud Boy* has many more outlets.

FLA: Is the conceptual process in writing a children's book—say, figuring out certain combinations of text and visuals—the same or different from the comic book?

RM: It's similar in that you are trying to tell a story with so many pages and in sequence of events. I do thumbnail sketches and enlarge them to see how the story is working with both comics and children's books. In comics you can have as many panels as you'd like to convey an idea, and in children's books the panels are pretty much the pages, at least for me. So I think in children's books it's a bit more of a challenge of trying to convey a clear story with the standard amount of pages, which are generally twenty-four and thirty-two pages.

FLA: Is *Cloud Boy* Latino or multiethnic in any way?

RM: The only thing is that I tried to depict a variety of children playing on the hills that bookend the story. I didn't want to show their faces in hopes that kids could see themselves as one of those children. Other than that, it's a book that deals with art and shapes in clouds, subjects that hopefully can be enjoyed by people everywhere.

FLA: Will we see more of the children's book and comic book in the future?

RM: I would like to. I have a few more stories I'd like to share. It might be awhile before I get to them because of the kids' books, but I'm figuring out how to put the pieces together along the way.

Rafael Navarro

Rafael Navarro was born in 1967 in the border town of Nogales, Mexico. He notes jovially that due to a technical glitch, he is registered as having been born on August 21, when he was actually born on the 19th. After the age of two, Navarro spent the majority of his life in the United States—in the sleepy barrio of Bell Gardens, which abuts East Los Angeles—only going back and forth across the border once or twice a year for summer vacation. Mostly Mexico came to inhabit, as he says, his dreams.

By the age of seven, Rafael had become enamored of comic books. It wasn't those issues of *Spider-Man*, *New X-Men*, and *Tomb of Dracula* that all his peers were reading that did it for Rafael, although later they did. While comics like *Archie* were passed down to Rafael, it was at his local liquor store, Tick Tock, that he first saw the eye-catching, flashing red, white, and blue of *Captain America* (issue 183, in which he appears on the cover crucified). Frank Robbins's artwork jumped out from the stand. Navarro also found himself drawn to the legendary Jack Kirby reprints of the '60s issues of *Captain America* (*Marvel Double Feature*) and anything by Jim Steranko—all of which turned him permanently in the direction of the comic book world.

That these comic books were created by real people turned on a light for Navarro: he realized for the first time that he didn't have to aspire to be a marine, a fireman, or a plumber, but could be a professional comic-book creator like Stan Lee and Jack Kirby. So not only did Navarro continue to read comic books, but did so with an eye to studying and practicing the art form. They also inspired and enlightened him to read more.

After graduating from Bell Gardens High School, and with his heart and soul in comics and his eyes set on training in sequential art, he attended Woodbury University in Los Angeles. He was unable to afford Joe Kubert's School of Visual Arts in New York. At Woodbury, he majored in graphic design, but designing logos wasn't exactly what he wanted to study, so he moved on to see what he could learn from Otis [College of Art and Design], Cal Arts, and Cerritos College. (This is what Rafael refers to as his "Bruce Wayne period of education.") All of his experiences, including graphics, life drawing, watercolor, and oil paint, would later play a role in his own comic book storytelling.

In 1988, he took a pencil test at DC that led to a freelance career as a comic penciler; he has worked also for Marvel and Dark Horse. While he left comics for animation—and he continues to work as a storyboard artist for various animation studios—it wasn't long before he began to create his own comic book, *Sonambulo*.

Having lived most of his life in and around Los Angeles (after Bell Gardens, he moved to La Habra, then Whittier), he likens himself to fictional detective Philip Marlowe, in that no matter where his work takes him, his base of operation will always be the City of Angels. He continues to live in Whittier, where he creates *Sonambulo*. His Web site is www.sonambulo.com.

FREDERICK LUIS ALDAMA: Jack Kirby's, Frank Robbins's, and Jim Steranko's superheroes had a big impact on you as a kid. Do they still play a role in your work today?

RAFAEL NAVARRO: They were my comic book superhero 101 experience. They led to where I am now. To this day, I still go back to it. I've been a scholar of this genre ever since. You have to always go back to the basic fundamentals to understand how things are made, how the rules work, so you can remember how to break them when the time comes. Even today, I stop to go pay homage to them. As far as I'm concerned, the new comic books produced today all pretty much look alike.

FLA: Why the comic book as a vehicle to tell your stories?

RN: My first love has always been comics; my second is animation. With comic books, it's a primal thing. The way it's told with pictures and words taught me—inspired me—to read and to tell stories.

FLA: At what point were you aware that there weren't any Latinos in comic books?

RN: Noticing Latinos concerns (representation or otherwise) in the comic industry happened as an adult, when I was sophisticated enough to realize such things. In my first year of college or so, I began to expose myself to nonmainstream comic books. I think Robert Crumb was one of the first cats that put me into that spectrum. Around that same time of the '80s, pioneers like the Hernandez brothers really brought it home like you wouldn't believe. For the first time, I was reading comics that were literally speaking to me. Every time I opened an issue and saw its background characters, I felt they were drawing my family.

Los Bros proved that Latinos in comics could be done—that you could tell a story from the perspective of what you know. That's why, when it came to creating my own, instead of doing just another macho, long-john-underwear story, I'd write from my own cultural perspective.

FLA: Is this when *Sonambulo* arrived on the scene?

RN: *Sonambulo* is this giant burrito that wraps up all the things I've always loved, either from my culture or just stories in general. From Mexican luchadores, folklore, to horror, sci-fi, and noir films—especially noir. He's Mexico's equivalent of the U.S. superhero, the luchador: an ordinary person that becomes larger than life once they put on their mask. They disguise themselves to protect their own personal lives and family. Creating a luchador superhero was also a way to bring in rich indigenous and folkloric Mexican culture.

I don't want to get too much into the origin of his hereditary and cultural power. He'll discover this later. To a certain point, I've already introduced these elements, but I am going to explore this idea of who he really, truly is and why he's got this wacky power and why he can't sleep, in much more detail later in the series.

FLA: Can you talk about your experiences with trying to break into the market with *Sonambulo*?

RN: When I created Sonambulo in 1996, there was no market. The independents were around, but it was the mainstream comics that were calling the shots. We all know how the story ends for one of the first successful independent superhero comics, Whizz Comics' *Captain Marvel*.

Ten years ago here, there was no market for a luchador comic book hero. In Mexico, the luchadores were the norm, even celebrated like the samurai in Japan, but here they weren't even known. So I thought, what the heck, I'm going to create a noir-atmosphered, larger-than-life luchador who will represent everything I have learned and loved in my life.

The important thing was that he would be a Latino. He would be a person that has walked in the same kind of shoes that I have and that I'm familiar with.

This is the inspiration that drives me to create *Sonambulo*.

It's ten years later, and I see that Marvel and DC have created Mexican-wrestler comic-book superheroes. Dark Horse has done their version too. If I'm to blame for any of that at all, whatsoever, I'm grateful for that.

FLA: Did you have to establish your own publishing machine to get *Sonambulo* out?

RN: At the time, I was freelancing for Dark Horse, so I seriously considered taking it to them. Eventually I chose to just do it myself because, like most creators, I'm a control freak.

Independent comics are not just done because one can't find a publisher. It's to have as much control over the comic as possible. If you have a job and income independent of the comic book, you have a greater degree of artistic expression. This is its creative strength. This is the main reason why I continue to draw *Sonambulo*. In fact, I'm doing it right now.

After ten years of publication, it's finally reached a financial advantage, but I never went into it thinking of profits as its reason and purpose. I will continue to create *Sonambulo* for as long as I get at least one fan letter that asks about how I might end a particular story line. That's good enough for me. Movie deals and everything else—I mean, that's just icing on the cake. I don't count on it, but if it's going to happen, cool. It's another incentive to continue to work.

FLA: With a job and a life, how do you manage to make time to create *Sonambulo*?

RN: After a long eight to ten hours a day working for someone else at the studio, it is really hard to get motivated to do my own work. But it can be done. The first half of the *Sonambulo* books were squeezed into those couple of hours right after work. I'd be in bed by two or three AM, then be back up again for another day working on the *Rugrats* show. It gets taxing after a while, but that's why you have to pace yourself.

If you really, really want something, you make the time and make the sacrifices. Right now I'm on hiatus from this particular show for three-four weeks, so I'm using the time to get my book done. After which, I'll have to go back and report for duty at some studio. God willing, when I do get home, I won't be too tired to finish the book that I'm currently working on.

FLA: How about your creative process, from conception to the inking of the final line?

RN: Some people have this fantastic gift where they can just sit down and start writing what's going to happen: act 1, scene 1, panel 1 is an establishing shot of the top of a building. Enter, a luminous, mysterious figure. Cut closer to character. Character revealed to be the villain. People can do that really out in their head. They establish a script and a strong structure then draw it panel by panel from there. For me, I'm lucky if I might remember my name after I get out of work.

I'm a visual person by nature. So I do a breakdown of how I think it's going to work. I give myself a certain amount of pages I'm going to be doing—usually a thirty-two-page book—and try to get to a certain point of the story and explanation by this final page. I might also decide to hold certain explanations till the next issue. I have some backstory ideas and structures already in mind that I develop along the way. And I revise, too, as I go along. Sometimes the dialogue sounds really funny when I read it out loud on its own, but then when I actually put it with the images, sometimes the verbiage doesn't actually fit what you've got going there. On the spot, I revise the dialogue. I redraw, rework, rewrite till the last minute. If I were working with a company, I'd be driving them crazy, literally on the eleventh hour, pulling a certain scene out and reworking it completely because it didn't meet my expectations.

At the same time that I like to keep it pretty free for revision till the very end, even as late as the inking, I keep in mind a certain structure and schedule with a deadline.

FLA: Does this sense of a basic structure also mean you have an overall vision for the series?

RN: Even among the seeming chaos of filling in the gaps and building his mythology, I have some kind of structure, including a sense of an ending to this character's life and career. But there are a lot of questions I haven't answered yet. That's half the fun of creating the book. I'm constantly thinking of different things. So I have an idea of the overall structure, but then I need to add things, like embellishing his background. Then there's the future. What's going to happen tomorrow? Who knows? You can only figure this out once you arrive at that next bridge that needs crossing.

FLA: You mentioned the luchadors and film noir as influences. What about other media?

RN: I love telling stories by laying things out like a film: the establishing shot, cut to a medium shot, then pull back, then cut to a close-up, all for dramatic purposes. I love the whole creative process of film. Filmmakers like Fellini, Leone, Orson Welles, Fritz Lang, Howard Hawks, Akira Kurosawa, Federico Curiel from Mexico, David Lean, David Lynch, and Robert Rodriguez—even B-movie guys like Ed Wood—have all had a major impact on my work.

Take Sergio Leone, who could take the most insignificant moment in mankind's history—some petty little duel between some bounty-hunter-drifter guy from Iowa, a Mexican bandit, and a vicious, cold-blooded killer out in an insignificant cemetery in the middle of the Civil War, over $20,000 in gold—and make it seem like the single most important clashing of gods over the fate of the universe! Now, that, my friend, is storytelling.

FLA: Literature and other arts?

RN: As far as I'm concerned, García Márquez is the Faulkner of Latin America—of my culture. I'm grateful to have discovered him at an early age. And there's Dostoevsky, Maxwell Grant aka Walter Gibson, and Louis Rhead. Then there are the true anime masters like Ozamu Tezuka and Mitsuteru Yokoyama, the creators of Junguro Taite (*Kimba*) and Tetsujin 28 (*Gigantor*)—two of my favorite comics characters of all time. Culturally, they're from another part of the world, but they're all following a similar philosophy and tapping into similar thought patterns: we are all here for a reason.

FLA: Latino comic book authors that have inspired?

RN: Los Bros Hernandez's slice-of-life stories written from a Latino perspective were wonderful. They were profound. And still are. You could feel the tragedy, the joy, the transformation. You could feel these characters living and breathing as if they were people you knew.

FLA: You complicate fairly conventional romance and adventure narratives?

RN: I don't think I have an actual method. If I take certain genres and mix them up or put characters in weird situations, it just happens. Life is complicated to begin with. And if you're going to tell a story that's defined as a romantic story, just as in life, as you proceed, things happen along the way: a death in the family; a big, giant robot army comes down from space to destroy your home; the IRS comes down upon your small business. This will have an effect on the moment and the situation of the romance story. That's what complicates it.

FLA: Your plots tend to be quite complex, not just going from A to Z, but from A to R to B to C . . .

RN: Then you jump back to Q. Stories just take me that way along this nonlinear path. I mean look how Tarantino begins *Pulp Fiction* chronologically in the middle of the actual story and has chronologically the beginning of the story in the middle.

When I start a story, I usually know the ending just as I'm about to put down the very first stroke of ink on the paper on that first page. I just don't know the middle. So it's just a matter of figuring out along the way how to get to the ending.

FLA: When you're doing the story itself, do you have that ideal audience in mind, the audience that picks up on all of your twists and turns, references, and so on?

RN: When I first started *Sonambulo*, ten years ago, the only audience was myself. There was no market for this weird, abstract character of a luchador detective who has the ability to read people's minds. Now I have a fan base that challenges me in the letters that they write. They expect something weird and different from me. In return, I try to challenge them by giving them something different along the way. I try to answer to those readers who want something bizarre, all while creating something that pleases myself.

Right after I did *Ghost of a Chance*—a fairly straightforward romance with a little bit more depth of character given to Sonambulo, a glimpse into his own soul and a forlorn love—I began receiving letters and e-mail from female fans. I gave him a forlorn love that never saw its final coming until the very end. It was quite refreshing at the time for me, eventually increasing my fan base.

FLA: Can you talk about your use of point of view and voice in *Sonambulo*?

RN: Unless I'm cutting to different scenes where I shift point of view, most of the stories are told from Sonambulo's first-person perspective—as per the classic, Chandler's Philip Marlowe tradition: "It was on a cold night in December in 2004 when I saw her. She walked into my office at three in the morning, and I had nothing better to do, so I stood there and I just gazed at her. And I was trying really hard not to look at her breasts."

FLA: How do you conceive of the way the voice interacts with the visual images?

RN: Sometimes I write the story down in a script form that I then print out and follow. Sometimes I just work it out as a storyboard visually, allowing the visual itself to carry the story forward without narration or dialogue. It depends on the scene. Sometimes less is said by just action alone. But there are other times when something has to be addressed fully and wholeheartedly with every honest word you can possibly think of at that moment.

Therein lies the true storytelling art: to know the difference between subtlety and something bombastic.

FLA: Sometimes you use gutters more prominently and others less so. Sometimes your panels vary radically in shape and size.

RN: That's the beauty of the design features of comics. Animation storyboards have page after page after page, three panels per page, of the same shot with slight changes. Comics, on the other hand, work with more design elements. As long as you follow certain visual conventions—in American comics, it's left to right—you can design anything.

I like doing traditional shots: the long rectangular shots to establish a scene, then cut closer to introduce characters. But I also like doing weird, abstract shots, like extreme close-ups of a character's face.

If you can actually tell a story in a way where you can cut to those extreme close-ups to show drama and tension and emotion and also establish enough prior background information in a long shot without losing your readers, then you're doing a good job.

FLA: The rhythms of your cuts and edits create a certain mood?

RN: Yes, but there's also the lighting that creates ambience. Film noir is wondrous for that. With small budgets, it was all about lighting: lighting in specific ways a figure standing in front of venetian blinds to convey that striking sense of drama.

FLA: Each character has his or her own voice that can also capture a certain mood?

RN: It's all about the art of language and how this conveys the psychology of character. If the character's surly, then I'll use a language and approach the scene in that emotion. I always thought of Sonambulo as a self-educated guy. With this comes a certain confidence in self-experience: he's very comfortable with himself and confident about where he stands on issues. He's this simple, two-fisted guy with a semirighteous view of the world. At the same time, he knows he's flawed, that he does the best he can then moves on. Then there are the other characters, like the intellectual professor. He's stuffy, but he's also just as human as the next guy: his heart problem, lost wife, and he files his taxes. He's got to deal with all the other day-to-day trivialities as everyone else.

The beauty of creating a certain world with these characters and their own inner complexities is really fascinating. And just when you think you know the character in one scene, in another interaction with another complex character, he shows you a different side. At this moment, he's actually something else.

FLA: In the issue *Mexican Standoff*, Sonambulo addresses the audience: "By now you're probably wondering how this will end. Me too." You play with tense here and elsewhere.

RN: This is a personal nod to the film noir that's usually told in a past tense. In *Double Indemnity*, Fred MacMurray comes into the office, and he's been shot, and he knows he's bleeding to death, and he sits down, and he starts recording this message to his partner, played by Edward G. Robinson: "Remember that girl I told you about. Well, you know . . . By the time you read this, I'm probably going to be dead. So, therefore, I'm going to tell you what really happened . . ." At the same time that I pay homage to this narrative device in noir, there's this sense that Sonambulo is the storyteller, but one who doesn't have the power to determine the end of the story. He's in a crappy situation, and he also wants to know how it will end.

FLA: You use black-and-white and not color?

RN: Most mainstream comics are designed for color. Therefore, in the production and design, there are a lot of open spaces, flat shots, outlines that are going to be filled with color. It's the coloring-book story approach to layout and design. On the other hand, if you're working with black and white, you can add a little bit more detail or black certain things out, pick up a silhouette.

I would like to have the possibility of marrying both. Just as there are some books I would have loved to color, there are others where it would be a complete mortal sin if I colored them.

From the very beginning I knew with *Sonambulo* that I would be working in a black-and-white format. So I went out of my way to specifically design it in a noir fashion, to use lighting to create the atmosphere and sense of suspense.

FLA: Why give Sonambulo the power to read dreams?

RN: All artists are all dreamers to some extent. I've always been fascinated with the subconscious, analyzing the symbolism of dreams. I always liked the idea of a character who could actually read people's subconscious. Sonambulo became that figure—a merchant of dreams, a custodian of the subconscious. Whether he wants to or not, he just knows you. He probably knows you better than you do yourself because he knows your hopes, your dreams, your fears, your most hidden, innermost thoughts. This is quite a power—to know you even before you do. He uses his power to get clues, to get a better idea who he's dealing with, and to get to the truth.

FLA: Sonambulo is sympathetic to the plight of others, but he's also an old-school macho.

RN: He's open-minded, but he's also a fundamentalist, in the sense that he falls back on old values of good and bad. But at least you know where he stands on things, to some extent. And sometimes, you know, half the fun is just chasing the riddle itself. Sometimes you'll never have the answer. And like I said, you spend your whole lifetime trying to find out a certain answer, and in the end you still don't find out, but it was fun chasing and pursuing that thought at the moment. And that's Sonambulo too. His path is uncertain in this strange new world, but he has his old-school values to fall back on.

Sonambulo's Strange Tales, Issue 1

FLA: You're a young creator, and Sonambulo's a sixty-something luchador detective.

RN: I'm of another era and mental decade than Sonambulo, who is from this late-1940s–early-1950s period. He came before the sexual revolution, and the biggest element of fear in his world were Nazis. I wanted him to be sort of progressive, but at the same time, I have to keep in mind that I'm trying to capture an old-fashioned mindset.

FLA: Often a good comic book story is one where the villains are as complicated as the heroes.

RN: True. In the first story line, the greatest villain really wasn't cult leader Eugene, who had this weird, cryptic, satanic power of being able to resurrect mindless starlet zombies. There's something creepy about this, sure. But the biggest villain was the senator. He was complete trash. According to the world's point of view, he's a benign man, a man of God, a man of great respect. Yet we know that he does these vile things on the side. It's about telling stories that introduce the flawed world that we live in.

FLA: Moving readers is also an important ingredient for the comic book story.

RN: I'd say so. If you can use words and images to strike an emotional chord or trigger those primal instincts of anger, sadness, happiness, then you're doing a great job. If you can do this with the written word and draw pictures that move your reader, that is power.

Without question, my ultimate goal is to move my readers. To convince them that my fictional world actually exists—that I'd been there and back, and that they've experienced and felt this world with me—that is my ultimate goal.

FLA: Are there certain ingredients that make the comic book world Latino?

RN: Michael Aushenker created a comic book, *El Gato: Crime Mangler*, about

YOUR BRAIN ON LATINO COMICS

a gorilla-sized Mexican wrestler living in the 1930s. It's impressive and funny as all heck! I absolutely loved it! Yet Mike is Jewish. Not that it actually matters, but I mean where did all this fantastic cultural influence come from?

I don't think you have to necessarily be an Eskimo—it might help—to write a book about Eskimos. You don't have to be a Latino to write about Latinos, but it helps. If your heart's in it, then it doesn't matter who you are doing the storytelling.

FLA: Current and future projects?

RN: I'm currently finishing up the final issue to the *Sonambulo* story line, called *Mexican Standoff*. I'm wrapping up this one-shot full-color comic book, *Mac Afro*, for another independent publishing company, Atomic Basement. It's as if blaxploitation director Melvin Van Peebles was given the *Blade Runner* script and an endless budget, and made it from the perspective of 1972. Its funky Los Angeles in the future, and visually one of the single greatest things I've ever done. I've just contributed to the anthology, *Hot Mexican Love*, where I visually adapt Marty Robbins's tragic western song "El Paso" into comic book form. On the day-job level, I'm about to embark on a new animation project from the creators of *Mucha Lucha* called *Los Campeones de la Lucha Libre* for Univision.

FLA: Any last comments?

RN: Sleep is for sissies, remember that!

Anthony Oropeza

Anthony was born in Kansas City, Missouri, in 1969. A third-generation Mexican American, he grew up in a mixed Anglo, Latino, and African American neighborhood or district known as Argentine. A product of a divorce and a single-parent family, he, with his three younger siblings, was raised by his mother from the age of about six. His mother is from Kansas City, Missouri, and his father is from Kansas City, Kansas; their parents were bilingual. Because of the farming industry, meatpacking industry, and railroad, many Latinos were drawn to Kansas City. Oropeza's grandfathers worked for the railroad and steel industries, while his father worked for the railroad for thirty-seven years, and his mother worked over twenty-six years as a bundler for a local corrugated-box company. It was working at that corrugated-box company one summer in 110-degree heat that made Oropeza decide to finish college. At the time, he could never figure out how his mother endured the heat and cold of that factory for so many years. Now, a father himself, he understands.

At a young age, Oropeza wouldn't buy comics, but rather looked at hand-me-down coverless comic books (those sold for a nickel) of the army-comics variety and also *Captain America*. He was fascinated by the artwork and drawings of the superheroes more than the written part of the story. That the good guy would always win the day, whether a superhero or a soldier battling evil Nazis, appealed to his nascent ethical sensibility.

In his twenties, while taking communication classes at Rochurst College, a local Jesuit school, and becoming attuned to questions of audience demographic, he realized one day while in a comic shop that among the sea of Marvel and DC comics there were a few local African American independents and some Asian ones (ninjas or karate fighters), but absolutely no Latinos. He wondered why there weren't any superheroes with a similar skin color and ethnic background. This is when Oropeza decided to create a superhero

YOUR BRAIN ON LATINO COMICS

who would represent someone from his cultural background and neighborhood. On the drive home from that comic shop, he came up with a name for this superhero that would work in Spanish and English: Amigoman. Then he began to fill out the character: his background, occupation, age, biography, psychological profile, experiences. Would he make him Cuban, Mexican, or Dominican? he asked himself. What kind of costume would he wear? All of these decisions were also shaped by his developing sense of what type of audience he would like Amigoman to appeal to and how he would like to affect in particular ways this audience: how they would see him, and what they would think or feel about him.

After years of development, while the author-artist was going to college and holding a full-time job, Oropeza's Amigoman was born—the first Latino superhero from the Midwest. Oropeza continues to live in the Kansas City area, where he works as a Web development coordinator for a local parks and recreation district, and also continues to produce *Amigoman*, available via his website (www.amigoman.com), and to make guest appearances at local schools and libraries, speaking to kids about teamwork and being creative with your ideas via a comic book. He also conducts free art classes for local kids once a week at the local Argentine library.

FREDERICK LUIS ALDAMA: Is Amigoman Mexican American?

ANTHONY OROPEZA: I don't really specify his Latino ethnicity. I want all my readers to be able to relate to him and his social environment first, so I leave this open-ended. The Latino element is important, but I want the readers to understand larger issues: that he's from a blue-collar working family and that he grew up without a father. Relating to his ethnic origin is secondary in this sense.

FLA: Where did you learn the comic book craft?

AO: I'm mostly self-taught. I'm still learning the art of storytelling. I've never taken a writing class. I picked up bits and pieces from other comic book authors that I've met and who participate in our local comic book club— when I can attend. I also listen to interviews with authors of scripts on TV and read books from the library on, say, how to write the DC way. Because my time is limited, I pick up tidbits here and there. This is how I learn the shortcuts on writing the story.

FLA: The visual art?

AO: I learn by studying what the pros do. I would buy comic books and study their design, layout, and style. I've also learned a lot from Lorenzo Lazana [artist and collaborator], who's done a lot of my pencil work in the last few issues. He's helped me understand why certain angles are used and their effect on the reader. The graphic design skills—color and layout, for example—that I learned in college have also helped shape my visual-art technique.

But I'm still in the learning phase. I'll probably still be learning till the day I die when it comes to the comic book.

FLA: You mention "the pros." So has Marvel or DC influenced your style?

AO: It was the great artwork of both. I didn't really pay attention to names of inkers and artists. I was more into their overall style.

FLA: There are moments when *Amigoman* feels very cinematic.

AO: First of all, I love movies. I like dramas. I'm addicted to TV, and would watch a movie every day if I could. If I had the money, time, patience to direct, I'd try to make a movie. Comic books are a very short version of a movie: like the director who controls how the audience sees the film, the comic book creator does the same for the reader. There are also the angles that work similarly, like the close-up. And in making film and comics, there's the writing, drawing, and storyboarding to make the character work and the story fit within a certain amount of pages.

FLA: Can you talk about the process of creating *Amigoman* specifically?

AO: In general, the process is like this: idea, story outline, script, thumbnail sketches, and edit, edit, and edit, get thumbnails to Lorenzo, then ink his work, scan art, clean up art, place text, proof text, place noncomic pages and edit and proof and proof and edit and pray we have not missed any misspellings and somebody buys a copy.

Right now I'm working with three story lines, including Amigoman's origin story (how he becomes this vigilante out to find the killers of his grandfather). Already I had to figure out if I wanted to make a two-part series or a three-part series. If a two-part series, then how many pages?

I have to understand what my canvas is, then work with it. This will also determine how much dialogue I'm going to use. You can only put so many words in there before it starts becoming too text heavy. The choice of dialogue should be precise enough that it gets my message across effectively. And this choice of dialogue is shaped by my audience. I'm beginning to redo some of the adult-oriented issues (eighteen-to-thirty-five-year-olds) for a younger audience (ten-to-fourteen-year-olds), so the story will be the same but the dialogue and the artwork will be different. There are also other sorts of revisions. I'm redrawing and reediting the earlier issues from 1996 to 2000 with the idea of republishing them in Spanish.

FLA: Was *Amigoman* for a younger audience?

AO: At first, no. The book was set up for the eighteen-plus audience, but after the third issue, a couple of the libraries in the area started taking to them, so I started thinking about creating issues for fifteen-year-olds and younger—and now am in the process of creating something for the two-to-five-year-olds. Our *Frankenstein* book has a "K+" rating so parents know that it's okay for their five-year-old to read one of my comic books. Being able to see that the younger audience is starting to take to my book has made me rethink and adjust to that audience.

FLA: You first began creating *Amigoman* in the early 1990s, then took a break to return to it only recently.

AO: Working with a great artist like Lorenzo has made me want to take my time in putting the revisions of the earlier issues out—from the redoing of the layout to the editing of the English and getting the best translations into Spanish. I want them done as well as possible.

FLA: Difficulty breaking into national markets?

AO: Right now, yes, it is difficult. No one knows of me yet, and I don't have the connections I need. I also need to put out better books and promote them well. And I don't feel that what I have today is ready for national publication. But our work is getting better. If I'm going to submit something to a publisher or marketing company, I have to show them the best work that we can put out. I'd have to show them a complete package: the books, the story, style guide (images of all the characters, their colors, from eyes to skin to clothing), and the environment that my characters live and work within (buildings, schools, house, car). I'll also need the kids' books as well as other projects, say, an *Amigoman* CD-ROM for learning Spanish. Right now I could take them some comics and an idea, but that's not enough. They want to have certain solid stuff before they'll look at you, and I'm not ready yet. But we will be soon.

FLA: Who is your main audience?

AO: Right now, the kids in elementary, junior high, and those who go to the local libraries. But hopefully we'll hit all age groups. Our *Amigoman* story has the potential to reach all audiences of all ages and races.

FLA: Amigoman teaches history at high school and is for the most part a pretty regular guy.

AO: The media has thrown us these images of Latinos as drug dealer, gangbanger, thief, fat, sloppy, bean-eating stereotypes. Today, too, we're seeing more Latinos of a less stereotypical character. Of course, they are all pretty boys or very beautiful women, but they are better roles. So I wanted readers, the viewers, to see that we are not all gangbangers or drug dealers;

that we might be high school teachers who finished college, like to watch baseball, work out, eat protein shakes, read books, etc.—all the stuff that white America does.

For the young readers, my goal is to provide them a positive role model with Antonio Alvarado and with Amigoman. That if you are in a bad spot, you can still find a way to pick yourself up. That you can finish high school and do something positive with your life even if your past is a little tarnished.

In the case of Antonio's grandfather, I want the readers to see that even if you are trained one way—he's a military guy—you can choose to learn other ways of life and other cultures. He learns martial arts and uses Confucius's sayings to teach Antonio.

FLA: Do you consider *Amigoman* to be doing the work of a kind of cultural literacy?

AO: I grew up in a Latino neighborhood with a Latino family, but we listened to '50s and '60s rhythm and blues. My dad would listen to Frank Sinatra and Spanish music, and my uncles played the oldies and all R&B and soul. In junior high and high school, I was exposed to rock and roll, and in the '80s I was a teenager with the birth of rap. I enjoy reading Confucius. I love to read about famous people, and have been intrigued with the concepts behind martial arts and love all different types of art. And being exposed to not only my brown culture, I have been exposed to the white, black, and even Asian cultures as well. It's this kind of fusion of cultures that I hope to bring to the reader.

FLA: You use a lot of techniques—panel layout, shading, and lighting. Is this to give an overall mood to *Amigoman*?

AO: Yes. Because I work with black-and-white, like a Hitchcock film, it is the lighting that sets the mood. If it's a happier mood and the characters are outside, then the inking's not going to be as heavy.

As far as the panels, nowadays I give Lorenzo the thumbnail layout of the different views (bird's-eye view or worm's-eye view) and a script. He'll read the script, and if he thinks that it needs to be a different angle, or a close-up, then he will make that adjustment. He then pencils it in. If he can pick up on the mood, he will put the black in there where it needs to be, whether it's in the background, foreground, or on the character. If he doesn't, then I'll try to figure out where I need to put more, say, black in. Because he understands the story line, he understands the story and the characters. For the most part, everything Lorenzo's done is right on. He's a great talent.

FLA: Why black-and-white instead of color?

AO: It costs a lot of money to print in color. I don't have a large enough fan base to support this, so I print them out in black-and-white in small bulk, then send them out. Even in black-and-white, with a minimum print run of a thousand copies it comes out to about two bucks a book; with color it would cost me three-fifty a book. It's just not cost-effective to do color for the everyday working class.

At least with the black-and-white I can focus on producing quality books with a good story and good artwork that people will want to read.

FLA: How do you build your readership?

AO: Its promotion, promotion, and promotion. The Internet has helped, but it's usually after I make an appearance somewhere and introduce and explain the story of my character. Comic conventions don't really work, because they are on weekends, when the younger readers are out playing soccer or baseball. That's why I go to the libraries or schools to reach the kids. I offer the books at cost or free and also give them free coloring pages or bookmarks. Of course, it is more work, and it is time-consuming, but, you know, the kids are enthusiastic and I love talking to them about my book and showing them our artwork.

FLA: Why the picture of Cesar Chavez in Antonio's study?

AO: Comic book artists do this all the time. They'll try to sneak something in there like a drawing of a friend or relative in a crowd for that reader who will notice it. Also, the image of Cesar Chavez tells the reader something about the character: that he has respect for Latino cultural history, and like an African American might post a Dr. Martin Luther King Jr., our character posts up someone like Mr. Chavez. He was a great man.

FLA: How do you imagine the panel and gutter working together?

AO: I attempt to make a page that will stand alone. Drawings and the panel layout should be effective. You can have fifteen rectangular panels all stacked up on each other on one page, but the artwork within it has to be effective and has to work within those panels. If not, you change the panels. And if you were to keep the artwork, you change the design of the panels. Or vice versa. You change the artwork to fit within the panels.

I can draw five or six different pages, the same page, five or six different ways with different panel layouts, and only two will be OK. Then you have to determine which of those two is the best.

FLA: The way you stylize the characters?

AO: Some comic books are written as real life. The army ones were lifelike, but others I grew up with weren't real life. They still had a moral to the story, but they were less realistic. My comic book characters have ups and downs, and they struggle. But the way I draw them is a little cartoonish because I didn't want them to come off as real life. It's still a comic book.

FLA: Do you have a sense of responsibility as an author-artist—Latino or otherwise?

AO: Yes. Visiting schools and libraries and meeting seven-, nine-, fifteen-year-olds has given me somewhat of a sense of responsibility. I have started to take them into consideration—as well as their parents—when I write a story. I just want to put out a book that's positive so that, regardless of what race you are, you'll know that everybody has problems but that they can be worked out to get to a better place.

Of course, my character, Amigoman, becomes a vigilante. He doesn't really want to be a vigilante, he's not out to kill, he just wants to find the killer (or killers) of his grandfather. He does everything in his power to find the killers the right way. Only once this fails does he put a mask on to become a vigilante superhero.

FLA: Latino comics today?

AO: For about the last seven years or so, the comic book world has become more diverse. And with Latinos becoming the fastest-growing minority population, this has impacted the representation of Latinos in the media generally. There are not a lot of Latino cartoon and comic books, but they will be coming. I don't write *Amigoman* only for the Latino community. It's an attempt to reach the mainstream.

FLA: Future projects?

AO: I want to translate, redraw, and put color covers on the first three books that I originally did in English, years back. I want to continue working on the bilingual kids' *Amigoman* books, then submit them to a publisher. I have laid out a bilingual comic book on CD that gives the user the option of translating from Spanish to English and vice versa. The ultimate goal is to try to get an animated series, create a line of *Amigoman* products, and then invest the money back into the district of Argentine, where I grew up. But I need to do more work and to work with good, reliable people.

FLA: You have a nine-to-five job and you produce *Amigoman*?

AO: I love doing what I do when it comes to the design stuff and working with Web sites and graphic design at my current job. I need to pay the bills. I was a stay-at-home dad for a while, and it killed me financially, and it hurt my relationship with my kids' mom. And now, with a full-time job, attempting to produce freelance sports art and Web design and graphics work on the side with my small graphics company (AO ART 5), and being a daddy, is a tough gig. I am up until one or two some nights working on projects. I still don't know how my mom did it with four of us. And with all I have on my plate, I have to make time for the *Amigoman* work. I have to hire and pay my artists and translator and then eventually the printer to print the book. All that comes out of my pocket. It's not only time management— it's money management and being creative when working with others.

And what helps keep me going? There are times I wish I could just work my nine-to-five, come home and relax, and go to work the next day. But I guess it's not in my blood. I've always got to have a project to work on. Of course, my girlfriend still doesn't understand that I have something in me that says I have to produce something creative and work on projects, but that's a whole different story in itself. But on the flip side of that, everybody I know is always asking about *Amigoman* and how it's coming along. Everybody is always real positive, and I am really thankful for that. Many of them say it's going to hit, just keep working at it. My brother, who doesn't talk much to me, told me to keep it up, and he also feels it will hit big soon. He actually loaned me the money to purchase the trademark for the character.

And the teachers and kids I talk to at schools and libraries love it and take to it like fish to water. That's the kind of stuff that motivates me. If I were twenty-two, single, and with no daughter, I would take a part-time job and devote myself full time to *Amigoman*, but I can't do that. I have too many responsibilities.

Peter Ramirez

Peter Ramirez was born in 1960 in Brooklyn, New York. Raised primarily by his Puerto Rican–born mother on public assistance, he grew up mainly in the Bronx as the second eldest of three brothers and three sisters. His father, also from Puerto Rico, wasn't much in the picture while he was growing up, so Ramirez acted as the unofficial father figure of the household.

From a young age, Ramirez had a passion for drawing cartoons. It was a way to escape the gritty reality of living in a broken home just below the poverty line. He and his mother and siblings struggled to survive on welfare in the barrio, where Ramirez endured many horrific experiences, such as witnessing the murder of a man just feet away from where he was standing. Comics had a healing value for Ramirez. With a mother who kept a tight rein on Ramirez and his siblings, he wasn't allowed to spend time hanging out on the streets. Instead, he would read comic books and comic strips from the newspapers, and draw. He had an uncanny talent at being able to look at a comic book visual then re-create it identically freehand.

Ramirez was the only one in his family to take up comic book art seriously. After graduating from high school, he earned a BA in graphic design from Long Island University (C. W. Post campus). He was the first person in his family's history to attend and graduate from college. In college, Ramirez was the cartoon editor for the school's *Summit* magazine. In *Summit*, he debuted his first comic strip, *LOUIE*, which followed the adventures of an ornery cartoon character trying to escape his comic strip world. After college, Ramirez went on to work as a political cartoonist for *HOY*, New York *Newsday*'s sister Spanish-language paper, for over 2 years. Here he created political cartoons that touched upon local, national, and international left- and right-wing topics.

While he had a day job as a police officer, his true passion was the creating of comic strips. While working as an undercover narcotics investigator for the New York City Police Department's Organized Crime Control Bureau, Ramirez was badly injured during a "buy and bust" operation in Brooklyn. Unable to continue on the force, he took on the role of stay-at-home dad. This freed up some time, and he was able to create the comic strip *Raising Hector*, which was syndicated by Tribune Media Services.

Ramirez currently lives with his family on Long Island, New York. *Raising Hector* is syndicated in newspapers across the United States and abroad in both English and in Spanish. His work can be seen on his website, www .raisinghector.com, as well as at www.comicspage.com.

FREDERICK LUIS ALDAMA: Can you speak to some of your early experiences with comic books or comic strips?

PETER RAMIREZ: When I'd get my hands on a comic book, it was a rare gift, and I would read it front to back. I wasn't that concerned about race. We lived in poverty, and the comics were a way for me to escape this.

FLA: Was race or ethnicity an issue?

PR: I do remember the Latino character Tarantula in the *Spider-Man* comics. He had all these tattoos, and he was the bad guy. All the Latino characters seemed to be villains.

FLA: How did you come up with the idea of creating the strip, *Raising Hector*?

PR: I didn't create *Raising Hector* to fill a gap by making a Hispanic comic strip. It was more inspired by my own experiences of having to make the transition from macho cop to stay-at-home dad. I thought this transition would be a piece of cake. If I can fight crime, I can stay home and wash the dishes. As time went along, I discovered that it wasn't so easy. That's when I sat down, took a look at members of my family, the gender-role reversal with me and my wife, and then began to conceive of *Raising Hector*—a Latino comic strip for English-language papers.

I could have easily created a strip that fell back on a lot of old stereo-types, but I didn't want to do that. I was sick and tired of seeing Latinos in the media portrayed negatively as drug dealers, junkies, criminals, low-lifes. Rarely do you see them being portrayed in a positive light. I wanted to create a strip that would let the world know that Latinos nowadays are captains of industry. We're professionals, retired cops at home raising kids, and so on.

I felt it my responsibility to enlighten and educate by creating a strip that portrayed a complete family like my own: grandparents, parents, and a son.

FLA: Why the comic strip and not a comic book?

PR: I love the healing power of its laughter. I can work through my own issues, and by sharing it with others and bringing the readers joy, I bring myself great happiness.

FLA: Did you have any formal comic-strip-art training?

PR: Fresh out of college, I studied for six years with Bill and Bunny Hoest, creators of the comic strip *The Lockhorns*. I told Bill I wanted to be a comic strip artist, and he took me under his wing. He not only taught me the art aspect, but he also taught me what to expect from the business end.

FLA: Can you speak to issues of production with *Raising Hector*?

PR: The latest U.S. census statistics indicate that Latinos are the fastest-growing population, and our spending impact is steadily rising. So from a numbers point of view, a Latino comic strip seemed to be the way to go.

Before I submitted the strip to the papers, I wanted to get a feel for how readers would take to it, so in 1999, I started a Web site and then contacted a lot of different colleges and other organizations. I'd invite them to go to the Web site and read the strip and tell me honestly what they thought. I was pleased and mildly surprised at the positive reactions—especially from non-Latinos.

Once it was all ready to go, I approached the syndicates. Unfortunately, they weren't interested. So I self-syndicated.

Around the time when *Raising Hector* came out, there were two other Latino strips. There was Martha Montoya's comic strip called *Los Kitos*, about cutesy animals, and *Baldo* was launched about six months later, after I launched mine. I knew of others that were trying to get their work recognized, but basically we were it.

FLA: *Baldo* was syndicated relatively quickly. Are there certain comic-strip ingredients that the syndicates go for more than others?

PR: *Baldo*'s main character is a teenager, so the marketability is easier than a paunchy, late-thirties– early-forties main character, Hector. But obviously there is more than enough room for *Baldo*, *Raising Hector*, and ten other comic strips. We all offer something a little bit different. We all have different stories; they all should be heard. Instead, they get their one Latino strip and that's it. They say they don't need any more.

FLA: So what happened when you went to the syndicates?

PR: One offered me a development deal, and I worked several months on fine-tuning the artwork, and at the end of the development stage, they decided to pass on it. And another small syndicate offered me a contract, but they were asking for me to have the same workload that I did when I was self-syndicating it. I had just recovered from major surgery, and so I told them it was too much work and that I just could not do it. Had it been a big syndicate, it would have been different.

It didn't help that I made a lot of noise about the fact of there being hardly any nationally syndicated Latino comic strips, that we didn't have any representation. I think that shaking this tree alienated me from the syndicates. It wasn't a question of selling the strip. A gentleman who works for some of the biggest newspapers in the world told me that I could sell this thing with my eyes closed.

Now, I'm happy to say I've recently signed a syndication agreement with Tribune Media Services, Inc., one of the world's largest newspaper syndicates.

FLA: Up till this potential break, how have you been able to stay afloat with *Raising Hector*?

PR: I was fortunate that this wasn't my bread and butter. I had my police pension that would help support my family, along with my wife, who is the executive assistant to the editor in chief for *ESPN Magazine*. This separate monetary income has allowed me to keep my hand in the creating of the comic strip.

FLA: Why the title *Raising Hector*?

PR: Well, because of the new situation that Hector finds himself in. He has no idea of what his new job is, and he's basically starting from scratch. So it's like everybody's taking a hand in raising him, teaching him the new responsibilities that come with the shift from macho-cop breadwinner to stay-at-home dad. He's the baby. And it's everybody's job to raise Hector. I chose the name "Hector" to honor a friend and fellow police officer who was tragically killed in the line of duty.

FLA: Can you break down the process of imagining, developing the story, writing, drawing, and inking the strip?

PR: The story is easy because it's autobiographical. Whenever my son or I screw up, I get a gag out of it. I've got various notepads all over my house, and whenever a gag pops into my head, I write it down or record it.

I also always keep in mind that people go to the comic strips to read, enjoy, and then move on. They don't want to spend a lot of time thinking about a gag. There's really no reason for them to sit there and contemplate world events while reading the comics section. They go there to have a good time. So everything has to be fast and funny.

You can't get too technical with the drawings, and timing is important. It's like you're doing stand-up comedy but with pictures, so you have to develop a rhythm. That's why I keep my drawings pretty simple: so the words have a punch-line effect.

I use my computer, and I draw everything by hand. A lot of guys use specialized computer equipment like digitizing tablets, where they'll draw it directly onto the tablet and pop it onto the computers. I pencil everything out, make sure it's the way I want it, and then I take out the old tried-and-true artist's pen that you dip into the black ink, and I draw it out. Of course, I incorporate a little bit of modern technology, using the scanner to move everything into my computer. But I do this more to save time than anything else.

FLA: Cartoon images rely on drawing types that allow the reader a ready identification of the character's personality—if they're good, bad, or whatever. Are there ways that you complicate the Latino types in the strip?

PR: I'm just describing my life through the life of the characters. If it turns out that I'm dispelling some stereotypes, then that's the way it is.

My goal is to make people laugh so they can identify positively with the characters—rambunctious children are rambunctious children in any culture—then maybe enlighten them about Latinos. I want to show our similarities and then our differences. We all can slip and fall on a banana peel, but it's how each culture handles it that makes each of us different. So while the reader's getting a laugh out of it, they may end up learning something about Latinos.

FLA: Some of your inspirations and influences?

PR: Marvel comics. I started collecting comics as a kid; today I have about 7,000 comics in my collection. Comic strips that have been a big influence include Bill and Bunny Hoest's *The Lockhorns* as well as Schulz's *Peanuts*. When Charles Shulz died, I was invited to draw a strip in his memory, and had my drawing included in a memorial book dedicated to Mr. Schulz—the original cartoon is on display at the Schulz Museum in California. I'm also a big fan of Bill Watterson's *Calvin and Hobbes* because he incorporates humor with a message. There's laughter—the reactions on the faces—at the same time that there's these serious words of wisdom that come out of an eight-year-old boy and his stuffed tiger. They convey a message and get the reader thinking. That's what I'm trying to emulate in *Raising Hector*.

FLA: You mentioned your love of Marvel comics. Why not tell stories in the comic book form?

PR: The comic strip's humor is important; it's always been very healing for me and the reader. Whether in grade school, or in college on a message board, or with a Magic Marker on my dorm-room wall, people just enjoy laughing at all my little cartoon drawings. I knew from my response and those of others to my cartoons that comic strips and not comic books were what I wanted to do.

FLA: The setting is vague, and so are the cultural particularities of the Latino family. They could be Puerto Rican, Chicano, or Cubano . . .

PR: No. I didn't specify the city or the specific cultural identity of the family, but I do mention specific cultural traditions in terms of holidays like Cinco de Mayo and address their historical significance. If I can find something good to say about a given Latino tradition, then I'll pass this on to the readers. It's a form of cultural literacy.

FLA: What kind of audience do you have in mind when you're creating the strip?

PR: People my age. First- and second-generation Latinos. Migrants from Puerto Rico, Mexico, or whatever country who all find themselves in the same type of situation I have found myself in: first generation born in the U.S. with parents who still try to hold onto old family values and traditions and with kids that try to move us forward into the future with their iPods and Internet. You feel as if you're being pulled in all sorts of directions. My hope is that the reader will identify with the cultural push and pull that Hector deals with daily.

FLA: You create both multiple-panel strips and the single-panel strip *The Deep End*. Is there a different process in terms of how you imagine the visuals and the text working?

PR: I like being able to control the action, movement, and pace of the longer strip story. The single-panel strip can be great too, but, really, it's a way for a newspaper to conserve space. It's why newspaper syndicates love the single-panel comic strips: because you can have at least two single-panel strips in the same space that you might only be able to have one multiple-panel strip. The more single-panel strips you can fit on a page, the more they sell, and the more money they make.

With *The Deep End*, I wanted to capture in a single panel different scenarios when you find yourself in the deep end of things, when you react differently to normal. So I take everyday occurrences, then figure a caption that will say something funny about the situation, then figure out a drawing that will work with the caption to deliver the punch line, the gag. Sometimes I start with the drawing, then develop the punch line.

FLA: You talked about humor as a source of healing.

PR: I want my drawing to capture the mood: the humor or sadness or whatever. There's no special sound effects here, so I rely on the drawing to deliver the mood and the punch line.

FLA: The strip is shorter than the comic book, but is there still room enough for the characters to experience a transformation?

PR: Basically, there are two types of comic strips: those where the characters do age, like Lynn Johnston's *For Better or For Worse*, and the others, like Shulz's *Peanuts*, where the characters remain eternally young. Just as I've changed, so too is there change in *Raising Hector*. At the same time, I don't want to slow the reader down with too much transformation. They've got to be able to get to the punch line.

FLA: What makes a comic strip Latino?

PR: I think it's how you appreciate and represent Latino culture. The importance of family is central to being Latino as well as that craziness of being pulled by the old and new generations. I'm not sure if you could come up with the gags that convey these unique feelings and cultural pressures if you weren't Latino.

FLA: We've certainly made great strides in terms of self-representation, but we still have a long way to go.

PR: Yes, they still have Anglos writing Latino and other multicultural characters. It's sort of like Al Pacino playing Tony Montana—as if audiences wouldn't know the difference between an Italian and Cuban?

FLA: Current and future projects?

PR: While my main concern is still *Raising Hector*, I'm still fine tuning *The Deep End* to send out to the syndicates. I have some other family-based strips in mind, but haven't decided whether or not to make them Latino. I may venture back into creating political cartoons, something I did for two years for a local New York paper.

Fernando Rodriguez

Fernando Rodriguez was born in El Salto, Michoacán, Mexico, but was raised his entire life in San Jose, California, with his younger brother and sister. He started reading comic books in the first grade when he discovered a local paper-recycling warehouse, where he found dozens of heroes, resplendent with intergalactic fantasy and lore. Several of these comics—*Avengers*, *Iron Man*, *Prince Namor*, *Spider-Man*, *The Surfer*, *Hulk*, *X-Men*—would become the foundation for his literary and art appreciation as well as the springboard for learning and sharpening his own comic-book storytelling craft. He realized his goal of creating a Latino superhero in 1993 with his series *Aztec of the City*. More recently, Fernando added two new comic book titles to the Latino super-hero fold: *Adelita: Tales of Aztlan* and also *Super Latino*.

Fernando lives in Rosarito, Baja California, Mexico, where he continues to create *Aztec of the City* and *Super Latino*.

FREDERICK LUIS ALDAMA: Can you speak to some of your inspirations?

FERNANDO RODRIGUEZ: There was an article in the *San Jose Mercury News* in late '92 that totally influenced me. It was about two young black kids (nine and twenty-two years old) who, out of Oakland, California, created, wrote, and did the art for their self-publishing venture of a comic book they called *The Cipher*. After that, I bought four issues of *BrotherMan* by the Simms Bros from Dallas, Texas, and that pretty much did it for me, because I saw how these African American contemporary visionaries sought to put black heroes, black stories into the comic book realm.

Also about that time, I'd been reading a lot of Ostrander's DC *Spectre* and DC's *Deadman* series—and *Dr. Strange*, with his ghost-like abilities—that I think drew me towards the spiritual concept origin of *Aztec Of the City*. I did this knowing I could somehow tie the Aztec with Cuauhtémoc down the road, because I'd read back in '87 *The Conquest of Mexico*, by Bernal Díaz, and how the prince was ultimately hanged. Like Eastwood in *Hang 'Em High*, rebel Aztecs trailing Cortés's minions could have cut the prince down, saving his life. And later they would draw from him the vial of blood preserved through the ages, which would contribute to the resurrection or rise from the coma of Tony Avalos in modern-day America.

Tales of Aztlan, Issue 1

Inspirations too came from a well of books, especially those on Latinos and Natives in professional football, like Engine Joe Kapp and Jim Plunkett. I thought with a comic book title, *Tales of Aztlan*, I could tell those same biographical stories in comic book form. I thought, too, of Cesar Chavez, but was stonewalled with some rhetoric about trademarks and such by the corporation and family members that run the show now. So I ended up printing my first *Tales of Aztlan* about the legend of La Llorona.

FLA: Other influences?

FR: I grew up watching pre-cable black-and-white shows like *Time Tunnel*, *Land of the Giants*, *Twilight Zone*—Rod Serling, too, was an idol of mine—as well as the early animation cartoons *Fantastic Four*, *Sub-Mariner*, *Captain America*. I also watched with regularity *The Herculoids*, *Speed Racer*, *Space Ghost*, *Bugs*, *Daffy*, *Ultra Man*, *Batman*, *Green Lantern*, *Shazzam*, *Wonder Woman*, and *Baretta*.

FLA: Why the revising and redoing of *Aztec of the City*?

FR: There were three redoings. The artwork in the volume 1 series sucked. High school students were calling and complaining about why I'd made Tony Avalos a traditional blue-collar construction worker and not some doctor, lawyer, senator, white-collar hero. In junior college, after showing Kasey Quevedo, my Chicano cultures professor, volume 2 of *Aztec of the City*, he nonchalantly tossed them on his desk and said, "That's no Aztec. An Aztec can't fly nor can he speak English. His language would be that of Nahuatl, and La Llorona too . . . He wouldn't speak Spanglish either."

So after hiring a new artist, Ernie, I set about putting together a series of stories and heroes that would originate in *Aztec of the City*, then spawn

YOUR BRAIN ON LATINO COMICS

their own titles. Hence the creation of the cousin of Avalos, Tony Torres, as the Super Latino. Ernie suggested that Torres be a nuclear physicist, but I wanted to make him a former convict who uses his fighting abilities to return to society as a better person. So I did. Right from the beginning, he's a psychologically complicated character. For example, upon reentry, he's faced with a restraining order from his ex-girlfriend—the mother of his daughter—and constant surveillance by a parole officer. He also faces a difficult mainstream unwilling to give him a chance. He can't find gainful employment. His street smarts and prison savvy would enable him to combat the everyday forces that plague our neighborhoods. For example, in the *Super Latino* premier, titled "Crystal Meth Madness," he saves a childhood friend gone astray by the drug which is sweeping across the nation.

Ernie proposed that Torres should have some kind of powers. So in *Aztec of the City*, issue 2, Torres gains finger-emanating Taser abilities while on a custodian job search at the Stanford Linear Accelerator Center in nearby Palo Alto, California. I also created the character, Dynamis (the same Greek word origin as "dynamite"), who is a homely, hard-working nuclear physicist who is transformed into a hot babe after a laboratory accident. Post-lab-accident, she has Wonder Woman–like powers, and her lab partner is facially (Dr. Doom–style) disfigured, gaining the power to touch the ground and make the earth tremble. He becomes Torres's nemesis, known as EarthQuake.

FLA: Can you speak to your process from conception to creating *Aztec of the City*?

FR: Certainly. The process has evolved with the different versions. I first semi-draw the comic book on letter-size paper, giving the text and visuals. Then I go over the drawings a few times. I put the script down on computer and send it out as a written, play-like draft. In the original, Kasey used to do thumbnails first, then went blue line, pencil, and then ink. He was also afforded the luxury of redrawing the same story. With this new *Aztec of the City*, Ernie has had to create fresh new drawings. Lastly, because we all work full-time, I decided to ease the stress on *el artista* by not imposing a predetermined deadline or printing date.

FLA: How do you know if your visuals and text are conveying what you intend to readers?

FR: Once I've got my sketch-style art and the dialogue down, and the story finished, I'll have a test group of people—including some comic book aficionados, those who read novels, and regular joes—read it and give me feedback. That has worked tremendously well in helping me fine-tune and revise the comic book to make sure I'm conveying the intended meaning and effect.

FLA: Can you talk about the creating of El Salto Comics and the production end of *Aztec*?

FR: I'm the cofounder of El Salto along with my brother, cousin, and his wife. I asked my brother if he wanted to be on board with the original *Aztec of the City*; he could always draw better than me. I also thought two bros hammering it out would be good promo. But he hated issue 1. It didn't help matters with my brother, *primo* [cousin], and so on, that issue 1 didn't arrive to the book signing till the last hour of the press conference. I told them and others that, sure, the book wasn't all that great, but at least it was there in hand to bash and criticize rather than some sketches on my wall or desk with me dreamily saying, "Some day, maybe some day there'll be a Latino hero." To cut a long story short, because of tensions and bickering, I dissolved El Salto and proceeded as sole proprietor with full control over all creative projects. My goal: to eventually run a stable of artists creating books that speak to Latinos at-large. That would provide work for minority artists. I want to be a Mexican Stan Lee with my Sanchez, Gomez, and Robledos.

FLA: Why choose to tell your story in the superhero genre?

FR: I chose the superhero genre because that's all I've known. Sure I read *Veronica and Jughead*, *Archie*, the *Freak Brothers*, and *Mr. Natural*—all that type of stuff—but I have always loved the hero epics.

I decided to bring the natural and real with the superheroic, creating heroes who wore costumes that would be plausibly worn in the real world. I didn't want many world-conquering bad guys. I wanted to portray the daily struggles of Latinos. This was the obstacle—a villain of sorts—that they had to fight to overcome.

FLA: When creating *Aztec*, who do you imagine as your audience, and does this differ from your actual audience?

FR: When Kasey and I set about redoing *Aztec*, I had in mind third or fourth graders, that age when I had first fallen in love with comic books. So there's no cursing, and there's no profiling of guns. I've found great support for my work in adult literacy and English as a second language classes that I've visited—as well as a few libraries. Teachers, instructors, tutors all heavily support the magic of comic books that entice first-time readers to actually read. I include some Spanglish here. Now, I use the same word in both languages usually in the same word bubbles, therefore providing translation on the spot. Of course, some words, like "Mexica" and "Xochti," need a narrator's boxed-in help.

What happened is that those nerdy comic book fanboys at the Comi-Cons found *Aztec of the City* insulting. It was too tame for them. So the new *Aztec of the City* is edgy. It's possibly the first comic book story where there's a restraining order given to the superhero. It also seeks to address that modern-day epidemic of breakups, divorces, family-custody issues, and so on.

FLA: Ups and downs of the profession?

FR: In 1996, my son's mom vowed to take me back and give our relationship another family try only if I agreed to give up making comic books. So I gave up the comic book world. In 1998, we took our son and niece to the San Diego ComiCon, and others were encouraging me to return to comics. In 2003, after moving back to San Jose, I printed the 5,000 copies of *Adelita: Tales of Aztlan*, one of the first Chicana superheroes. The comic book passed with flying colors.

FLA: How do you create rhythm, pace, suspense, a sense of danger in your stories?

FR: Bottom line: I come from that silver age of comic book storytelling, along with Javi Hernandez, Rafa Navarro, and Richard Dominguez. I've always been better at tracing than drawing. So when creating my comics, I've tried to learn as much as possible about visual and story technique: how to do the camera-angle-type shots (bird's-eye, worm's-eye, close-ups, establishing shots) and write dialogue, especially. I took courses in photography and writing to help me sharpen my skills.

FLA: Why your choice of characters?

FR: I created and went with working-class characters because Latinos in general have been predominantly working-class. We're the ones who've always picked the fruit. At first, the Aztec could fly. He spoke English and used his Aztec warfare ensemble to defeat the bad guys. But I wanted him to be physical and directly connected to the power of the earth. He's a silent, Nahuatl-speaking Prince Cuauhtémoc who is unable to comprehend the society he now finds himself thrust into. He moves about at night while his alter ego, Avalos, sleeps, or wanders about whenever Avalos falls unconscious due to his post-coma medical injury. His powers now are more Captain America and Daredevil, who fight with semi-superhuman athletic training and prowess. Aztec is thus skilled in the use of all his warrior weaponry.

FLA: But he does have some type of superpower?

FR: I chose to limit the powers of the new Aztec to make it *X-Files* believable. The further into Mexico Avalos wanders, the more prone he is to become like Cuauhtémoc, the legendary warrior who was done in by Cortés in Mexico City, known then as Tenochtitlan. So his powers are rooted in the earth and have a mythic dimension.

FLA: You use very little Spanish in your comic books?

FR: Although I can read and write Spanish, I don't enjoy reading a comic book story in Spanish and English.

FLA: How about humor in your work?

FR: I got the comic book humor from Spidey's wisecracking jargon while combating the bad guys. Stan Lee proved you could balance the action-fantasy adventure with a few laughs.

FLA: Why the legend of La Llorona for issue 1?

FR: Inspired by Rafael Navarro's use of La Llorona in *Strange Tales of Sonambulo*, her story was clamoring to be told in *Aztec*. She's such an obvious choice as nemesis.

FLA: Is there significance to some of the names you've chosen for your characters?

FR: Why create fictitious combination names like Frank Fernandez, Juan Jimenez, when I could readily name them after actual *raza* that I've known. It has worked out well.

FLA: How about character transformation?

FR: All the characters will experience transformations and growth.

FLA: Should there be a place in your comic book worlds to convey values of good and bad?

FR: While I haven't had the sixty-odd-issue runs that can blur the lines between good and bad—I have the Mob and La Llorona, who are simply bad—I do believe that comic books can be the medium for identifying the difference between good and bad. A fine blend of action, suspense, and great storytelling technique can do this in interesting and subtle ways.

FLA: Choice of setting?

FR: Like Stan Lee, I wanted to go with *our* Latino world as the premise and locale for *Aztec of the City*. So I picked San Jose. It has its fair share of crime, teenage angst, and melodrama, with gangs like the Norteños and Sureños fighting over turf. I didn't want to glorify, but at the same time I wanted my comic book story to reflect this real, everyday world.

FLA: Is this where the element of social critique enters?

FR: Giving it an urban setting meant necessarily that I would need to center-stage issues like homelessness. It's a prevalent problem in San Jose. And in the new *Aztec of the City* appears a scene with Torres verbally objecting to police harassment and the killing of a ninety-eight-pound Asian lady. This

 YOUR BRAIN ON LATINO COMICS

isn't so much social critique as it is simply reflecting our everyday reality: bang bang, another minority dead at the hands of those sworn to serve and protect. In some of the other stories, like the mini-four-pager "El Coyote," I portray a smuggler who outwits and outfoxes both the U.S. Border Patrol and the Texas-Arizona Minutemen.

FLA: In the ten-plus years that you've been creating Latino comics, has the audience demand changed?

FR: I've noticed since the first publication of *Aztec of the City* that both Latino and Anglo readers want more than your run-of-the-mill non-Hispanic comic book. They hungered for something new, unique, and different. Since then, I've noticed more and more Latinos wanting to identify and connect with their cultural past: writing themselves as Xicanos with an *X*, desiring to know more about the Nahua language and Aztec, Maya history. My stories satisfied that hunger.

FLA: Is there a Latino comic book market today?

FR: I think there *is* a Latino comic book market today. Before, there wasn't even a ghost town of Latino comics. At the top of the successful frontier is *El Muerto*, the Latino *The Crow* that's been turned into a feature film with Wil Valderrama as the lead. And of course there's Richard Dominguez with *Team Tejas* and *El Gato Negro*. He's a dynamic artist whom I told should move from lettering his stories freehand like the days of yore and go with computerized fonts like everyone else. He also brought to light the 1977 *Relampago*, an insightful, eye-opening discovery of the first Mexican American superhero. And there's Lalo Alcaraz's zany antics and humor-filled political satires. And, of course, Rafa Navarro, who's *the* artiste extraordinaire. He's funny, savvy, and continues to create his Blue Demon–Santo tribute, *Sonambulo*.

But we've all felt the sting of Diamond and Capital City Distribution because they've decided to ignore us guys. So how many of our stories will readers actually get in their hands?

FLA: Have we moved beyond stereotypes in the mainstream?

FR: I don't know. As a kid, I thought it was cool having the Frito Bandito representing us brown folk in TV commercials, and back then the only Hispanic I saw was Ricky "Desi Arnaz" Ricardo. For a while, DC even had a Puerto Rican superhero, Firebrand. And sure, there are more Latinos in the mainstream, like Cartoon Network's recent *El Jefe*, with his leaf blower that reminds me of the joke about Davy Crockett and Daniel Boone's last words at the Alamo: "What're these landscapers doing here?"

Although we have pioneered a new frontier of Latino comic-book heroes, we have yet to arrive. Neither I nor anyone else's books and characters have become recognizable players in a comic book store. But with our rich, concise stories that attract the minions to our line of heroes, I think we're closer to cracking that safe.

One day kids and adults will speak of Sonambulo, El Gato, El Muerto, Aztec, Super Lat, and Montijo's Inferno with the same zeal that they mention Murdock, Parker, Von Doom, Blake, Stark, Steve Rogers, Wayne, Kent. For now, it's just a lot of hard grunt work chasing that tangible dream.

FLA: Current projects?

FR: I've continued to create, revise, and reevaluate the *Aztec* series. To continue to develop the *Super Latino* comic book series. The introduction of the new comic book, *Mestizo*, a story about a fugitive character who is both Aztec (mother) and Spanish (father)—the nation's first *mestizo*—that is set in the year 1537.

Right now, I'm waiting anxiously to print *Aztec of the City*, volume 3, number 1, praying the books will disappear from the shelves and propel the rest out from the shadows and into the hands of readers nationwide.

FLA: Any last words?

FR: There has been a growth process in what I feel is God's plan for me to write, create, and develop comic book stories. If I were to perish tomorrow, all of this would die with me.

 YOUR BRAIN ON LATINO COMICS

Bobby Rubio

Bobby Rubio was born in San Diego at the Balboa Naval Hospital in 1971. Robert and Lucila Rubio are his parents. He is the oldest of three sons; Anthony and Ronald are his younger siblings. Rubio grew up with a strong sense of his Filipino cultural roots. His parents would speak Tagalog in the privacy of their home, but didn't insist that he learn. Self-identifying as Filipino American, Rubio grew up in a multiracial San Diego. He attended Robert E. Lee Elementary School, Bell Junior High School, and then Morse High School. His choice of career as a traditional animator and cartoonist would eventually lead him back to his growing-up experience.

After graduating from high school, he worked as a freelance comic book artist (an adaptation of *Friday the 13th's Jason Goes to Hell* for Topps Comics, penciling a short story, "Scraps," for Dark Horse Comics, among others) before attending junior college—a stepping-stone to Cal Arts (California Institute of the Arts). After three years at Cal Arts, he landed another penciling job with Dark Horse, this time penciling a Godzilla story. Afterward, he interned with Jim Lee at Homage Studios during the second round of a Homage Studios talent search. Restless to work in animation, Rubio interned with Disney Feature Animation, putting comic books on the back burner to pursue an animation career. He began on *Pocahontas* as a cleanup artist, and then was promoted to an in-betweener for *Hunchback of Notre Dame*. He got his break when he worked as assistant animator on *Treasure Planet*, for which he was eventually promoted to animator. After learning storyboards at Disney and working on *Tarzan 2*, he left the company to work for Nickelodeon on the animated series *Avatar* as an assistant director and storyboard artist. In his free time, he returns to his first love, comic books.

He continues to self-publish his comic book *Alcatraz High* as well as work

as a story artist for Pixar Animation Studios. His official website is www
.alcatrazhigh.com.

FREDERICK LUIS ALDAMA: What were your first experiences with comic
books?

BOBBY RUBIO: As far back as five years old, I remember liking comic books. I
liked the Super Friends. I also had a Superman costume. I didn't really get
into it until I was, like, probably in elementary school. In fact, my friend
Fred Rubio, myself, and a couple other friends started our own little comic-
book company in sixth grade: RRAM Comics, an acronym made up of the
first initials of our last names. This was also when I started to do my own
comic books. Our teacher, Mr. Edwards, was very encouraging, letting us
do our own comic strip and put it up every week or so. The first character
that I did was five-two and called the Charger (referring to the San Diego
Chargers), and his alter ego was Filipino. My father was an electrician, so
he probably was the inspiration for that character.

My favorite comic book that I picked up, and the artist that I really dug
at the time, was George Perez—his facial expressions and his dynamic artwork. I still love his work. And it was *The New Teen Titans*. It was issue 39
that got me, the one where Robin and Flash quit. It had a great cover: both
walking away.

FLA: At what point did you know that you wanted to go into this profes-
sionally?

BR: I knew I wanted to be a comic book artist since sixth grade and RRAM
Comics. I enjoyed the freedom of doing my own thing, creating my own
world, creating my own characters. I couldn't see myself drawing *Spider-
Man* or *X-Men*. I just wanted to do my own thing. My mother was supportive of my artwork and always encouraged me. She herself was self-
employed as a clothing manufacturer. I know that I got my independent
nature from her, and so it is easy to see that my first comic book out would
be a self-published book.

FLA: At Cal Arts, what would you say was the most important experience
for you?

BR: The people that become your friends and later on become your connections. The guys I know from Cal Arts all ended up at different studios, like
Disney, Pixar, DreamWorks, Cartoon Network, and Nickelodeon.

But there are other ways to approach this. My brother Ronald didn't
go to college or the Cal Arts route. He went to one of those academy art
schools and built up his portfolio. He's done well in animation. He got a job

at *King of the Hill* and worked his way up; he's going to be director at *King of the Hill*. Meanwhile, I went to Cal Arts, and I had to pay back student loans. And he has no student loans to pay off.

FLA: How about your experiences as a Filipino in the profession?

BR: There's nothing to compare it to. I mean, I don't have a sense that I was treated any differently than white or Mexican guy. In the beginning, I remember how great it was that there was a Filipino, Whilce Portacio, working on *X-Men*. Whilce worked out of Homage Studios. And when I started my internship with Homage Studios in 1994, it was diverse among the artists. You had Joe Benitez, Billy Tan, Dave Finch, Matt Broome, J. Scott Campbell—all different races. And I felt we were all treated the same.

FLA: What did you learn at Homage Studios?

BR: The comic book artist's lifestyle. It was a bullpen with a hierarchy setup: clusters of pencilers, colorists, and inkers hanging out with each other in groups. I was hired on as a penciler. They wanted me to start off doing pin-ups and trading cards. I did help Jim Lee, though, with layout on *Savage Dragon*. He swapped with Eric Larsen, who got to do another Image character. Jim noticed that some of my perspective was a little off, and he gave me some pointers. He also gave me some pointers as far as trying to make things more dynamic.

FLA: Your central character in *Alcatraz High* is Latino?

BR: I always saw Miguel as Mexican. I never imagined him any other way. That's just how I saw him: a Latino as a hero. But I also wanted him to reflect me in a small way, so I didn't make him totally bilingual. I'm Filipino American, but don't speak my native language fluently. I know a few words here and there. Culturally, Miguel's in between, like me.

FLA: When did you first conceive of *Alcatraz High*?

BR: I came up with *Alcatraz High* in 1986. My girlfriend at the time, now my wife, was going to this brand-new high school in La Jolla in San Diego. She later joined me at Morse High School. They called it something like University City High School. It was built out of all bricks, and you couldn't see the windows. The few you could see were tinted. I was joking around that she went to Alcatraz High because it had all bricks, and that name stuck. With the name, you immediately get an image of this school with a Big Brother mentality.

FLA: Did you know that you would return to this initial concept and create a comic book, *Alcatraz High*?

BR: Actually, no, I didn't. It was a toss-up: either *Alcatraz High* or this multicultural superhero idea. It was my brother Ronald who told me I should do

Alcatraz High. He said that there are a million superhero comics, but that at least *Alcatraz High* would put my work outside of that. He thought it would play up to my character-driven strengths.

FLA: Can you speak a little to the process of getting *Alcatraz High*, issue 1, out into readers' hands?

BR: It's easier to do a comic book when you've got a day job that pays pretty decently. I didn't really have a lot of expenses at the time, so I just used my own cash. I also used some of my connections within the comic book industry. I drew up the comic book, and then had someone print the book. Then went to the San Diego ComiCon. I'd been going since I was thirteen, but now with my own comic. My game plan: to get publicity. It's always been a dream of mine to do my own thing.

It's not paying the bills, but it's been successful enough for me to continue. And I've been getting acclaim from peers and also people in the industry—to make me actually feel that this is a viable product. My goal right now is to get at least four issues done before I actually distribute it nationwide, because it's a five-issue story arc. I have this feeling that the fans don't want to wait a year for each issue. At the moment, I haven't gone full distribution. It's still strictly just comic convention and Internet sales. By the way, my brother Anthony did my website, and I think he did an amazing job, considering I didn't give him much to work with.

FLA: So how do you pay the bills?

BR: Storyboarding right now for Nickelodeon.

FLA: What about other storytelling forms?

BR: There is something fantastic about being a comic book creator. You can control the form and produce worlds. It's not that I'm not a team player. When you're in animation, it's all about working with others: I do the storyboards, somebody else writes it, another colors it, and yet another directs. But I think I feel most rewarded when it's mostly me. That's what *Alcatraz High* is. Comic books are your pure vision, my own vision. Those are my drawings on there. That's the way I want those guys to look. That's the way I want them to talk. There's something satisfying about that. I mean, sure, I would love to see *Alcatraz High* as a live-action movie someday. But that's Hollywood, and I have no control over what gets made in Hollywood.

FLA: How about when you work with a letterer or colorist on *Alcatraz High*?

BR: I'm not picky when it comes to the lettering. As long as it reads and it looks kind of like what I asked for. And as far as colors, I do remember the first time I saw the cover and the interpretation of my idea: it didn't match what I imagined. But how can someone see what's in my head? With issue 3, Mike Greenholt did the interior color as well. My initial reaction: too bright. But then we would argue, and he would tweak it, and I would listen to his suggestions. There were some of the things he did that he brought to the table that I would have never thought of. Coloring is one of my weaker points. The collaboration process is fantastic when it's between friends, you know. It's give-and-take, and so I enjoy that. But at the end of the day, because it is my book, if I did tell Mike, "I want it red, not blue," I'm sure he would make it red and not blue.

FLA: Can you describe your writing, drawing, inking process a little?

BR: I get an idea, then I do it the Marvel way: come up with a basic plot, draw out the visuals to get a sense of story flow, then add dialogue. The dialogue's easy for me because I talk like the guys in the book.

FLA: You have a keen sense of how the visuals alone can tell a story?

BR: That's my Disney training. In storyboards, you're supposed to be able to look from across the room and tell exactly what's happening in that shot. And so I was always trained to do the clearest, most simple, concise way of telling visually what is going on in that situation. But this is no Disney picture. It's more Disneyesque-looking characters living in a Japanese-anime-type world: characters riding around in robots, and with a more hard-core story line. My style is evolving to a fusion of Disney and Japanese anime.

FLA: Why the choice of colors?

BR: In issues 1 and 2, the colors were more vibrant. I wanted to pull people into the book. I also wanted the colors to reflect the light-hearted sense of the book. If I did use dark tones and sepias, I think people would go into the book thinking it was going to be a drama, and it's not. It's so not a drama. It's light-hearted action-comedy. It helps steer people in the right direction. If they see *Alcatraz High* as a cold, dark tale of a high school where everyone wears orange jumpsuits, this wouldn't be visually as fun for me to draw. I'd rather have fun drawing cheerleaders and giant robots—to play up my strengths with character facial expressions.

FLA: What about other technical aspects, like your sense of panel and gutter layout?

BR: My style has a more storyboard feel than a comic book. I'd never want to break up an emotion or the action by flipping the page. I'd always want to keep that sense or that sequence within that page. I'll keep the romantic feeling that leads to action; I won't put them both on the same page. I'll try to put in romance and keep the reader in that state when they're reading that page, and then they flip over and then start the action. When I lay out my pages, sometimes plot point dictates page layout, but also emotion:

what the character and reader should be feeling at this particular moment. It's also about pacing of emotion and action.

Because my book is around twenty-four pages, I know that I have plot points that I have to hit. So if I needed to introduce the character Dayton in issue 1, I knew that I didn't want to introduce him halfway through the book. I wanted to introduce him as soon as I could. So he's on the fourth page or so. That's what dictates layout: emotional pacing and plot lines.

FLA: Do you have an ideal reader in mind?

BR: Not really. I guess I'm trying to please myself first. If I think it's funny, I hope other people will think it's funny. I try not to appease fourteen-year-old girls, say, by putting in more Dayton. I try to just tell a story that I want to tell and hope that other people like it.

At least a third of my real readers are female. I thought they'd take a look at the cover with a cheerleader, or flip through and see a locker-room scene with girls, and be turned off. I was surprised find out that I have female fans who come back and say they love the book. Of all ages, too. It's PG-13, so I cover the cuss words with asterisks. And I've got readers as old as sixty. I think it appeals because of the artwork and because everyone can relate to being in high school. I also have Latino and many ethnic-identified readers. Latinos who have come up and said they know Miguel: "I recognize that guy." He's real enough to Latinos. He's definitely real to me.

FLA: Is there room for social critique in your comic book world?

BR: I might touch on little things here and there, like the fact that kids bring guns to school. But I'm trying to address it in a fantastic way. Some comic books can work well as a place to bring up politics. If that's your strength as a writer, if you can show your views, and do it in an entertaining way—Alan Moore's good at this—then why not the comic books medium. Alan Moore works like that. But I'm not that guy. *Alcatraz High* to me is a pop-corn kind of movie. I'm not trying to make a statement. I'm just trying to entertain people.

FLA: You mentioned that characters and facial expression were one of your strengths. Can you elaborate?

BR: I design my characters the way I see them. With Miguel, I always saw him as kind of a handsome guy, but not too handsome. I wasn't necessarily trying to make him very ethnic-looking. I wanted to make the principal look older, statesman-like. That he's Caucasian is of secondary importance. I design them less according to racial stereotypes and more based on how they are as characters. Steve's a very shy type. I draw him with big eyes, so he looks scared and/or nervous all the time. I draw his face rounder to give it a quality of innocence. Miguel, on the other hand, tends to be more tall and sleek-looking, so he's more an action-type guy. In this sense, I follow that character-design philosophy: squares as more stable and blockier, circles as softer and more innocent, and triangles—Miguel's face—as active and more action-oriented.

FLA: How about Latino representations in the comic book mainstream today?

BR: That Jaime Reyes is the new Blue Beetle means we've come a long way from Vibe. There's progress. And they're bringing back White Tiger.

FLA: Which comic books are you reading right now?

BR: *The Astonishing X-Men*, by Joss Whedon and John Cassaday, and the *Ultimates*, by Mark Millar and Bryan Hitch. Both books are outstandingly written, with amazing artwork. I'm also eagerly waiting for George Perez's *New Teen Titans* graphic novel to come out. But these days I've got to be picky. I have a son now, so I really can't spend as much as I used to on comic books.

FLA: Are you working on developing another comic book?

BR: There's that superhero one I've mentioned. And actually I do have an ashcan [a cheaply produced comic used to establish copyright] out that I put out last year that had two projects that I'm considering. I still might. And I can tell you the titles because it's written in the ashcan: *Robo Brigade*, about five bad-ass evil robots who are inherited by this little boy, and *4 Gun Conclusion*, about a bounty hunter who has two mechanical guns attached to his back and two sidearms, hence he has four guns. That will be a dark action-comedy.

FLA: Are these new comic book worlds multicultural?

BR: My world will always be multicultural. Even if the lead character is white, I will definitely make the world multicultural. I just don't understand comic books that don't have Latinos, Asians, and African Americans. It's as if there are no Latinos or African Americans in New York? Come on. If I can, I'll always draw them in the background at the very least because they belong as much as the next guy and because it makes the world of your story more believable.

Carlos Saldaña

In 1954, Carlos Saldaña was born in Los Angeles, California. He grew up in and around downtown LA and considers himself a native Angeleno. Born the second eldest among six brothers and sisters, he was raised by parents who had immigrated from Zacatecas, Mexico.

At an early age, Saldaña was already fascinated by comic books and cartoons—even puppeteering. Not only did he learn how to read comics at an early age, but he also started to understand their value, collecting mainstream U.S. (*Pink Panther*, *Donald Duck*, and *Mickey Mouse*), Mexican (*The Family Baron* and *Capolina*), and even Japanese comics (*Astro Boy*, *The Amazing Three*, *Gigantor*). He had an uncanny sense that they might be valuable later on in life. They were, in more ways than one. They offered him guides to learning the art of drawing and telling stories—his father had given him a big roll of butcher paper to work on—which he would later develop in high school and college.

While at Los Angeles City College and then the Los Angeles Occupational Center and Cal State–Los Angeles, Saldaña took courses in advertising and commercial art (and music). He also began to send out his cartoons to newspapers, magazines, and syndicates. Rather than rely on syndicates, he decided to publish his own comic book. In 1990, he self-published *Burrito: Jack-of-All-Trades*, which featured a little burro named Burrito and his zany misadventures.

Today Saldaña still lives in Los Angeles, has a nine-to-five job working for the government as "the computer guy," and continues to create his *Burrito: Jack-of-All-Trades*. His website is www.toonist.com.

FREDERICK LUIS ALDAMA: Growing up, were you surprised at the lack of Latinos in comic books?

CARLOS SALDAÑA: No. Because I would read Mexican comics, I never really considered a lack of Latinos in cartooning.

FLA: At what point did you decide that you were going to go self-publish a comic book?

CS: Even after five years and rejection number ten-thousand-something, I didn't give up. I had met other independents who had made it on their own, and they taught me how to self-publish, so I decided to go for it. By 1995, I actually had managed to distribute *Burrito* nationally and internationally. To my surprise, *Burrito* did great on the East Coast and internationally. Places like Boston, Philadelphia, Baltimore, France, Switzerland, Germany, and so on. I was only hoping to get a little success in California, maybe Texas.

As I was in the beginning stages of my publishing business, I read about a guy in Texas that was going to put out a comic book too, titled *El Gato Negro*. It was Richard Dominguez. We got in contact with each other, and we've been pals ever since. Soon after, Rafael "Sonambulo" Navarro came on the scene, then others. It was an encouraging time.

FLA: You had initially wanted it to be syndicated?

CS: I had already tried to publish other projects, mostly gaggers, with newspapers and magazines, and then I tried to get *Burrito* comics picked up and published, but it didn't go anywhere. I don't think funny Latino animals were on top of the hit parade. The comic publishers all loved *Burrito*, but the main issue each had was how to market it, because nothing like it has ever been made.

FLA: When did you come up with the idea of creating the comic book character Burrito?

CS: This happened on September 27, 1990. I wanted to create a funny animal, something I hadn't done before. Now, because the mouse, the cat, the dog, the frog, the chicken, the duck were all taken, in the first sitting I settled on the burro—a little burro, a burrito. I got him right from the first drawing. Suddenly, the world of funny animals opened up for me. Of course, trying to get him published would be another matter altogether.

FLA: Is this when you helped establish PACAS [Professional Amigos of Comic Art Society]?

CS: We formed PACAS in the early 1990s, mostly to create a forum for networking. Everybody had different characters and ideas they were trying to publish, and so we formed a strong camaraderie. Reflecting back, PACAS members were the barbed-wire cartoonists. What I mean is, we consciously or unconsciously knew that we were going to lay our bodies on the barbed wire so that the younger cartoonists and writers of our genre could succeed. I can say that it worked, from the printed page to even Disney. Our reward is not to be forgotten. It was a good effort, but it's in a dormant stage right now.

CAPS [Comic Art Professional Society] also helped foster camaraderie with other independents. Because the artists had already traveled this road, they told me what the pitfalls were and what to look out for. If ever there was a group that showed unselfishness, it was CAPS. It's my cartoon academy. I am still honored to interact with great cartoonists and call them my friends.

NCS [National Cartoonist Society]: I've been a proud card-holding member in good standing since 1990.

FLA: Do you collaborate—guest editor and such—on projects?

CS: As far as guest editors, I'm a notorious bad speller, so I get somebody to look at it and go over it. It really helps to have someone go over, even revise, the work. Someone will approach me, asking if I have room in my book for a story that will take up a few pages. If I like it, I'll publish it. Mostly, I work alone.

FLA: Big distributors for the work?

CS: When I came in, there were four big distributors: Diamond, Capital City Distribution, Friendly Franks, Heroes World. I've heard horror stories about them, but all of them were kind and helpful to me. They all led me by the hand and showed me how the comic book business worked. Today, it's a one-horse town. That's the way it is, and there's nothing I can do about it.

FLA: So you sold *Burrito* out of the trunk of your car?

CS: Yeah, you hit the pavement and try to sell them in any way you can. It's a product, so you do what you can. I have to put on all the hats: selling out of your trunk, at ComiCon festivals—you name it, I'll be there.

My dad told me one time, "You're a businessman, and business is the way that you make it. Nobody else." So when it comes to struggles, I cannot point fingers at anyone but myself.

FLA: Inspirations and influences?

CS: Anything from the underground comics to Marvel, Disney, Japanese manga—even independent animated film. In terms of style, I steal from everybody and from everywhere. Once you've studied enough styles, you can adjust and refashion them to your own particular project. I developed the style that best works for a particular character and a particular project.

FLA: What kind of audience do you have in mind when creating *Burrito*?

CS: As universal and general as possible. I don't use dirty words. I want to reach three-year-olds to 103-year-olds. I've got kids of my own, and I've got to be able to show it to them. I'm not built to write the other—trashy—stuff. Even though there are quick bucks in the other stuff, I just can't get into it. It does not appeal to me. It still gives me a charge when someone writes me, saying that they found my book in Japan or Chicago, or some teacher read my book to their students, or soldiers passed around my book in some distant battlefield.

FLA: How about the process?

CS: I'm a one-man show here. I can only afford one writer or one penciler, one inker, one public production manager, one editor, and all of them are me. When I'm creating *Burrito*, I'm first trying to capture the story. The story's the most important thing. Then I start working it out and massaging it, and sometimes even changing the story. Then the drawings just flow out. Then I do the penciling and identify where the breakups capture that certain flow of the story. It just can't be random pictures. And if it's not important, I don't put it in. The longest part of the process: I have to find that great ending. I usually come up with a big twist that takes the reader in a direction they least expect. Then I do the tighter penciling, the inking, and finish up with the lettering. Because up till the very end, I might change the wording.

Every time I make a comic, I make sure it stands alone. Burrito's bullet-proof serape is the only constant throughout the stories. I don't like stories that continue on in a series format. When I was a kid, I could never get the continuing story because I didn't know when they would come out or if it ever would come out. So when I create a *Burrito* story, it's a whole story compacted into one issue.

FLA: How about the use of black-and-white, panel layout, framing, lettering, and so on?

CS: For me, every line, panel size and layout, every page is important and creates a specific style and mood. Framing and lettering create a certain rhythm. The placement of gutters can slow or speed up the story sequence and help add the sense of action and suspense. Sometimes I don't want to make the simple square grid, because it looks boring. And then sometimes it calls for a square grid. Then I do a big splash page if I really want to make a point.

Even though I use black-and-white, I also use cross-hatching and point dotting to use gray scales to convey what I would be able to do if I were using color. In black-and-white, shadows are important. They help "color" the page and to give it depth.

FLA: I noticed a shift in your style from issue 1 to issue 2.

CS: Style is both a constant and changing process for me. I actually did issue 2 first, but at the last minute before going to press, I switched issues. It had changed, and by the time I got to issue 5, *Burrito* had matured into the style that it would follow more consistently. I mastered inking with a brush.

FLA: You mentioned that *Burrito* is aimed at a general audience. Does it aim to educate or convey certain universal values?

CS: As a burro he gets kicked around a lot, but eventually even a burro will stop and say, "Enough!" Importantly, he uses his wit to get himself out of problems. I throw in some history, too, to educate the reader a little. I feel, if you're going to read something, you might as well get something out of it.

I'm not one of these political guys. Mostly my purpose is to entertain and not to shoot down anything or have any hidden agendas. Its sole purpose is to be a comic book and to entertain.

FLA: Burrito travels to different places and different historical moments?

CS: Yes, he can be anywhere, any place. He's anachronistic. He's a time traveler. He's free to go anywhere. That's the beauty of *Burrito*.

FLA: You sprinkle some Chicano slang and Spanish into a mostly English written comic.

CS: I write the way I talk.

FLA: Why do you write on the cover of issue 2, "Written in English?"

CS: Especially for the earlier issues, it was important for me to let the comic book retailer know what product they have in their hand so they'd know how to rack it. Otherwise, they will put it in the foreign section or who knows where.

FLA: Burrito has a degree in nursing from Stanford?

CS: That's in the third issue. In another issue, he's an explorer: in issue 5, Burrito "discovers" Europe first. He can be anything, any occupation. He's a jack-of-all-trades.

FLA: How does Burrito differ from other animal characters?

CS: I never set out to make Burrito a cute animal. Also, there are certain things that bug me when I see certain other comic book or cartoon animals: Donald Duck having a roast goose for Thanksgiving; Quick Draw McGraw, the horse, riding another horse. Burrito, when he does eat, he'll have a cookie because it makes sense.

FLA: Where's Burrito today?

CS: He's still here. In fact, he's right next to me. I'm doing the gallery piece—a poster of Burrito—for an exhibit with Laura Molina, Rafael Navarro,

Javier Hernandez, and some other people. And *Burrito* is still looking for corporate sponsors. *Burrito* is published out of pocket. My pocket. It has no ads, and it's tough to continue. The comic book is nationally and internationally distributed, so it seems to be too big for local sponsors and too small for the big sponsors. One day Lady Luck will appear.

FLA: Current and future projects?

CS: I've been adding Flash animation to my website at www.toonist.com as well as making that gallery piece and writing comedy. Mostly, I just can't wait to retire from my good government job so that I can go at this full-time and put out *Burrito* in full force. It's coming up real soon.

Wilfred Santiago

Wilfred Santiago was born in Ponce, Puerto Rico, in 1970. He grew up both in Ponce and further north on the island in San Juan. As he grew up, he would also spend time in the United States with family members and with his mother in Maryland before she divorced her second husband. In 1990, Santiago settled in New York.

The only comic the teenage Santiago read consistently was *Mad* magazine. The first dollar he spent on a comic was to buy *The Amazing Spider-Man* (issue 320), mainly because of the "funky" artwork. Being drawn to the visuals became the main criterion for his attraction to certain comics and not others. It wasn't until he read Moore's *Watchmen* that he began to become interested in the author-artist. This would become an important criterion for Santiago: how the creator made an impression on him. So while he never followed titles, he did attend to who the author-artist was. With this in mind, he also considered how much the comic book was going to be worth.

Even before comics, Santiago was extremely interested in art, specifically painting. He has been drawing ever since he can remember. His artistic skills would later be developed into his unique visual and verbal storytelling style, seen especially in his short stories in *Pop Life* and also in *In My Darkest Hour*. He recently published with Fantagraphics the graphic novel *21*, which follows the life of Roberto Clemente. His website is http://www.wilfredsantiago.com.

FREDERICK LUIS ALDAMA: When there are so many different ways to tell stories available out there, why choose to tell stories in comic book form?

WILFRED SANTIAGO: It's cheaper than making a movie. I'm sure someone has said this before.

FLA: How might other media, like movies, help teach readers—Latino or otherwise— how to read comic book stories?

WS: Movies probably have the most influence on how one might read a comic if they are new to the comic book language. Movies and comics are both ways of telling stories visually, but there are elements of comic books that are unique to that medium. In terms of the content, there are more similarities between film and comics than differences.

As a Latino, I probably related to comics the same way I related to movies. Although the way I relate to both movies and comic books has changed over the years.

FLA: Has your biographical experience informed your stories?

WS: There are always biographical aspects in one shape or another. Personal experiences and the people I've met through the whole creative development of a book like *In My Darkest Hour* played a very essential part in terms of what's in it. Some of it is completely made up, while other elements and characters are real. It's a fictional journal, an elaborate photograph.

FLA: Can you speak to your experiences in the profession as a Latino?

WS: It's been interesting. It took some years to understand the particulars around me and what it meant to be a Latino, not just in the business, but in the U.S. It was really exciting in the beginning to meet people with different cultural and socioeconomic backgrounds. Having in mind the first job I landed was with Milestone Comics, which wasn't exactly a typical comic book publisher.

FLA: Was it difficult for you to break into the market? Can you make a living from your work?

WS: It wasn't difficult for me to break into the market. However, once the focus went to alternative comics, the money became an issue.

FLA: How about working at Milestone?

WS: In a way, I didn't fully appreciate the opportunity I had when working with Milestone. At that time, I hadn't fully committed myself to working in comics. I did learn a great deal about the ins and outs of the business. On the other hand, what I did with them sucks, and I wish it didn't exist.

FLA: Can you speak about the history and conception of *In My Darkest Hour*?

WS: I started thinking about it around the whole millennium thing. There were many questions and anxieties, and it was a moment of transition for me, although I can't tell if the times had anything to do with it. Omar is a reflection of his society: medicated, obsessed with consumption, image, and perhaps very afraid and in a permanent state of anticipation.

FLA: What about some of your other projects, like *Pink*, *The Thorn Garden*, and *Pop Life*, with Ho Che Anderson.

WS: *Pink* was fun to do. All those projects before *In My Darkest Hour* were a great learning experience, but they are really bad. I didn't have any idea what I was doing, so I'd rather not talk about it.

FLA: In the acknowledgments to *In My Darkest Hour*, you mention comic book authors Ho Che Anderson and Ivan Velez but also Daniel Guérin, Howard Zinn, Noam Chomsky. Omar reads García Márquez. Other influences that come to mind?

WS: Dave McKean, Bill Sienkiewicz, José Muñoz, too many comic book authors to name. Pop culture has always been a big influence. Music and movies are always present. Anything coming out of the tube. Anything that interests me in the moment affects my work. Dreams were also an essential part in creating the content and the whole disquieting feel of *In My Darkest Hour*.

FLA: How about genres? I think of how you break the mold of the romance genre by providing a look into the gritty interior landscape of Omar's mind and then creating a "happy" ending.

WS: I wasn't thinking much about genre when I was creating it, although I knew it would have a romantic element to it. The "happy" ending, just like the concept of happiness itself, is up to individual interpretation. Omar does what he has to do to go on. Does that constitute a "happy" ending? That's not for me to decide.

FLA: In many ways, Omar's romance is pretty conventional: a couple who aren't supposed to be together split up and then reunite.

WS: Because for Omar, human existence is pretty much doomed, and we're all just waiting. For a person like him, a relationship is almost an anchor to some normalcy, an opportunity and a challenge to his own impulses, questions, and views.

FLA: You use other techniques to break with comic book storytelling conventions, especially when your panels explode with irony. I think specifi-

In My Darkest Hour

YOUR BRAIN ON LATINO COMICS

In My Darkest Hour

cally of the explosive panel portraying a grotesquely muscled, bald Captain America.

WS: There are critical events that collectively pull us out of our routines, affecting our lives. And a lot of times there's nothing else for us to be but spectators, and you can be sure the powers that be will always give us a show. Once we get some sort of closure, we go back to our routines. At least that's how Omar sees it.

FLA: Can you speak a little about your process of drafting, writing, imaging, inking, and so on?

WS: Each project is approached differently. Aspects like style, size, tools used, etc. vary, depending on my intent. There's not really a specific process or rules. Some of *In My Darkest Hour* was drawn and written simultaneously, and that goes with my original intention to create more of an emotion than giving a linear story to the reader.

FLA: You've worked alongside Ho Che Anderson ("Faith at 30" and "The Boob Barrier" in *Pop Life*). What are the pros and cons of collaborative work?

WS: Collaborating with other creators is a great learning experience more than anything else, but once the need to try new things comes in and you also realize the possibilities, it can get a little crowded. Also, I never really planned to write. That's something that sort of happened organically.

FLA: The choice of visuals and lettering for a cover is very important in setting the mood?

WS: The *In My Darkest Hour* cover was inspired by a tanka called "Gone":

> *I sit at home*
> *In my own room*
> *By our bed*
> *Gazing at your pillow*
> —Hitomaro, AD 700

It really summarizes in a simple way the isolation and loneliness amidst the chaos that is Omar's life.

FLA: Why set *In My Darkest Hour* mostly in Chicago, with a short stint in New York?

WS: I'm living in Chicago, and before that I lived in NYC for seven years. Had I been in Alaska, I probably would have used it as a location.

FLA: Filtered through Omar's eyes, we encounter a society that's been desensitized to extreme violence and psychic trauma.

WS: There's a need for Omar to pause, to get answers, but the world stops for no one, and his attempt to understand the human condition has simply left him with scarier questions and a stronger feeling of powerlessness. He also expects the worst to happen, whatever that is. Most people prepare for emergencies or tough times. Omar gets ready in case things go well.

FLA: Why the use of flashbacks and multiple plot lines?

WS: Yes, there are multiple story lines. At one point, some of these story lines converge, while others intersect and never meet again. The intended effect on the reader can best be described as "walking on Jell-o," an analogy of Omar's mental and physical experience.

FLA: Both the visuals and the text tell a story. Sometimes the visuals and the text are in tension or conflict.

WS: True. Those conflicts are sharpest when Omar enters or exits his dreams or visions, like someone who hasn't slept for days seeing things differently. In some cases, the visuals might depict his dream state while the text occurs in his waking life, and vice versa. At moments, we are seeing Omar's dreams and visions through his memory and internal dialogue. So there's always an interchange between those layers.

FLA: I understand that a lot of this is the intuitive skill of the great comic book author-artist, but do you have an effect in mind when you play with the visual and the textual-verbal elements?

WS: The book is built on scenes. There are many different effects that I was going for, depending on the scene. *In My Darkest Hour* begins in the morning with Omar lying in front of the TV. Later he's working at the museum, and in the end pages he's back at his place in front of the TV. Nothing really happens. Everything you see in between has already happened. Everything you see is in his head, and the interplay of the words and text is an important part in trying to communicate this in the narrative.

FLA: How do you envision the relationship of the visuals with the verbal-textual elements?

WS: It goes back and forth. Sometimes it's the visual that carries the weight in the panels, sometimes the text.

FLA: How do you decide to divide one panel to the next with the specific placement of a gutter?

WS: Things like panels, gutters, etc. to me are like nouns, verbs, adjectives, or whatever composes a sentence, and a sentence itself can be put together in a variety of ways to articulate the same idea. So my first question is, what am I trying to say? Then I arrange my sentences in the most effective way I can think to communicate whatever it is I'm trying to communicate.

FLA: Your use of black-and-white, sepia, photographic collage, painterly impressionism, lettering font and size, shadows, facial expression, backdrop, blurred lines, and so on make for a unique Wilfred Santiago style.

WS: Sometimes it's intuition. Sometimes the purpose dictates the execution. Many parts of *In My Darkest Hour*'s visual sequences were carried out in stream-of-consciousness fashion.

FLA: You have a remarkable control over the story's pace.

WS: I intended for the book to have the spiral, progressive acceleration of a flushing toilet. That's the best way I can summarize it.

FLA: Your choice of artist palette?

WS: In *In My Darkest Hour*, I used two colors chosen not only for how they stand by themselves, but how they relate to each other.

FLA: How about your play with perspective, sometimes even telling the story through the eyes of a character?

WS: This is very important because a lot of times I want the reader to get inside the head of a character. But the visuals are more about how a person might remember something rather than what he or she saw.

FLA: How do you convey laughter, anger, sadness, frustration?

WS: There's not much of a thought process here. I imagine the scene and take a mental picture of it and try to interpret it. Sometimes you work around the character's environment rather than the character to suggest something.

FLA: Is it possible to employ the conventions of comic-book stylization of human face, body, anatomy generally to undermine negative stereotypes?

WS: I do try to co-opt all those stereotypes from comics, TV, movies, and other media that we all grew up with and learned to love. Not just visually, but in the way the vocabulary is employed in my work.

FLA: You include many Latino characters, but with the exception of Sonia, most only speak English.

WS: There are also many Latinos that are somewhat embarrassed about the way their Spanish sounds, and they don't speak it. When I lived in Brooklyn, the circle I hung out with were mostly Latinos who did speak English, but between each other we mostly talked in Spanish. With people from Colombia, Nicaragua, El Salvador, Puerto Rico, it was an interesting kind of Spanish, borrowing words from each other's countries—mostly dirty.

FLA: This is not a happy, tortilla-eating family.

WS: Yes, Omar's family is not exactly a Goya commercial, with everybody dancing from the kitchen all the way to the dinner table. Family is important for Latinos, but to Omar, he sees his as the foundation of his pathos and something to disassociate himself from.

FLA: There's the full-page panel of an amputated, tied and bound, grotesque body that conveys a sense of fragmentation, imprisonment, alienation.

WS: Omar's body and what he does to it is a reflection of what's going on inside, and it is that vision and its significance that feeds his self-loathing. He's trapped in an unwanted body and mind.

FLA: On the one hand, we see a decrepit society through Omar's eyes. On the other hand, he himself is no saint. On one occasion, he remarks, "We all rot. Soon I'll be nothing. Why bother with the triviality of ethics that are nothing more than man's invention?" Can the comic book convey a complex sense of right and wrong?

WS: Omar questions society's priorities and definition of good and bad. These very concepts come into question, and therefore the way he sees himself. There's also a deep religious background, like in most Latino families, but by the time the story takes place, Omar has lost his faith long ago, and that black hole left is still within him. I don't see why comics wouldn't be the place to discuss those issues.

FLA: On the one hand, Omar is immoral, and yet there's a strong undercurrent of religious moralism.

WS: You can get Omar out of the church, but you can't get the church out of him.

FLA: Yet the so-identified pagan rituals of Santeria—the gods Ochún and Chango are mentioned—are also important?

WS: These things are part of Omar's childhood and are not rare in Latino culture. It's important for him to strip this off because he's in a state of metamorphosis, and like most of his past, this is one more thing to purge.

FLA: *In My Darkest Hour* has a strong grounding in current events—the Gore-Bush election, 9/11 and World Trade Center—and yet is a story that's primarily character driven. How might the use of both complicate our reading of the character and his actions?

WS: To people with cognitive dysfunction or a mental illness like bipolar dis-

YOUR BRAIN ON LATINO COMICS

order, schizophrenia, or whatever, everyday details can have an impact on their ability to work, go to school, to deal with relationships. An event the magnitude of 9/11 for someone like Omar would be of most significance. For that moment, Omar is pulled back from his revamped life. Remember, this happened right after he and Lucinda get back and move in together.

FLA: Omar lives in a society that's more interested in doling out pills than reflecting on itself or figuring out deep psychological issues. The story conveys a strong social critique.

WS: It has a lot to do with a personal sense of powerlessness. All a person can do is vote and do a thing here and there, but where we live, what we eat, how we are educated, maybe even how we behave is very much in the hands of a small group of people, which most of us are not part of, either by accident or design. There's also the internal struggle between the material and spiritual. To what extent do you go to satisfy your aspirations before betraying your own principles? The point is they are my own principles, not religion or political alliance, but my own views as a human being trying to survive. A lot, if not most, things considered bad are acts of selfishness, and to Omar, mathematically, individuals will always go with what each considers is best for him or her. He would love to live in a dissimilar world, but he knows it's not happening in his lifetime. Not to mention he's probably convinced he'll witness Armageddon.

FLA: What type of audience do you envision reading your comics?

WS: Open-minded, inquisitive, nonconformist humanists of all ages, sexes, and backgrounds.

FLA: Critics have talked about a "healing" that happens at the end of *In My Darkest Hour*.

WS: I think Omar ends in more of an emotional limbo. I'm not sure that constitutes healing, especially when you consider his other option is self-destruction. I leave it to the reader to make what he or she will of the ending.

FLA: Others have identified your work as modernist. Would you consider your work modernist?

WS: I think so.

FLA: Yet other critics have commented on your "street aesthetic" and your "rapid, hip hop barrage of panels."

WS: Maybe that perception is related to my cultural or socioeconomic background versus what some expect to come out of a comic book.

FLA: Are there particular ingredients—character, style, etc.—that make a comic book Latino?

WS: The word "fiesta" on the cover? I haven't given much thought to that. I mean, are Alan Moore's comics American or British?

FLA: Being identified as a Latino comic book author-artist can be good and bad?

WS: This is so subjective. The Latino label can be beneficial now, and the next day it can work against you.

FLA: What's your sense of the state of Latino comics today?

WS: I don't read many comics, but the more aware I became (and still do) of my cultural background, the more rocky my relationship with the industry and comics becomes. Most Latinos working in the industry are assimilated to the American culture, and I consider myself part of that group. It took a conscious effort to say, "Why not write about things closer to me, closer to the world I live in?" This is pretty different from what the average comic book reader is accustomed to. Sure, some might find no interest whatsoever in some of the topics that affect Latinos and other so-called minorities or what they have to say, but that's their shortcoming.

I don't think there's a state of Latino comics because at this moment there's not really a Latino market for comics. But once we take over, that might change.

FLA: Current and future projects?

WS: I just finished collaborating on an anthology for Dutton Books, *Dead High,* and I'm in the developing stages of my next graphic novel, *Raul: A Latin Opera.*

Ivan Velez Jr.

Ivan Velez Jr. was born in 1961 in the Bronx, the place his parents had migrated to from Puerto Rico in the 1950s. Velez and his two younger brothers were raised in a Spanish- and English-speaking household largely by their mother and with help from his maternal grandparents. As part of his family's "big novela story" (his words), he recently discovered that his father had a daughter born out of wedlock and raised in Puerto Rico.

Ivan's mother, a paraprofessional working in education, had a voracious appetite for stories, including comics—a passion she passed down to Velez. He would devour *Archie*, *Richie Rich*, old DC comics such as *Superman* and *Supergirl*, and Action Comics. His mother would buy him kiddie, superhero, comedy, and even horror books. His father would read the cowboy and war comics and stay away from the rest. Velez read it all. He especially loved the DC mystery titles.

From the time he was a young boy, Velez has written stories. He would build on and re-create world myths that he knew well. His mother gave him a huge dictionary of Greek myths, and read fairy tales to him and his brothers at night. He also began drawing at an early age. Later, he would make it a habit to translate into comic book form films he had seen. *Enter the Dragon* was one he remade several times.

He studied illustration at Syracuse University in 1979. After graduation in 1983, he tried to figure out what to do with himself.

Velez continues to write scripts, work on his novel *Opaline's Secret*, make films, and create comic books. He won several awards, including an American Library Association award, for his first editing job, on *Dead High* (Dutton Books). He used a Xeric grant to publish the first volume of *Tales of the Closet*. He also works as a youth specialist, art instructor, and career prep guy at places like the Hetrick-Martin Institute, the New York Public Library, the

South Bronx JobCorps, and the Bronx Museum of the Arts in New York City. His short film *Malaguena* will be on the festival circuit at the end of 2008. His website is www.planetbronx.com.

FREDERICK LUIS ALDAMA: Was there a moment when you were growing up that you realized that Latinos were not being represented in comics?

IVAN VELEZ: Back when I was a kid, you just didn't think about Latino representation. You were just happy to see people with black hair and brown eyes. That's the way we connected with the characters.

The whole Latino thing wasn't even something I was aware of until I was in my teens. Then it hit me hard, like a pile of bricks. Particularly when the popular, big, giant-sized *X-Men* came out. They had all these international people, but no Latinos. There were so many of us around, so why were we excluded?

In college, I was naïve about how racial prejudice worked in mainstream culture. I went to this really nice private university that was full of rich white kids. I didn't even know what to do with myself. I felt so odd and different.

I realized for the first time how limited people's perception is of Latinos, how mainstream America made us feel invisible or out of place. In high school, I had been recognized for being talented, excelling in my classes, but in college, all of a sudden I was reduced to a stereotype.

FLA: Were your studies at Syracuse University useful in any way?

IV: This was in the late 1970s, before graphics software, when it was all by hand, with a lot of cutting and paste-up. My technique was all over the place, so I didn't make the first cut for the illustration program. So I took film. It was great, and I was good at it, but I was scared of it: "who am I to make film?" After a semester of film studies, I was invited to join illustration. I took it. Now I regret the decision. I wish I had stayed in film.

But it was my daily comic strip while at university that taught me the most. It was more than a dirty joke a day. It was more like a soap opera with continuing characters. Its characters were more diverse—Latinos and gays—than those at the university. People kind of freaked out. For instance, when I created a character who was a football player who came out of the closet, the football team chased me for a whole week to beat me up. I saw myself changing the way I wrote the characters so that the strip could teach people things about the world. It was this comic strip that was my biggest training in college.

FLA: Why tell stories in the form of the comic book?

IV: Comic books are very close to my heart. It's where I always retreated to when I was young. There was nothing like a comic for me to just disappear whatever was going on. And it stuck with me. I seemed to communicate better through comic books than other forms.

But I'm learning from other storytelling forms, too. I finished my first short film a year ago. I know that being a cartoonist helped that process a lot. Every shot I did was almost letter-perfect to the storyboard. The cartooning also informs the writing of my first novel, my script writing, and everything else I do.

FLA: What was your first moneymaking, breakthrough comic book project?

IV: Just before I finished college, I saw this ad in the back of the paper for a gay youth agency. I was myself dealing with my own sexuality, so I dropped into the agency to talk to somebody. After attending some discussion groups and doing some illustration work for them, I got the idea of doing a gay *Archie*. Back then, coming out of the closet made you feel pretty alone. So I thought that if I could get a comic book like this into teenagers' hands, this might help. Lying on my stomach in front of the TV, I created twenty-five pages in two weeks. It just came out of me. People at the Institute for the Protection of Gay and Lesbian Youth liked it.

So I started doing a comic book called *Tales of the Closet* that got a lot of attention. It went to all the high schools in New York State, and a few in other states. It went to some organizations, CBOs [community-based organizations], libraries as well as bookstores.

I had never gone to a comic convention before, but I had met Howard Cruse, and he invited me to sit next to him at his table. I decided to take *Tales* with me and circulate it. At the convention, people would pick up the comic, find out what it was about, then drop it and go away. Three feet in front, behind, and to the side of me was totally empty of people. It was like I had a force field around me.

This was the late 1980s–early 1990s, and there was still only a tiny percentage of people of color at the convention. There weren't any characters of color in comics. It seemed weird to me. If comic book authors are going to sell to the populace, shouldn't the characters look like the populace? This was around the time I started thinking about sketching a superhero team of color and calling them some sort of crew. I would start them in the past and bring them into the present day and give them a legacy. I was really thinking about the Negro Baseball Leagues.

At my second time at the convention, Dwayne McDuffie introduced himself and said he was starting a new company, Milestone Comics. He liked my work and wanted me to try out *Blood Syndicate*. Was it bravery and innovation on his part, or was he not finding anybody to work on the book?

So I started working for Milestone. They had a bunch of characters of color, but no Latinos. I think they may have had one, a maid. So I made Tech-9 a Puerto Rican, and turned Fade and Flashback Dominican. I added South Americans and Central Americans, and even included Caribbean blacks, like Masquerade, who considers herself West Indian, and not African American. I added Asian ethnicities, like Koreans, and added a Chinese heroine that I had created for my own team and brought in with me, a decision I came to regret. I wanted to complicate their identities. I noticed that when you did characters of color, they were simplified: black characters wouldn't also be Hispanic, and vice versa. They all had something very pointed and singular about their ethnicity. We are not all one type of Latino or one type of black in this country, so I wanted to mess with the differences. I'm proud that I also got to design a few of the costumes that played to, but didn't exaggerate, their identities.

FLA: I think your work in *Blood Syndicate* was inspired. Did this have to do with the freedom given to you in your work environment?

IV: It was a good, nurturing environment—at first. Once CrisCross came on board, it really seemed to click. He'd walked in off the street, but when I saw his samples, I knew this was the guy. He showed emotion without going overboard, and his drawing style complemented my writing. It was juicy.

I look at it now, and I see stuff we both could have done better, but it was pretty good for what it was.

FLA: Working for Milestone, were you able to make a living?

IV: I was also working another job as educational-materials coordinator, illustrating posters, pamphlets, and doing AIDS and sexuality trainings.

At Milestone I first got paid to move things around for them. I added a little to their bible, mostly background info about the cultural history of Dakota and the Blood Syndicate. It took a little while to get to the first scripts because they couldn't find artists who wanted to do *Blood Syndicate*. I think maybe the artists were a little nervous about who I was because I had done a gay comic book.

Once it got going, I was doing up to four books a month for Milestone. That was enough to live and give money to my family. It was a nice life. Plus, I would go to conventions and people would be really nice to me. Someone gave me a bottle of champagne at my first signing. It just felt so good to be noticed that way. I was, like, the Latino who got to write comics. And the fan mail I got was just amazing. I also started making enough money to quit my other job. It was a great three years.

FLA: At Milestone, was its sponsorship by the corporate DC Comics ever an issue?

IV: The guys who ran Milestone had to maintain a certain image. They dressed in suits every day and tried to maintain a big-business image. But some people at DC would sometimes slip and treat the Milestone guys very unprofessionally. There was this tension in the air with DC. The sales department wasn't reaching the sales they were supposed to—with their tired marketing—and so the relationships with the creative talent would become strained. Milestone fought really hard to keep their head above water and to keep their relationship with DC civil, but the numbers didn't work out. They even changed the paper, more glossy, to try to get a larger audience. They started to get anxious about every little detail. I think eventually the editors moved to DC to save costs. They're licensing characters for cartoons now, which is a great big step for them.

FLA: All these tensions and financial expectations led to the death of *Blood Syndicate*?

IV: It ended mostly because there was tension between the creative people like myself and the editorial staff. Bob Washington was too eccentric, and he was also doing a new team book that he was really invested in, but got axed from. The way he left that situation was pretty rough.

I created a lot of characters for the *Blood Syndicate* series, would sign these new-character agreements, and never see the paperwork again. Then the editorial management was changed, and I was told to my face not to expect any more new character agreements for new characters. That was the beginning of the end for me. They promised a lot in the beginning— prorates on the characters we created if they were used in cartoons, toys, and such—but in the end, didn't deliver. If they ever do a movie, I know I'm not going to see a red cent. So I left Milestone not on such good terms.

FLA: They took your characters without giving you credit?

IV: Yeah, or they changed them so that they would be unrecognizable. But what could I do? They said they had no evidence of any paperwork for my contributed characters. Then they said they created characters that I knew I had added to the team: Boogieman, Dogg, Aquamaria, Iota, Mother from System, so many more. My influence was very strong on any character in *Blood Syndicate*. But I had already left, and I knew that our relationship had been so torn up that I knew nothing good was ever going to come out of my work for Milestone after that.

FLA: After Milestone, you freelanced for Marvel and DC?

IV: I did *Eradicator* for DC for almost three years. I worked on *Ghost Rider* for Marvel as well as other little pieces here and there. There were editors at both who liked my work in *Blood Syndicate*, and so they hired me on. That was nice because I never had to look for work. They always came and got me.

Working for DC felt like I was doing things in a void. There were a lot more limitations to what you could do. You had to deal with a whole set of characters that were already done, and follow what DC wanted. Working at Marvel was even worse. I felt like the assistant editor and some of the staff was hostile to me. I'm a Puerto Rican guy. I'm a big guy. I'm a Bronx guy. And I'm a gay guy. And I came from nowhere, unlike everybody else there, who had to go through internships and assistant positions before being able to do anything. I was lucky security didn't follow me around when I'd go in to meet with the editor and give him my work.

Marvel didn't work with full scripts, so I would never fully get a feel for the character. When I got Ghost Rider, his continuity was so messed up that the character didn't seem true to me. To understand the character better—he's this guy who is basically stuck in a hole until he is ready to come out—I tried to fix the continuity right away, so I gave him a back-story. I also found ways of sticking color into the book because it was a pretty white book. With the backstory, I made his wife a dark Latina from the Caribbean. I moved him into one of my old neighborhoods in the Bronx and created a supporting cast made up of characters of color.

It was all a big mistake. The first problem was that I kept getting this really bad art that was totally inappropriate for the writing. This happened after the first artist left for greater things. The following artists couldn't do any of the subtlety or the darkness that the scripts required. And they started getting sloppy with the colorist: a character's hair that was brown from day one, like Ghost Rider's girlfriend, would all of a sudden be blond in another issue.

The artist has to go with my writing flow, or it doesn't work at all. I mean, a lot of *Ghost Rider* failed because the artist just couldn't get my rhythm, the point of my panels, the emotion, and the little clues here and there. The Marvel production line: you just take it and you run, and you have a deadline, so sometimes people crap out stuff and Marvel doesn't fix it. They never go back and reorder the art or correct it. By the time I got a good art team on the book, my rhythm was gone.

And I have to admit, I never got a really good grip on the character, at least not until the end.

YOUR BRAIN ON LATINO COMICS

FLA: Did this also coincide with that big downturn in the comic book market?

IV: *Ghost Rider* had kept up his sales numbers until I got the first replacement artist and the sales dropped 50 percent. This was a time when many series kept folding, and staff was being fired left and right.

After *Ghost Rider* got canceled, that was it. I could not find work for the life of me. It was, like, a very hard time because you don't get unemployment insurance. Man, was I depressed.

FLA: Did you pitch any Latino characters to the mainstream comic publishers?

IV: I pitched this really nice team to the new (and only) Latino editor at Marvel. They didn't bite, but a year later I saw something very similar come out, which happens all the time, because ideas have a way of coming to different people at the same time. I've always wanted to do characters of color in a team. But DC, Marvel, even Vertigo just didn't see it. Not Eurocentric enough, I guess.

FLA: What happened to your work after the slump in comic book publishing?

IV: I went through a really hard time, thinking that comic books were not for me. I couldn't thrive or be supported during this downturn. I was in a hole, a midlife crisis of sorts. To get out, I started thinking about what was important to me: representing people, issues, and putting things out. I realized that I had to do my own comic book. So I applied for a Xeric grant. They gave me the grant, and so I could start putting *Tales of the City* out there.

FLA: Can you think of any Latino comic book authors who have been an inspiration?

IV: I've been following the work of Los Bros Hernandez since the mid-'80s: *Love and Rockets*, *Palomar*, *Hoppers*, and *Speedy*. It's all amazing shit. I mean, you sit there and you're totally absorbed by these beautiful, simple, almost perfect drawings. The characters are so alive, you read them and forget where you are. You're in these characters.

I wanted to aspire to this level of story, where you would suck in the reader right away, and have them live these lives. I'm still working on it. I'm unlearning that impulse to drop in an explanation or commercial every ten pages or just leading the reader into one expected money shot.

FLA: Other inspirations?

IV: All the Hong Kong kung fu movies I would watch as a kid—those double features at the movie theater—had a big influence. Today, it's the Korean films. They pull you in all these different directions, and they make the characters, even the bad ones, so human. I think that's something that's helped me work on this crime-novel kind of comic book that I'm doing right now.

FLA: There's a telenovela-melodramatic feel to *Blood Syndicate* and also *Tales of the Closet*.

IV: I always lived with my grandmother, who would sit all day watching the soap operas. She would tell me what was going on, and even though it didn't really match, her story was always better than what was going on in the telenovela. This influenced the way I wrote and saw things. The old telenovelas are very histrionic: all this suffering, and where these women have to go through so much shit and always have to fight.

FLA: In each of your stories, you mix it up: adventure, epic, melodrama, and so on.

IV: You don't want the reader to get bored or to guess where you're going. In my film, I'll be doing a melodrama one minute, then a ghost story, then sentimental, horror, then crime drama—all in twenty minutes. And that's very attractive to me. I like to be surprised and pulled. Overlaying genres makes the story more interesting.

As far as characters, I'm a real believer that once a character is created, they should pull you in directions you don't necessarily want to go. They should surprise. You can try to fit them in a box and control them, but once you do that, they become flat, they don't move anymore. For the characters to keep moving and breathing, you have to let them push you in another direction or another situation. The characters I created in *Blood Syndicate* surprised me all the time.

FLA: Do you have an ideal audience in mind when you make these shifts and create these surprising characters?

IV: If you notice everybody else's day-by-day lives, you see these shifts constantly. I want my reader to feel as if the characters are real and true—to take a look at it and see what's really there. I know that everyday life is not as smooth as it looks in the movies, especially in Hollywood, where everything's on these tight rails. I mean, in my own day-to-day, I experience a couple comedies, some melodrama, and horror.

FLA: Can you talk about the creating of *Tales of the Closet*?

IV: I was basically doing therapy on myself, working the kinks out of that stuff inside of me. It was wishful thinking. It was fantasy.

The target audience was supposed to be teenagers, but every adult who read it had a stronger reaction than the teenager. Most of my fan letters came from adults. There was a big portion of gay and lesbian adult readers who felt cheated: how come I didn't get this kind of stuff when I was younger?

Now I think there's so much gay culture that, just like, say, the Latino canned culture, you now get the canned gay culture in the media: only stories about the one stereotype—prissy, clean, pretty, reckless, fashionable, flippant—that stands for all gay culture. And it's the same thing with black culture. I don't want my books to be like that.

At the same time that I don't want my work to fit into this, it has to compete with that gay—and Latino—canned culture out there. So it doesn't quite fit. This is probably why the book is picked up by a lot of middle distributors, but not the big ones like Barnes and Noble.

FLA: You use different narrative voices and image styles to create different moods.

IV: I'm not as practiced, and I haven't developed as many skills as I could have, but I do my best to let the story dictate what I can draw. So a lot of that change or shift of mood is what I can handle as an artist. If you notice, a lot of my stuff doesn't have a lot of backgrounds in it. This is partly due to

Tales of the Closet: Volume 1

a lack of time to do the research. That's why I focus so much on the faces and the body language—one of my trademarks. I really only want to draw things that breathe.

FLA: How are the sales of *Tales of the Closet*?

IV: I have 75 percent of the books still in my bedroom, mostly because my marketing is still word of mouth. The second book received some nice reviews; people liked it even more. This helped its sales. I just have to find the right marketing technique.

FLA: Can you talk about your comic book storytelling process generally?

IV: OK. I'm very loose when I draw. The inking is what ties it together. I used to use really cheap tools—whatever dollar marker I could find I used to use. But now I'm actually doing pen, ink, and brush, which takes a lot longer.

The most important thing to me is the characters. I'll sketch the characters out, come up with a couple of names, and then draw the faces out. The ones that click are the ones that look natural. Then I build the story around them. I then figure out the basic story outline: what happens in the key scenes are the ones I see in my head first and that I jot down first and play around with. I have to justify the scene, taking longer to get to a certain scene. It's like putting a puzzle together. That's why my stories seem to be a little twisty. It's like you're putting a puzzle together.

FLA: Panel layout and gutter placement?

IV: This is something I had to learn more and more as I went on. When I first wrote comics, I just shoved the panels together, using them more like scenes. I would group them together and use the gutters as an afterthought to separate the scenes from each other. That's why the panels look like they're shoving each other all the time. Howard Cruse asked me why I was doing this, telling me that I needed the gutters. I tried using more gutters, but then went back to shoving scenes together. For some reason, it flowed better for me. I know the gutter is very important—it's that empty space that the reader connects with—but if I have a gutter, I'd rather fill it black. Those empty spaces should indicate a total shift of time.

FLA: *Blood Syndicate* was in color, and *Tales of the Closet* in black-and-white?

IV: Color is like the music score in the comic book: it can make it feel somber, or bright and exciting. But you learn what you can do and work within your material constraints. I couldn't publish *Tales of the Closet* in color. There's something beautiful, though, about black-and-white art. There's something really pure about having to use the black line to set everything: the mood, the pacing, everything. The fact I never expected *Tales* to be color did change it a lot. It's very scratchy.

FLA: Comic book storytelling requires the use of certain identifiable visual types, but is there a way to complicate certain ethnic or Latino—gay or otherwise—types that have become stereotypes?

IV: People think of this country in black-and-white terms, and everybody in the middle doesn't count. So you combat this in your writing and drawing by portraying the shades in between. The shades and layers are so much more interesting to me—ethnic white characters too.

You can do a lot by complicating facial expressions: a little twitch can say a lot about what the character is thinking, feeling, or experiencing. CrisCross was able to capture the subtlety of what the characters were feeling and how certain ethnicities have a different way of expressing themselves facially. But the kings of this are the Hernandez Brothers.

FLA: Your stories move the reader emotionally?

IV: There's something really empowering when you actually make a person feel something, either from watching your character or from an event. This is the whole point of doing cartooning. You want to get into the mind and body of your reader, where you can convey a feeling and message. It's my way of reaching the world.

There's a certain melancholy about many of my characters. They have that feeling that something's wrong with the world or with themselves— something's muted—that I think most people feel at some point in their life. We remember something that made us cry more than anything else. I remember reading that scene in Gilbert Hernandez's *Palomar* when the character goes up in flames at the end. I didn't expect it, and it made me cry. This is the touching and poignant stuff that you want to capture.

But you want to mix it up too. To have your audience get angry and sad and happy and—well, you just don't want to get stuck like the histrionic telenovelas, where the pacing is so predictable. I want my readers to cry when they're not expecting to cry.

FLA: While you tell stories that engage your readers and even offer an escape, there's still that strong sense of opening up your readers' eyes to real-world issues. I think in particular of the gay-bashing scene in *Tales*?

IV: That issue of *Tales* was hard for me. I was scared of going overboard. But I knew that the reader wouldn't get the point unless I showed just how unpredictable this violence against gays can be. So I made the issue unpredictable. It's stronger when it's not predictable.

FLA: It seems the mainstream comic publishers have taken an interest in Latinos. I think of Marvel's making the new Blue Beetle a Latino, and also their comic book *Araña*.

Tales of the Closet: Volume 1

IV: When they have Latino characters, it seems they only exist to validate a non-Latino character. They'll put a creative team together to write a Latino character, but not think to put an actual Latino on board. I think Araña is cute—if only her dad wasn't so damn rich.

Mostly, I've distanced myself from mainstream comics. I decided to not really look at comic books that closely right now. My negative experiences with Marvel and DC—and given that my writing is better than at least 70 percent of the mediocre stuff out there—make it just too painful. I don't want this bad feeling to get in the way of doing my own comic books.

One of my big aspirations since I was a little kid: to walk into a comic book store and buy one of my comics. And at one point I succeeded. I would walk in, buy one of my comics, then read it on the train—even occasionally catch others reading it on the train too. I thought I could live the life of a comic book creator.

I haven't given up. If they don't want to hire me, I'll hire myself. I'll self-publish and put myself out there.

FLA: What's your sense of the independent author-artist trying to work in the comic book industry today?

IV: Let's face it: comic books aren't making that much money. I mean a kid doesn't have three bucks to pay for twenty-three pages. There just aren't too many independent comic book authors who are making it. Instead, they're hiring writers from TV, from the TV world, these people who are screenwriters for television shows. The guy who writes *Black Panther*—I mean, he's got his own million-dollar movie production company. One of the guys who writes for comics is a TV scriptwriter for *Lost*. The guy who wrote *Buffy* writes one of the *X-Men* comic books now. The comic book companies want to get ties to Hollywood and keep themselves in the mix. So it's kind of pushing aside the aspiring comic book writers in favor of these guys who already have high-profile jobs.

FLA: Along with your comic book work, you are involved in youth programs?

IV: I'm involved in programs around the city, Bronx Museum of the Arts, Hetrick-Martin Institute. I'm teaching cartooning to a core group of pretty gifted, high-risk Latino and black kids. I'm teaching them how to see the world as reflected in their art and how to push forward. I taught them how to produce a product and how to market it themselves if they can't find a buyer. My life is so much more improved now that I'm actually able to help again in this way.

FLA: How about your current and future work?

IV: I've finished about 100 pages of my novel, *Opaline's Secret*, a story inspired by my love of Chinese ghost stories.

It's hard for an artist working full-time to get all the work done. I leave at seven AM, and I come home drained at eight-thirty PM. Basically, I need more free time.

Notes

PART I

1. Because comic books are so deeply rooted in the childhood experiences of many of us, examples abound of this confessional mode that kicks in when writing about them. In "Borders and Monuments," Jared Gardner recalls the homogeneous world of comic book shops before Los Bros Hernandez hit the scene. The confessional essays collected in *Give Our Regards to the Atomsmashers!* edited by Sean Howe, also offer pages upon pages of resplendent accounts on how comic books formatively shaped their identities.

2. *Third World War*, the longest-running feature in the British anthology *Crisis*, follows the adventures of a multicultural ragtag team that is hired to supposedly liberate a Third World country. However, what the team actually finds is that a multinational interest controls the markets of the country. While issue 1 sold 80,000 copies nearly instantaneously, *Third World War* ended its run with issue 53, and within a year the comic book had ended with issue 63. (For more details on the history of this comic and other British-mades, see Graham Kibble-White, *The Ultimate Book of British Comics*.)

3. In Mexico, 80 percent of all periodical publishing is in the form of comics for an adult audience; India produces thousands of comic book titles for all ages; in the Philippines, we also see the large-scale publishing of comic books, and over a million comic books are sold each week. For more worldwide comic-book reading habits and statistics, see Roger Sabin, *Adult Comics*.

4. Recall, too, that it was not until 1966, after sustained protests by black actors beginning in the early 1950s, that the racist *Amos and Andy* minstrel show (first broadcast on the radio in 1928) ended its run. It was the large-scale events of the civil rights movement that helped open doors to nonwhites moving into areas of study and work otherwise blocked; this in turn led to the overturning of demeaning characterizations and to a large scale assault on mainstream cultural representations. For more on the importance of the social in influencing comic and cartoon art, see John J. Appel, "Ethnicity in Cartoon Art."

5. Mario Saraceni considers the verbal to be visual: the shape of the lettering, panel, balloon, and caption box, all convey, like language, meaning. According to Bart Beaty, in Europe in the 1990s it was the author-artists "raised in art schools" who used "techniques borrowed from the fine arts" that "transformed the field of comic book creation" (*Unpopular Culture*, 7). Beaty continues, "No longer would comic book artists seek legitimacy in relation to literature, but in relation to the visual arts. This shift in orientation meant abandoning the novelistic ideal for one more closely related to the traditions of the artist's book" (7).

6. While forms like the novel, short story, and even film have all experienced their moments at the scholarly and media-pundit margins—I think of those arguments of yesterday and even today that novel reading is less serious than that of history, for example—the comic book has been played against these others as a lesser art form: comic books are for children and adolescents, and novels are for adults.

7. The comic book itself crosses borders. It has a massive appetite, metabolizing other storytelling forms such as Shakespeare's plays (*Othello* published by Workman in 1983, and *Macbeth* by Puffin Books in 2005, for instance), Dante's *The Divine Comedy* (Chronicle Books, 2005), and poetry (Lewis Carroll and Alfred Noyes, KCP Press in 2004 and 2005 respectively).

8. While cultural studies gained momentum in the 1980s in the United States, the identification of comic books as a site of conformity or resistance to so-called grand narratives (in this case, U.S.-identified imperialist hegemony) had already appeared in 1971, when Armand Mattleart and Ariel Dorfman published *How to Read Donald Duck*.

9. We see such moves also in the realm of film studies. I mention only one recent example of many here. In *Action Figures: Men, Action Films, and Contemporary Adventure Narratives*, Mark Gallagher discusses how popular cultural phenomena like film and literature "employ numerous strategies to define particular spaces and environments as settings for action and male agency, to reestablish men's privileged position in active space, and to code a range of activities as inherently masculine, even in the relatively rare cases in which women undertake those activities" (3). For Gallagher, such hypermasculine constructions are a response to "threats posed by economic and cultural changes affecting men's roles in the workplace and in the domestic space" (3).

10. Jeffrey Brown positions *Blood Syndicate* within an African American representational frame, yet the series is written by a gay Latino author, Ivan Velez Jr., who creates mostly Latino (and some gay) characters.

11. While scholars and critics such as Deanna Shoemaker and Doris Sommer consider code switching a form of political resistance, its role in society is much less dramatic. First, with each passing generation, code switching between Spanish and English is becoming less and less a feature of everyday speech acts of Latinos living in the United States. Second, in its social operation and function, it is simply a linguistic inflection that attaches to something much deeper: the expression of an idiolect (in this case, English with a peppering of words in Spanish) that spins out of our evolved universal grammar. Whether I speak in English or Spanish or in English

with code switches, what I do individually is to exercise my language faculty. We all have the same language faculty (universal grammar), it is just that I might be born into a community that uses English with a peppering of Spanish, so in my everyday activities I acquire a series of habits that set in motion the sensorimotor system that will allow the functioning of this language faculty to manifest itself in the pronunciation of a set number of distinct sounds.

12. For a splendid analysis of this moment and how the split-view narrative depicts both the Western outsider and the native inhabitants' worldview in order to disrupt too-easy binary characterizations, see William Nericcio, *Tex[t]-Mex: Seductive Hallucinations of the "Mexican" in America.*

13. In an interview with George Gene Gustines, Judd Winick remarks of the fan mail that says he is pushing social issues: "I always ask: which social agenda are you complaining about? is it the gay people? or the black people or the Asian people? After a while, it doesn't look like a social agenda. This is the world we live in" (*New York Times*, May 28, 2006).

14. Alcaraz both critiques society and also plays with the device of the comic strip story. *La Cucaracha* begins with a self-portrait of Alcaraz drawing a cockroach: "This is no place for you! [. . .] As your alter ego, it's my duty to explain that I've leapt off the page and right into your boring life. What a cheap story device! Eddie, you're Latino, right? Just say it's 'Magical Realism.' The use of the fantastical dreamlike imagery found in some Latin American literature" (7).

15. Comic books can be about anything in the world. Likewise, scholars of comic books can write about anything in the world. For example, in *Can Rock and Roll Save the World?* Ian Shirley recharts a comic book history by detailing the presence of music either as an influence or as part of the storyworld (Shirley spots an Aretha Franklin album in an issue of *Spider-Man*). And so in the mode of Shirley's work and others', we might as scholars decide to try to quantify the relationship between comic books and the making of a subcultural trend; as Dick Hebdige does with punk music and its subcultural look, we might discuss how Los Bros Hernandez's do-it-yourself, punk-informed *Love and Rockets* was reappropriated by a late-1980s British rock band that chose the name Love and Rockets.

16. I ask what Philip Sills would make of Cartoon Network's *Minoriteam*, which features a Tejano oil baron who turns into a superhero leafblower, as well as a Jewish superhero who gets aroused while chasing a giant shiny nickel. Asked in an interview with Lola Ogunnaike if *Minoriteam* might offend some viewers, cocreator Adam de la Peña responded, "I have no idea. We're really targeting Eskimos" ("Satirical Superheroes for the Rude Set," *New York Times*, March 18, 2006).

17. It has been pointed out that Peter Parker as Spider-Man authenticates his white identity by locating his superhero character within the Afro-Caribbean spider-trickster tradition (see M. Thomas Inge, *Comics as Culture*).

18. Since his first appearance in 1940 in *Flash Comics* (volume 1, issue 1), the Whip lasted fifty-five issues. He also made an appearance in DC's *The Big All-American Comic Book* (1944). In this installment, titled "Warpath," Rodrigo "Rod" Elwood Gaynor as the Whip is described by the narrator as "an Eastern dude" who lives on a ranch;

he is a Euro-Anglo incarnation of an earlier *criollo* Texan, Don Fernando Suarez, who fought for the rights of the poor Mexicans as El Castigo, or the Whip. Here, Rod Gaynor as the Whip sports a blue and yellow mariachi jacket, yellow cloth belt, red pantaloons, mask, and blue hat; with the wearing of the disguise, he acquires a heavily accented and truncated English: "Hello, Amigo, you are ver' seek man—you mus' lie down!" (263). He saves a "fierce, proud and prosperous people" (262) from corrupt white businessmen who try to dupe the Indians out of their land. In 1987, Roy Thomas and Mike Gustovich gave the Whip a Mexican American makeover (see *Secret Origins*, volume 2, issue 13).

19. In 2000, DC returned to the making of multicultural superheroes. The "Planet DC" conceit that informed the annuals of 2000 was the introduction of superheroes from Turkey, India, Japan, and Argentina.

20. DC and Marvel have featured other Latino characters, including Marvel's Brazilian-identified Roberto da Costa, the son of a CEO, introduced as Sunspot in the *Marvel Graphic Novel #4: The New Mutants* (1982) by Chris Claremont and Bob McLeod. And Judd Winick reveals that the father of Kyle Rayner (the Green Lantern) was a Latino in *Green Lantern* (volume 3, issue 150).

21. The creator of *El Diablo*, Gerard Jones, takes the opportunity to inform his readers that he grew up Anglo, but was fascinated by Chicanos and Chicano culture; this allowed him to bring a greater realism to his work. Ultimately, however, as he states, "None of that matters [because] the whole Latino thing, is just background. We're all just doing *people* stories here, human dramas and comedies that are only incidentally about place and race" (issue 1, 40).

22. *Blood Syndicate* hit a chord with its multiethnic readers; one fan wrote enthusiastically about how the characters "looked like me, talked like me, grew up around the sort of people I did" (issue 13, 32).

23. In issue 10, Fade expresses his deeply troubled fear of being gay: "But what if the others find out? Somebody musta heard the demon call me a faggot? What if one of the crew picks up on it? I don't think I could stand them looking at me and knowing" (32).

24. There is some radical gender-bending going on by comic book author-artists like Sandra Chang and other women of color. (Notably, Chang is a member PACAS, Professional Amigos of Comic Art Society, along with Laura Molina, Carlos Saldaña, and many other Latinos interviewed here.) In her series, *Sin Metal Sirens* (2001), we see an Asian American author-artist working within the sci-fi genre—a genre dominated by white male author-artists. Its full nudity and explicit sexual play align it also within the erotica storytelling tradition. The character Anodyne is supermuscled and smart; she is visually depicted as Asian—and ethnically intergalactic. As she travels across the galaxy to rescue kidnapped victims, she encounters adventures that reveal her polysexual ways. Nothing is off-limits. I might add that Chang also visually describes men-on-men scenes, lifting *Sin Metal Sirens* out of the lipstick-lesbian comic book realm aimed at the straight-boy fan club. While I disagree with the idealist thread of academic scholarship that considers cultural phenomena like comic books, film, and literature to have a direct effect on our material reality—the

Uncle Tom's Cabin phenomenon, I will say that if any cultural object might have such an effect, it would be erotica or, even more explicitly, pornography. Like the pocketbook pornography the GIs read and masturbated to during World War II (much of it published by Obelisk Press and written by luminaries like Henry Miller and Anaïs Nin), the rather sexually explicit visuals in *Sin Metal Sirens* might also immediately and directly lead to certain motor-cortex reactions in the viewer or reader, with definite material results.

25. In the 1990s television animated series *Captain Planet and the Planeteers* (TBS), there appeared the eco-friendly eponymous superhero who was formed by energy rings of earth, wind, water, fire, and heart and who protected the planet against forest clear cutters (Dr. Blight) and delta-waterway destroyers (Looten Plunder).

26. One can have a comic book that is told in the alternative mode, but published by nonalternative, mainstream presses like Warner Books, Random House, or DC. Andrew Dabb and Seth Fisher's *Happydale: Devils in the Desert* (Vertigo/DC) is alternative in that it follows the lives of an untold number of nonmainstream characters, including Latinos who speak only Spanish, midgets, Native Americans, Egyptians, amputees, mechanics into bondage, Siamese twins, and so on. At one point, the mayor tells Sheriff Duncan: "Need I remind you that this town was built as a haven for outsiders—people subjected to ridicule and violence by mainstream society?" (issue 1, 47). The alternative spirit infuses the work of African Americans Kyle Baker, Reginald Hudlin, and Aaron McGruder. Their satiric *Birth of a Nation: A Comic Novel* (Random House) is set in an East St. Louis so down-and-out that even the police department can't afford gas for its squad cars.

27. Just as Roberta Gregory chooses not to create an ethnic- or Latina-identified character, native Hawaiian R. Kikuo Johnson does the same in his *Night Fisher*.

28. Jaime's character Maggie is into superhero comics. On one occasion in the first issue of *Locas*, she mentions how she pulls out her "Doomsday depression emergency kit (six pack) and my favorite stack of super hero comics, I came across an old Ultimax comic I really never looked at in detail (the art wasn't very good)" (51). And as we know from the interviews here, Jaime and Gilbert often gorged themselves on the massive piles of comics passed down by their mother and older brother Mario.

29. For an interesting discussion of the history of the rise of alternative comics, including the so-identified first graphic novel, *A Contract with God* (1978), see Stephen Weiner, *Faster than a Speeding Bullet: The Rise of the Graphic Novel*.

30. There have been several interesting non-Latino noir adaptations. I think of Paul Karasik and David Mazzucchelli's adaptation of Paul Auster's postmodern *City of Glass*, as well as Martin Rowson's noir adaptation of T. S. Eliot's modernist classic, *The Wasteland*. Rowson's work has the mood and tone of hard-boiled noir. The back-cover blurb mentions how Los Angeles private eye Christopher Marlowe is led into a "web of murder, deceit, lust, despair, and, coincidentally, a frantic quest of the Holy Grail. Doped, duped, pistol-whipped, framed by the cops, and going nowhere fast, Marlowe enters a nightmare world where Robert Frost, Norman Mailer, and Edmund Wilson drink in the gloom of a London pub, where Auden is glimpsed entering the men's room, where Henry James, Aldous Huxley, and Richard Wagner

share an ice cream aboard a Thames pleasure steamer, and where, out of luck and out of clues, Marlowe finally tracks down T. S. Eliot and Ezra Pound." There is also Spain Rodriguez's adaptation of William Lindsay Gresham's 1946 hard-boiled pulp novel, *Nightmare Alley*.

31. We see a more radical intermixing of storytelling modes and style with Jaime Piña's *Bad Latino Gazette*—a science-fictional zine-story in which Japanese-cartoon-styled drawing (Voltron and Robotech) meets cubism crossed with gender-bending erotica and a *luchador* wrestling free-for-all; its visually driven panels fill up with devils, marauding masked women and men, and Egyptian figures blasting light from their fingertips.

PART II

1. We know from everyday experiences that our individual and social memories are tied intimately to our system of emotions. The emotion center (the amygdala) and the memory center (the hippocampus) not only sit adjacent to each other, but neuroscientific research has determined that the firing of memory neural network occurs most dramatically when attached to strong trace emotions. Indeed, we can't talk about comic book genres—rules and form—without talking of memory and therefore also of emotion.

2. Comic books as a narrative vehicle for memoir and autobiography have been present since the '60s independents. Today, we see bookstore shelves filled with them. I think of Pete Friedrich's edited collection, *Roadstrips: A Graphic Journey across America*, which includes a variety of comic book vignettes that explore issues of identity within different social and cultural contexts in the United States. For instance, in one such vignette, Gilbert Hernandez announces, "I'm Proud to Be an American": "I was around eight years old when I figured it out that it was good to be a Mexican [. . .] I figured if blacks were often very dark and whites and Asians were relatively pale, at least in my neighborhood, that meant Mexicans were just right" ("Where at Least I Know I'm Free," 69). We also learn of Roberta Gregory's mixed Mexican and Anglo heritage in her story "California Girl": "My grandparents on my mother's side of the family were from Mexico. On my father's side, the relatives seemed like average white Americans" (71). And the many author-artists collected in *Autobiographix* demonstrate well that not all comic books are "about caped superheroes and spandex-clad bad girls," as its back-cover blurb declares. They run the gamut, as editor Diana Schutz writes, "from humorous anecdotes to poignant recollections to philosophical ruminations on life" (*Autobiographix*, 99). The collection invites the reader to feel directly the "physicality of the artist's hand across the page" (99).

3. As Patrick Hogan discovers of all narratives from all societies worldwide, it is the establishing of a romantic union that appears cross-culturally everywhere. Given that it appears to be "*the* prototype eliciting condition for happiness," it is not surprising that it "arises universally" (244). We plan, plot, and organize our lives with the goal of achieving fulfillment and happiness centrally in mind. That we shape our everyday life with a larger plot of happiness in mind is, not surprisingly, a pow-

erful determinant of prototype genres: romantic tragicomedy, heroic tragicomedy, and sacrificial tragicomedy.

4. Patrick Hogan clarifies how schemas fast-track our meaning-making processes: "When we read or hear the syllable 'mon' at the beginning of a word, we begin searching the lexicon for a 'fit.' When the topic is Wall Street, we will reach 'money' first; when the topic is animals related to apes, we will reach 'monkey' first" (56). And, such lexical networks, if not triggered regularly, will, Hogan continues, "drop quickly out of the buffer" (57). Hogan identifies three types of substructures within a lexical item that are at work in our everyday meaning-making processes: schema (a hierarchy of definitiveness: the conception of humans as organic), prototype (concretization of schema: the concept of men, say, as being those more different from women; sadness as sadder than average), and exemplum (specific instances of a category, say, man). We employ all three in cognition, not only when responding and interpreting the world and people according to abstract schemas, but also when referring to prototypes or salient exempla.

5. See also Patrick Hogan's recent essay, "Narrative Universals, Heroic Tragicomedy, and Shakespeare's Political Ambivalence," in which he is careful to distinguish his neurocognitive approach to global narratives (inclusive of Arabic, Persian, Sanskrit, and many other traditions) from that of a more Eurocentric structured and focused Jungian or Northrop Frye approach.

6. Prototype narratives (romantic, heroic, or sacrificial) are based on prototypical emotion scenarios that operate to prime or activate personal memories along with their associated feelings. Universally, our most prominent stories are also generated from the prototypical structures of our emotion concepts. Emotion prototypes—reunion with a loved one, for example—are shown to make for the strongest, most resonant memories because of our personal experiences and aspirations. This effects how comic book stories trigger the emotional network in the reader. When we read or write comic book stories, we are guided by prototypes of genre: standards of opening, characterization, etc. We are surprised when an author triggers an outcome different from the one we expect. As Hogan explains, emotion prototypes "will help guide our decisions as to what sort of story is tellable, what is of interest, what is valid, and what is effective and engaging. This is true whether the narrative in question is fictional, biographical, or historical; set in the form of an epic, a drama, or a novel. In each of these cases, due to the emotive purpose of the tale, emotion prototypes will provide central structural principles for the story, partially guiding its overall shape and outcome, its tone and so on" (*The Mind and its Stories*, 88).

7. The superhero can be stripped down to the following bare bones: an outsider to society, he uses his powers to ingratiate himself within society by defeating villainous interlopers. See also Richard Reynolds, *Super Heroes: A Modern Mythology*.

8. Memory, like almost everything having to do with human beings, is not only an individual phenomenological phenomenon or an individual neurobiological phenomenon, but also a social phenomenon. One can't explain comic books—their capacity to narrate verbally and visually—without taking into account that one's personal memory is at the same time a social memory. That is, an author like Wil-

fred Santiago adopts particular visual and verbal procedures to narrate the life of a depressed Latino character within a social context. Already here we have a social knowledge of what this comic book genre is—that it is fictional and not factual. And we are already exercising extensive historical and social skills in understanding that this is a character in a particular city in a particular historical moment: what it is like to be Latino in this time and space. We have to understand also the hundreds of other things that are givens in his everyday activities: the function of money, trains, houses, telephones, antidepressants, and so on. I think of *One Hundred Years of Solitude*, when eventually all the denizens of Macondo lose their memory: first the names of things, then the uses of objects and animals (they put a sign on a cow stating that it is used for milk), then the meaning of words. With a memory of language gone, that basic faculty upon which memory is based, then language and memory are ultimately lost. Memory is always at the same time individual memory and social memory.

9. When we turn a comic book page—or any page of narrative fiction, or look at any sequence from a movie for that matter—our brains are constantly telling us that this is not the real world. This must be a powerful product of our evolution. Already at a young age we know how to distinguish fiction from reality; it is because we know the difference that as children we can enjoy so much the make-believe worlds of narrative fiction.

Bibliography

Abbott, Porter H. "The Evolutionary Origins of the Storied Mind: Modeling the Prehistory of Narrative Consciousness and Its Discontents." *Narrative* 8, no. 3 (2000): 247–256.

Alcaraz, Lalo. *La Cucaracha*. Kansas City: Andrews McMeel, 2004.

———. *Migra Mouse: Political Cartoons on Immigration*. New York: RDV/Akashic, 2004.

Alcaraz, Lalo, and Ilan Stavans. *Latino U.S.A.: A Cartoon History*. New York: Basic Books, 2000.

Alvarez, David. *Yenny*. Issue 4, December 2005. La Mesa, Calif.: Alias Enterprise.

Amano, Jeff, and Ivan Brandon. *Ruule: Ganglords of Chinatown, Vol. 1*. Berkeley: Image Comics, 2005.

Anderson, Ho Che, and Wilfred Santiago, eds. *Pop Life: The Unbearable Truth*. Issues 2, 5. Seattle: Fantagraphics, 1998, 2001.

Appel, John J. "Ethnicity in Cartoon Art". In *Cartoons and Ethnicity*, 13–48. Columbus: Ohio State Univ. Libraries, 1992.

Avery, Fiona. *Araña: In the Beginning*. New York: Marvel, 2005.

———. *Araña: Night of the Hunter*, New York: Marvel, 2006.

———. *Araña: The Heart of the Spider*. New York: Marvel, 2005.

Barker, Martin. *Comics: Ideology, Power, and the Critics*. Manchester: Manchester Univ. Press, 1989.

Barkow, Jerome H., Leda Cosmides, and John Tooby. *The Adapted Mind: Evolutionary Psychology and the Generation of Culture*. New York: Oxford Univ. Press, 1995.

Barr, Donna. *Desert Peach: Out of the East*. Bremerton, Wash.: A Fine Line, 2000.

Barris, Jeremy. "Plato, Spider-Man and the Meaning of Life." In McLaughlin, *Comics as Philosophy*, 63–83.

Beaty, Bart. *Unpopular Culture: Transforming the European Comic Book in the 1990s*. Toronto: Univ. of Toronto Press, 2007.

Bell, Darrin. *Candorville: Thank God for Culture Clash*. Kansas City: Andrews McMeel, 2005.

Bongco, Mila. *Reading Comics: Language, Culture, and the Concept of the Superhero in Comic Books*. New York: Garland, 2000.

Brown, Jeffrey A. *Black Superheroes, Milestone Comics, and Their Fans*. Jackson: Univ. Press of Mississippi, 2001.

Campos, Mark. *Moxie, My Sweet*. Seattle: Finecomix, 2005.

Campos, Sam. *Pineapple Man*. Honolulu: SoloGraphics, 1997.

Cantú, Hector, and Carlos Castellanos. *The Lower You Ride, the Cooler You Are: A Baldo Collection*. Kansas City: Andrews McMeel, 2001.

———. *Night of the Bilingual Telemarketers*. Kansas City: Andrews McMeel, 2002.

Carrier, David. *The Aesthetics of Comics*. University Park: Pennsylvania State Univ. Press, 2001.

Chang, Sandra. *Sin Metal Sirens*. Seattle: Eros Comix, 2002.

Cheah, Sinann. *The House of Lim: The Year of the Monkey Collection*. Singapore: Comic Station, 1994.

Conway, Gerry, and Chuck Patton. *Justice League of America: Rebirth; Gangwar, Part One*. Issue 233, December 1984.

Crippen, Tom. "Sauntering through the Lands of Wonderful, Awful Dreams". *Comics Journal* 279, November 2006: 98–100.

Dabb, Andrew, and Seth Fisher. *Happydale: Devils in the Desert*. New York: Vertigo, 1999.

Dierick, Charles, and Pascal Lefèvre, eds. *Forging a New Medium: The Comic Strip in the Nineteenth Century*. Brussels: VUB, 1998.

Dominguez, Richard. *El Gato Negro*. Issue 2, 1994.

———. *El Gato Negro: Nocturnal Warrior*. Issue 1, 2004.

———. *Team Tejas*. Issue 1, 1997.

Douglas, Allen, and Fedwa Malti-Douglas. *Arab Comic Strips: Politics of an Emerging Mass Culture*. Bloomington: Indiana Univ. Press, 1994.

Eisner, Will. *Comics and Sequential Art*. Tamarac, Fla.: Poorhouse, 2005.

Englehart, Steve, and Joe Staton. *Millennium*. Issue 2, January 1988. New York: DC.

Espinosa, Frank. *Rocketo*. Vol. 1: *The Journey to the Hidden Sea*. Berkeley: Image Comics, 2006.

Fathi, Nazila. "Iran Shuts Down Newspaper over Cartoon." *New York Times*, May 24, 2007.

Fattah, Hassan M. "Comics to Battle for Truth, Justice and the Islamic Way." *New York Times*, January 22, 2006.

Foster, David William. *From Mafalda to Los Supermachos: Latin American Graphic Humor as Popular Culture*. Boulder, Colo.: Lynne Rienner, 1989.

Friedrich, Pete, ed. *Roadstrips: A Graphic Journey across America*. San Francisco: Chronicle, 2005.

Gallagher, Mark. *Action Figures: Men, Action Films, and Contemporary Adventure Narratives*. New York: Palgrave Macmillan, 2006.

Gardner, Jared. "Borders and Moments". *Iowa Journal of Cultural Studies* 6 (2005): 118–121.

Garza, Margarito C. *Relampago*. Issue 3: *America's First Mexican-American Super-Hero Battles El Pajaro Grande*. Corpus Christi, Tex.: Mesloh, 1977.

Gaspar de Alba, Alicia. *Velvet Barrios: Popular Culture and Chicano/a Sexualities*. New York: Palgrave Macmillan, 2003.

Gaudiano, Andrea M. *Azteca: The Story of a Jaguar Warrior*. Denver: Denver Museum of Natural History, 1992.

Giffen, Keith, John Rogers, Cynthia Martin, Kevin West, Phil Moy, and Jack Purcell. *Blue Beetle*. Issue 1, May 2006.

———. *Blue Beetle*. Issue 6, October 2006.

Goldberg, Myla. "The Exquisite Strangeness and Estrangement of Renée French and Chris Ware." In *Give Our Regards to the Atomsmashers! Writers on Comics*, edited by Sean Howe, 197–207. New York: Pantheon, 2004.

Gonzalez, Dave. *The Homies*. http://www.homies.tv/comics_harras_01.htm

Gordon, Ian. *Comic Strips and Consumer Culture, 1890–1945*. Washington: Smithsonian Institution Press, 1998.

Gregory, Roberta. "California Girl." In *Roadstrips*, edited by Pete Friedrich, 71–76. San Francisco: Chronicle, 2005.

———. *Life's a Bitch: The Complete Bitchy Bitch Stories, Vol. 1*. Seattle: Fantagraphics, 2005.

Gröss, Daerick. *Murciélaga, She Bat*. Issue 1, August 2001. Studio G.

Gustines, George Gene. "Straight (and Not) Out of the Comics." *New York Times*, May 28, 2006.

Harvey, Robert C. *Accidental Ambassador Gordo*. Jackson: Univ. Press of Mississippi, 2000.

———. "Describing and Discarding 'Comics' as an Impotent Act of Philosophical Rigor." In McLaughlin, *Comics as Philosophy*, 14–26.

Hatfield, Charles. *Alternative Comics: An Emerging Literature*. Jackson: Univ. Press of Mississippi, 2005.

Hernandez, Eli. *Americo*. In *Iguana*, vol. 1, no. 1 (2005).

Hernandez, Gilbert. *Chance in Hell*. Seattle: Fantagraphics, 2007.

———. "I'm Proud to be an American Where at Least I Know I'm Free." In *Roadstrips*, edited by Pete Friedrich, 69–70. San Francisco: Chronicle, 2005.

———. *Love and Rockets X*. Seattle: Fantagraphics, 1993.

———. *Luba: The Book of Ofelia*. Seattle: Fantagraphics, 2005.

———. *Palomar: The Heartbreak Soup Stories*. Seattle: Fantagraphics, 2003.

Hernandez, Gilbert, Jaime Hernandez, and Mario Hernandez. *Hernandez Satyricon: Love and Rockets, Book 15*. Seattle: Fantagraphics, 1997.

Hernandez, Jaime. *Locas in Love*. Seattle: Fantagraphics, 2000.

———. *Locas: The Maggie and Hopey Stories (Love and Rockets)*. Seattle: Fantagraphics, 2004.

———. *La Maggie La Loca*. *New York Times Magazine*. April 23, 2006.

Hernandez, Javier. *El Muerto: The Aztec Zombie*. Issue 1, 2002.

———. *El Muerto: Mishmash*, 2004.

Hillsman, Don, and Ryan Monihan. *By Any Means Necessary: The Life and Times of Malcolm X; An Unauthorized Biography in Comic Book Form*. Narragansett, R.I.: Millennium, 1993.

Hogan, Patrick Colm. *The Mind and Its Stories: Narrative Universals and Human Emotion*. Cambridge: Cambridge Univ. Press, 2003.

———. "Narrative Universals, Heroic Tragi-Comedy, and Shakespeare's Ambivalence." *College Literature* 33, no. 1 (2006): 34–66.

Horn, Maurice, ed. *The World Encyclopedia of Comics*. New York: Chelsea House, 1998.

Howe, Sean, ed. *Give Our Regards to the Atomsmashers! Writers on Comics*. New York: Pantheon, 2004.

Iger, Jerry. *Sheena 3-D Special*. El Cajon, Calif.: Blackthorne, 1985.

Inge, M. Thomas. *Comics as Culture*. Jackson: Univ. Press of Mississippi, 1990.

Inzana, Ryan. *Johnny Jihad*. New York: Nantier, Beall, Minoustchine, 2003.

Johnson, R. Kikuo. *Night Fisher: A Comic Book Novella*. Seattle: Fantagraphics, 2005.

Jones, Gerard, and Mike Probeck. *El Diablo*. Issue 1, August 1989. New York: DC.

Juno, Andrea. *Dangerous Drawings: Interviews with Comix and Graphix Artists*. New York: powerHouse, 1997.

Kading, Terry. "Drawn into 9/11, But Where Have all the Superheroes Gone?" In McLaughlin, *Comics as Philosophy*, 207–227.

Kakalios, James. *The Physics of Superheroes*. New York: Gotham, 2005.

Kibble-White, Graham. *The Ultimate Book of British Comics*. London: Allison and Busby, 2005.

Kuper, Peter. *The System*. New York: DC, 1997.

Laffrado, Laura. "Postings from Hoochie Mama: Erika Lopez, Graphic Art, and Female Subjectivity." In *Interfaces: Women, Autobiography, Image, Performance*, edited by Sidonie Smith and Julia Watson, 406–429. Ann Arbor: Univ. of Michigan Press, 2002.

Lobdell, Scott, and Joe Madureira. *The Uncanny X-Men*. Issue 317, October 1994. New York: Marvel.

Luna, Joshua, and Jonathan Luna. *Ultra*. Issues 1–8. Berkeley: Image Comics, 2004.

Madrigal, Oscar "The Oz." "'Los Borrados': A Chicano Quest for Identity in a Post-Apocalyptic, Culturally Defunct Hispanic Utopia (A Reinterpretive Comic)." In *Velvet Barrios*, edited by Alicia Gaspar de Alba, 311–322. New York: Palgrave, 2003.

Mantlo, Bill, and Sal Buscema. *The Incredible Hulk*. Issue 265, November 1981. New York: Marvel.

Martinez, Jose. *The Chosen (The Americanos)*. Chico Comics, 1997.

McCloud, Scott. *Understanding Comics: The Invisible Art*. New York: Kitchen Sink, 1993.

McGruder, Aaron. *Public Enemy #2: An All-New Boondocks Collection*. New York: Three Rivers, 2005.

McGruder, Aaron, Kyle Baker, and Reginald Hudlin. *Birth of a Nation: A Comic Novel*. New York: Three Rivers, 2004.

McLaughlin, Jeff, ed. *Comics as Philosophy*. Jackson: Univ. Press of Mississippi, 2005.

———. "What If? DC's Crisis and Leibnizian Possible Worlds." In McLaughlin, *Comics as Philosophy*, 3–13.

Mellmann, Katja. "E-motion: Being Moved by Fiction and Media? Notes on Fictional

Worlds, Virtual Contacts and the Reality of Emotions." *PsyArt: An Online Journal for the Psychological Study of the Arts*, 2002. www.clas.ufl.edu/ipsa/journal/2002_mellmann01.shtml

Mills, Pat, and Carlos Ezquerra. *Third World War: Book I, Crisis*. Issues 1–2, 13–14, 17–18, 20–21, September 1988–March 1989. London: Fleetway.

Molina, Laura. *Cihualyaomiquiz, the Jaguar*. Insurgent Comix, 1996.

Montijo, Rhode. *Pablo's Inferno*. Oakland: ABISMO, 2004.

Morales, Gil. *Dupie: The Life and Times of a College Student as Seen through the Pen of Campus Cartoonist, Gil Morales*. Stanford, Calif.: Dupie Press, 1981.

Morales, Robert, and Kyle Baker. *Truth: Red, White, and Black*. New York: Marvel, 2004.

Morris, Tom, and Matt Morris, eds. *Superheroes and Philosophy: Truth, Justice, and the Socratic Way*. Chicago: Open Court, 2005.

Motter, Dean, and Paul Rivoche. *Mister X: The Definitive Collection, Volume One*. New York: ibooks, 2004.

Navarro, Rafael. *Sonambulo's Strange Tales*. La Habra, Calif.: Ninth Circle Studios, 1999.

Nericcio, William Anthony. "Artif(r)acture: Virulent Pictures, Graphic Narrative, and the Ideology of the Visual." *Mosaic: A Journal for the Interdisciplinary Study of Literature* 28, no. 4 (1995): 79–109.

———. "Autopsy of a Rat: Odd, Sundry Parables of Freddy Lopez, Speedy Gonzales, and Other Chicano/Latino Marionettes Prancing about Our First World Visual Emporium." *Camera Obscura: A Journal of Feminism, Culture, and Media Studies* 37 (1996): 189–237.

———. *Tex[t]-Mex: Seductive Hallucinations of the "Mexican" in America*. Austin: Univ. of Texas Press, 2007.

Nyberg, Amy Kiste. "'No Harm in Horror': Ethical Dimensions of the Postwar Comic Book Controversy." In McLaughlin, *Comics as Philosophy*, 27–45.

Ogunnaike, Lola. "Satirical Superheroes for the Rude Set." *New York Times*, March 18, 2006.

Oropeza, Anthony. *Amigoman: The Latin Avenger*. Issue 1, 2002. Kansas City: Strong Ave. Studios.

Pierce, Tamora, Timothy Liebe, Philippe Briones, and Don Hillsman. *White Tiger*. Issue 1, 2007. New York: Marvel.

Piña, Jaime. *Bad Latino Gazette*. Los Angeles: Yesca Nostra / Azteca Ace, 2004.

Ramirez, Peter. *Raising Hector*. www.raisinghector.com

Reynolds, Richard. *Super Heroes: A Modern Mythology*. Jackson: Univ. Press of Mississippi, 1992.

Robbins, Trina. *From Girls to Grrrlz: A History of Women's Comics from Teens to Zines*. San Francisco: Chronicle, 1999.

———. *The Great Women Superheroes*. Amherst, Mass.: Kitchen Sink Press, 1996.

Robinson, Lillian S. *Wonder Women: Feminisms and Superheroes*. New York: Routledge, 2004.

Rodriguez, Fernando B. *Aztec of the City*. Issue 2, May 1993.

Rodriguez, Spain. *Nightmare Alley*. Seattle: Fantagraphics, 2003.

Ross, Steve. *Chesty Sanchez*. Issue 1, November 1995. San Antonio: Antarctic Press.

Rowson, Martin. *Wasteland*. New York: Perennial Library, 1990.

Rozum, John, and Robert Quijano. *Kobalt*. Issue 16, September 1995. New York: DC/Milestone.

Rubenstein, Anne. *Bad Language, Naked Ladies, and Other Threats to the Nation: A Political History of Comic Books in Mexico*. Durham, N.C.: Duke Univ. Press, 1998.

Rubio, Bobby. *Alcatraz High*. Issues 1–3, 2003.

Sabin, Roger. *Adult Comics: An Introduction*. London: Routledge, 1993.

Sacks, Oliver. *An Anthropologist on Mars: Seven Paradoxical Tales*. New York: Vintage, 1996.

Saldaña, Carlos. *Burrito: Jack-of-All-Trades*. Issues 1–5. Accent Comics, 1995.

Santiago, Wilfred. *In My Darkest Hour: A Graphic Novel*. Seattle: Fantagraphics, 2004.

Saraceni, Mario. *The Language of Comics*. New York: Routledge, 2003.

Savage, William W. *Commies, Cowboys, and Jungle Queens: Comic Books and America, 1945–1954*. Middletown, Conn.: Wesleyan Univ. Press, 1998.

Schutz, Diana, ed. *Autobiographix*. Milwaukie, Ore.: Dark Horse Books, 2003.

Shainblum, Mark. *Angloman: Making the World Safe for Apostrophes!* Winnipeg: Signature Editions, 1995.

Shoemaker, Deanna. "Cartoon Transgressions: Citlali, La Chicana Superhero Avenges Neo-Colonialism". *Blackstream*, 2005: 105–118.

Sills, Philip. "Illusions: Ethnicity in American Cartoon Art". In *Cartoons and Ethnicity*, 51–64. Columbus: Ohio State Univ. Libraries, 1992.

Skilling, Pierre. "The Good Government according to Tintin: Long Live Old Europe?" In McLaughlin, *Comics as Philosophy*, 173–206.

Storey, Robert. *Mimesis and the Human Animal: On the Biogenetic Foundations of Literary Representation*. Evanston, Ill.: Northwestern Univ. Press, 1996.

Trillo, Carlos, and Eduardo Risso. *Chicanos*. San Diego: IDW, 2006.

Velez Jr., Ivan. *Tales of the Closet: Volume 1*. Planet Bronx Productions, 2005.

Velez Jr., Ivan, and CrisCross. *Blood Syndicate*. Issue 17, August 1994. New York: DC.

Velez Jr., Ivan, and James Fry. *Blood Syndicate*. Issue 2, May 1993. New York: DC.

Velez Jr., Ivan, and Wilfred Santiago. *Blood Syndicate*. Issue 35, February 1996. New York: DC.

Velez Jr., Ivan, and Trevor Von Eeden. *Blood Syndicate*. Issue 1, April 1993. New York: DC.

Weiner, Stephen. *Faster than a Speeding Bullet: The Rise of the Graphic Novel*. New York: Nantier, Beall, Minoustchine, 2004.

Wentworth, John B., and Homer Fleming. *The Whip*. In *The DC Comics Rarities Archives, Volume 1*, 262–267. New York: DC, 2004.

Wertham, Fredric. *Seduction of the Innocent*. New York: Rinehart, 1954.

Wright, Bradford W. *Comic Book Nation: The Transformation of Youth Culture in America*. Baltimore: Johns Hopkins Univ. Press, 2001.

Zunshine, Lisa. *Why We Read Fiction: Theory of Mind and the Novel*. Columbus: Ohio State Univ. Press, 2006.

Index

audience of *Palomar* series, 177; biography of, 171–172; *Birdland* by, 86–87, 179; *Chance in Hell* by, 18, 19, 172; characters of, 16, 62, 178, 179; comic books read by, 171, 172, 297n28; creative process and style of, 102, 175; current and future projects of, 180–181; and extratextual signposting, 89; and financial issues, 173; flashbacks used by, 176, 177; graphic novels by, *18*, 19, 172, 173–174; Roberta Gregory on, 169; "I'm Proud to Be an American" by, 298n2; interview of, 172–181; *Luba* by, 62, 96, 171, 176; and *Mr. X*, 173; and music, 172–173; on political commentary, 179; prototype narratives used by, 86–87; and racial scripts, 96; sexuality in comics by, 174, 179; on single-issue comic books and collected-book comics, 174–175, 180–181; *Sloth* by, 172, 173–174; on unique ingredients of Latino comic books, 179; verbal and visual narration by, 103–104, 169, 171–172, 176–177. See also *Love and Rockets*; *Palomar* series

Hernandez, Jaime: alternative storytelling mode of, 60–62, 64–65; biography of, 171, 182–183; characters of, 12, 182, 185, 188; on choice of comic medium, 183; comic books read by, 171, 182, 185, 297n28; creative process and style of, 175, 185; and financial issues, 183, 188–189; flashbacks used by, 182; Roberta Gregory on, 169; Gilbert Hernandez on, 181; *Hoppers 13* series by, 182; influences on, 182, 185–186; interview of, 183–189; *Locas in Love* by, 61–62, 64–65, 187; *Locas* series by, 8, 61–62, 64–65, 182, 187, 297n28; *La Maggie La Loca* by, 10, 98–102, 182; and *Mr. X*, 173; and music, 183, 184; *New York Times* Sunday comic strips by, 179, 182; *Penny*

Century by, 188; on romantic-tragicomedy mode, 187–188; sexuality in comics by, 186; storytelling style of, 6; on taking break from *Love and Rockets*, 188; on underground comics, 185–186; visual and verbal narration of, 98–100, 169, 182; and will to style, 101–102. See also *Love and Rockets*

Hernandez, Javier: on audience of *El Muerto*, 193–194; autobiographical stories and appearance of, in comics, 196–197; biography of, 190–191; characters of, 195–199; on choice of comic medium, 192; comic books read by, 192, 195–196; on comics distribution, 194; and comic strip form, 72; creative process and style of, 195–199, 201; day job of, 15, 194; ethical concerns of, 199–200; exhibit of works by, 269; and film adaptation of *El Muerto*, 15, 190, 197, 200–201, 255; on films compared with comic books, 8–9; future projects of, 195; on humor in *El Muerto*, 199; influences on, 190–193, 195–196; interview of, 191–201; on responsibility of comic book author-artist, 199–200; Fernando Rodriguez on, 253; on self-publishing, 194–195; on unique ingredients of Latino comic books, 200; visual and verbal narration of, 197–198; and work with aspiring comic book authors, 200. See also *El Muerto* (comic)

Hernandez, Lea, 195

Hernandez, Mario, 65–66, 171, 173, 297n28

Hernandez Satyricon: Love and Rockets, 66

heroes. *See* superheroes; *and specific superheroes*

Heroes World distributor, 147, 266

heroic tragicomedy, 86–88. *See also* narratives; superheroes

Herriman, George, 78

High School of Art and Design (New York City), 152, 153

Hispanic Business Magazine, 128, 130, 139

Hispanic Magazine, 193

historietas (serialized satirical short stories), 13

Hitch, Bryan, 60, 263

Hitchcock, Alfred, 238

Hitomaro, 273

Hoest, Bill and Bunny, 244, 246

Hogan, Patrick, 84, 86, 91, 298–299nn3–6

Hogan's Alley, 71

Hogarth, Burne, 144

Hogarth, William, 71

Homage Studios, 257, 259

homelessness, 23, 53

Homer, 19, 70, 154

Homies, The, 137

Homies, 76

homosexuality. *See* queer characters

Hoochie Mama (Lopez), 12–13

Hoppers, 182, 285

Horn, Maurice, 71

Hot Mexican Love, 233

Howe, Sean, 293n1

"How to Spot a Mexican Dad," 26

HOY, 242

Hudlin, Reginald, 297n26

Hulk, The (comic book), 145, 153, 156, 249

Hulk, The (film), 2

humor: of comic strips, 113, 125, 132–133, 134, 136, 243–244, 246–247; in *El Muerto*, 199; Fernando Rodriguez on use of, 254; and stereotypes, 132–133, 136

Hunchback of Notre Dame, The, 257

Icon, 14, 30

identification with comic book characters, 93–97, 208

Iger, Jerry, 11

Iguana, 56

illegal immigrants. *See* immigration and border issues

illustrated books, 9

I Love Lucy, 191, 255

Image Comics, 30, 58–59, 152, 202, 204

ImageTexT: Interdisciplinary Comic Studies, 10

immigration and border issues, 23, 25, 41–43, 58, 74, 129, 134–135, 155, 211, 247, 255

Impact Comics, 212

imperialism, 34–35, 66

"I'm Proud to Be an American" (Gilbert Hernandez), 298n2

Incredible Hulk, The, 31, 32, 33, 92, 196

India, 293n3

Indians. *See* American Indians

Inferno (Dante), 217

Infinite Crisis, 41

Inge, M. Thomas, 295n17

In My Darkest Hour: alternative storytelling mode of, 64, 69, 272–273; colors in, 275; creative process and style of, 273–275, 277; current events in, 276–277; dreamlike subjective realism of, 101; ethical issues in, 24–25; flashbacks in, 274; frame narration in, 82; history and conception of, 271; influences on, 272, 273; irony on, 272–273; multiple plot lines in, 274; Omar's reuniting with girlfriend at end of, 87; perspective in, 275; prototype narratives in, 87; reader-viewers of, 277; romantic element of, 272; setting of, 274; social context of, 299–300n8; visual and verbal elements of, 101, 270, 272–275; visuals in, 25, 64, 87, 272, 273

Institute for the Protection of Gay and Lesbian Youth, 281

Rodriguez, 254–255; and *Yenny*, 113.
See also capitalism; immigration and
border issues; imperialism
Popeye the Sailor, 152, 156
Pop Life, 61, 270, 271, 273
pornography, 297n24. *See also* sexual
themes
Portacio, Whilce, 259
Portishead, 205
Posada, José Guadalupe, 12
Power Man and Iron Fist, 31
Preacher, 205
Prince Namor, 249
Professional Amigos of Comic Art
Society (PACAS), 211–212, 265–266,
296n24
Prohias, Antonio, 131
prototype narratives, 84–88, 299n6.
See also narratives
publishers. *See specific publishers*
Puerto Rico, 111, 113, 114–116, 270, 276
Pulp Fiction, 228

queer characters: in *Blood Syndicate*, 59,
296n23; in *Locas* series, 182; in *Love
and Rockets*, 186; in mainstream
comics, 37, 38, 56, 59–60; in *Tales of
the Closet*, 24, 63, 281, 286–287, 289;
in *Ultra*, 59
Quesada, Joe, 39–40, 200
Quevedo, Kasey, 250, 251, 252
Quijano, Rober, 45
Quino, 19, 73

Rabelais, François, 9
race and ethnicity: African American
characters, 12, 29–30, 34, 45, 47, 78,
145, 234; Asian characters, 47, 56,
182, 234; in *Bitchy Bitch*, 169–170; Filipino characters, 202–203; in Latino
comic books/comic strips generally,
103–105; and racial scripts, 96; and
Rocketo, 161. *See also* multiethnic
characters

racial scripts, 96
racism: against African Americans,
293n4; Alcaraz on, 74–75; *Bitchy Bitch*
series on, 62; *Candorville* on, 78; Gilbert Hernandez on, 103–104, 179;
The Jaguar on, 214; *Love and Rockets*
on, 104; at MGM, 119; and reader
responses to Alcaraz, 29, 76; Velez
on, 280; and witch-doctor image,
19–20. *See also* political commentary
and social satire; stereotypes
Radiohead, 205
Raising Hector, 15, 76, 104, 243–248
Ramirez, Peter, 15, 76–77, 104, 242–248
Random House, 297n26
Rattner, Larry, 201
Raul: A Latin Opera, 278
Rawhide Kid, 60
Raymond, Alexander, 126–127, 162
raza art, 12
Raza Unida, La, 128
reader-viewers: adult readership for
comic books, 3–4, 293n3; of Alcaraz's
satire, 29, 76; of *Alcatraz High*, 262;
of *Amigoman*, 236–238; of *Aztec of the
City*, 252–253, 255; of *Baldo*, 133–134,
142–143; of *Birdland*, 179; of *Burrito*,
266–267; different responses by, to
Latino comic books/comic strips,
103, 106, 107; emotional effect of
visuals on, 91–93, 104, 106, 232,
289; empathy and identification of,
with comic book characters, 93–97,
208; of *El Gato Negro*, 149; of *Gordo*,
125–126; of Roberta Gregory's comics, 170; of *In My Darkest Hour*, 277;
of Los Bros Hernandez's comics,
177, 188; of *Love and Rockets*, 179;
of Luna Brothers' comics, 205–206;
and memory, 84, 91, 92, 96–97,
104, 106, 298n1, 299–300n8; mind-
reading capacity of, 95–97, 107; of
Laura Molina's comics, 213–214; of *El
Muerto* (comic), 193–194; of *Pablo's*

of, 213, 267–268; Web site of, 264, 269. See also *Burrito: Jack-of-All-Trades*

Sánchez, Alejandro, 12

Sánchez, Rosaura, 12

San Diego ComiCon, 50, 163–164, 253, 260

San Diego State University, 73

San Diego Union, 119

San Francisco Chronicle, 119

San Jose Mercury News, 249

Santeria, 39–40, 276

Santiago, Wilfred: alternative story-telling mode used by, 60–61, 64, 69, 272–273; on audience of *In My Darkest Hour*, 277; biography of, 270, 274; on breaking into comic book marketplace, 271; characters of, 275–276; on choice of comic medium, 270; on collaboration process, 273; comic books read by, 270; creative process and style of, 273–275, 277; current and future projects of, 278; dream-like subjective realism of, 101; early work by, 271–272; and ethical issues of *In My Darkest Hour*, 24–25; flashbacks used by, 274; frame narration used by, 82; graphic novel by, 270; influences on, 272, 273; interview of, 270–278; prototype narratives used by, 87; social context in work of, 299–300n8; on state of Latino comics, 278; on unique ingredients of Latino comic books, 277–278; visual and verbal narration of, 82, 87, 101, 270, 272–275; Web site of, 270. See also *In My Darkest Hour*

Saraceni, Mario, 6, 294n5

Sasse, Diana, 169

satire. *See* political commentary and social satire

Savage Dragon, 259

Savage, William W., Jr., 4

Savage Sword of Conan, The, 138

Savannah College of Art and Design (SCAD), 202, 203

schemas, 85, 86, 104, 299n4

Schmidt, Peter, 60

School of Visual Arts (New York), 152, 223

Schulz, Charles, 78, 246, 248

Schulz Museum, 246

Schutz, Diana, 298n2

sci-fi mode, 70, 296n24. See also *Rocketo*

Scott, Darieck, 12

Screen Gems, 120

Seduction of the Innocent (Wertham), 4, 10, 20

Segar, E. C., 78, 162

Self Help Graphics, 213

self-publishing, 168, 194–195, 217, 257, 265

self-syndication, 244

Serling, Rod, 250

Severin, John, 60

Sevier, Mary Frances, 119, 122, 124

sexual themes: in *Birdland*, 179; in comic books generally, 12–13; in Los Bros Hernandez's comics, 174, 179, 186; in Luna Brothers' comics, 207, 208. *See also* queer characters

shading, 177–178, 267, 275

Shadow Cabinet, 14

Shainblum, Mark, 60

Shakespeare, William, 10, 294n7, 299n5

Shazzam, 250

Sheena, 11, *11*

Shirley, Ian, 295n15

Shoemaker, Deanna, 13, 294n11

Shyamalan, M. Night, 205

Sienkiewicz, Bill, 272

Sills, Philip, 20–21, 295n16

Silo Roberts, 76–77, 102

Simms Bros, 249

Simon & Schuster, 216

Simone, Gail, 56

single-issue comics, 174–175, 196

Sin Metal Sirens, 296–297n24

Sloth, 172, 173–174, 177, 179

Smith, Jeff, 219

Smurfs, 112

social realism, 24–25, 46–47

SoloGraphics, 60

Sombra, 50

Sommer, Doris, 294n11

Sonambulo: characters of, 225, 230–232; creative process and style of, 226–229; cultural references in, 70; ethical issues in, 21–22, 29; and financial issues, 226; influences on, 224–225, 227–228; machismo in, 21–22, 231; noir conventions in, 67, 85; point of view and voice in, 229; reader-viewers of, 228–229; reshaping of genre in, 85; Fernando Rodriguez on, 254, 255, 256; villains in, 232; visual and verbal elements of, 228–231; visuals in, 67

Sorrows of Young Werther, The (Goethe), 94

Space Ghost, 250

Spanish language. See language

Spawn, 30

Spectre, 249

Speed Racer, 196, 250

Speedy, 285

Speedy Gonzalez (character), 71

Spider-Man: and Afro-Caribbean spider-trickster tradition, 295n17; Araña character in, 39; first appearance of Spider-Man, 38; influence of, on Latino author-artists, 144, 145, 153, 156, 191, 192, 195–196, 216, 223, 243, 249; music reference in, 295n15

Spiegelman, Art, 10, 14, 61

split-view narrative, 27–28, 295n12. See also narratives

Spy vs. Spy, 131

Stanford Daily, 73

Starman, 59–60

Star Trek, 215

Static, 12, 14, 30, 59

Static Shock, 59

Staton, Joe, 34

Stavans, Ilan, 69

Steinbeck, John, 123, 124

Steranko, Jim, 223, 224

stereotypes: and comic strips, 76, 114–115, 132–133, 136–137; in films, 119; Frito Bandito as, 255; and humor, 132–133, 136; of Latinos/Latinas, 43, 69, 71, 76, 114–115, 136–137, 237, 243; Fernando Rodriguez on, 255–256

Sticks and Stones, 98

Stormwatch, 60

storytelling modes. See narratives

Strange Tales of Sonambulo, 67, 232, 254. See also Sonambulo

Sub-Mariner, 250

Sugar and Spike, 166

Summit magazine, 242

Superboy, 166

Super Friends (television show), 31

Supergirl, 166, 279

superheroes: African American, 12, 29–30; blue-collar, 52–53, 235; characteristics of, 299n7; ecofriendly, 60, 297n25; Javier Hernandez on, 199; influence of, on Latino author-artists, 29; Latino, by Latino author-artists, 44–56; Latino, in mainstream comics, 31–44; luchador of Sonambulo, 225; Luna Brothers on, 208; mixed-race Latino, 38; multiethnic, 46–48, 50–52, 59, 87, 296n19; queer, 59–60; Fernando Rodriguez on, 252–254; scarcity of nonwhite, 30–31; scholarly approach to, 7; vigilante, 240; women, 11, 13, 16, 23, 38–40, 43, 56–59, 89, 208–209, 213–215; for younger reader-viewers, 55–56, 236–237. See also luchador (wrestler); narratives; villains; and specific comic books

Super Latino, 249, 251, 256

Super-locos, Los, 13